Australian
and New Zealand
Wine Vintages
Seventeenth Edition
2000

Robin Bradley

Hunter Agencies

First Edition	Nov. 1979
Second Edition	Nov. 1981
Third Edition	Sept. 1983
Fourth Edition	Aug. 1985
Revised	Dec. 1986
Fifth Edition	Sept. 1987

First Five Editions Published
  Under The Title:
  Australian Wine Vintages

Sixth Edition	Aug. 1988
Seventh Edition	Aug. 1989
Eighth Edition	Aug. 1990
Ninth Edition	Aug. 1991
Tenth Edition	Aug. 1992
Eleventh Edition	Aug. 1993
Twelfth Edition	Aug. 1994
Thirteenth Edition	Aug. 1995
Fourteenth Edition	Aug. 1996
Fifteenth Edition	Aug. 1997
Sixteenth Edition	Aug. 1998
Seventeenth Edition	Aug. 1999

National Library of Australia
ISBN 0 9577280 0 X

Produced by
Phoenix Offset Hong Kong

Film separations by
Eastern Studios Graphics Australia

Published by Hunter Agencies
Telephone 61 3 5368 6770

Preface to the 17th Edition.

It is now two decades since the first edition if the Gold Book appeared. 650,000 copies later, much has changed, so here are a few idle thoughts prompted by the compilation of this millennial edition:

Prices have in some cases increased markedly since the last edition, especially for premium Shiraz. Often such wines are sumptuously presented, designer-labelled, tissue wrapped and perhaps even boxed, velvet lined and personally delivered in a stretch limousine, but the quality does not always match the price or the marketers' aspirations. On the credit side however, the burgeoning respect - even awe - which this variety is commanding make it possible for some painstakingly made wines of extreme quality to be achieved.

I wish I could be as sanguine about Sauvignon Blanc. What an unrewarding variety it can be! At its best it is gently subtle in nose, urbane in palate, undercoloured and shortlived; at its worst coarse in nose, obvious in palate, undercoloured and shortlived. Yet it commands prices which Rieslings can only dream about (unless they are decades old Burings), and Semillons too must be wistful (unless they are Mount Pleasant Lovedales). I hasten to add that I do not allow my personal distaste for the variety to influence my "star rankings", merely that I gain little pleasure from drinking many of the wines wrought from it.

Merlot is becoming an important variety for us, not merely for blending with Cabernet but for its own distinctive flavours. I have no doubt that we will see more straight Merlots produced, particularly from some of the cooler areas which have annual difficulties ripening their Cabernet.

And welcome to another Gold Star wine - the superb Mount Pleasant Maurice O'Shea series of Shiraz. It is a big, old-fashioned Hunter Shiraz, in style quite unlike the elegant, satiny wines made by O'Shea himself, but substantial, complex and utterly satisfying.

You may note that the Gold Book has again put on a little weight. There are now some 360 makers, 1400 labels and over 12,000 entries, but I have no immediate plans to publish it in two volumes, A to K and L to Z

WineBase for Windows: Now generally accepted as the world's best cellar management software, WineBase has the good sense to include the Gold Book data as standard. To acquire a copy, contact Almost Vertical Software on (03) 9580 2100, or visit the Web page at *http://www.winebase.com.au*

And talking of Web pages, if you have difficulty obtaining a further copy of this book, or would like to have the Windows disk version of the book, with full search facilities, both are available at *http://users.netconnect.com.au/~goldbook/orderidx.htm*

How to use this book.

Wines are listed alphabetically by each maker's "short name", that is, the name by which the wine is commonly known to the consumer. Most wines listed are accompanied by reduced-scale versions of the current labels.

STAR RANKINGS: Each winestyle (label) listed is ranked out of a maximum of five stars. This ranking is my own, but is applied as honestly as I can manage, suppressing as best I can any prejudices, so that the star ranking reflects some of the earned respect for the particular label over the years of its production. If you disagree with my star ranking you are exhorted to ignore it and apply your own.

A few wines of supreme quality are given "Gold Star" highlighting. In their best years these wines are among the world's greatest.

At the other extreme, there are no "one star" wines in this book. It now seems wine-writers' convention that one star means undrinkable, (which should really be "no star"). But if I stay out of step with my colleagues it would be unfair to recipients of a one star ranking.

So what do these rankings mean? As a very broad and indeed over-simplified guide, something like this:

★	not applicable - see the previous paragraph
★★	basic, agreeable drinking
★★★	average to good quality
★★★★	very fine wines
★★★★★	the continent's best
✹✹✹✹✹	among the great wines of the world

VINTAGE RATINGS: These are out of seven, and are for the most part the makers' ratings. It is very important to understand that these ratings merely compare the specific wine being rated with itself in other years. A rating of "7" does not mean a perfect wine, merely that the winemaker has no higher quality aspirations for the label than are represented by that particular year's example.

BEST YEAR TO DRINK: By far the most useful entry in the book, this is intended to identify the particular year when, in the winemaker's opinion, you will derive the greatest pleasure from drinking the wine. I have sometimes been criticized for citing a particular year rather than a range of years over which the wine should be drinking well. But were I to ask winemakers for such a range instead of a year, I know that some drinking recommendations would come in as "now until 2010". This would be confusing, messy in print and completely wrong anyway.

There's a useful rule of thumb in considering wine development - that a wine improves for a third of its life, remains on a plateau for another third, and spends the remaining third declining gracefully into eventual feebleness.

The "Best Year to Drink" recommendation is an attempt to identify the middle of the plateau phase, not the extreme limit of the wine's longevity.

PRIOR: The word "Prior" does NOT mean that the wine is undrinkable, merely that the ideal time to have consumed the average bottle is prior to today. Some well-cellared bottles can still be superb.

CURRENT INTRINSIC VALUE: This is an arbitrarily derived estimate of value - not a price, nor yet a price recommendation. The formula applied to achieve these values allows for improvement in the bottle, inflation and the rating for the particular year compared with the average rating for the label, and effectively establishes a value to you the consumer, provided that -

(a) You feel that the current normal retail price is a fair one for the average wine of the series.

(b) The actual bottle under consideration has been cellared adequately (particularly important if the wine is of some age).

The formula ignores discounting, State pricing variations, star rankings and "rarity values". It does however continue annually to increase the value of a wine throughout its "drink now" life - a token acknowlegdment that most wine-lovers will value more highly an older wine still drinking well than a mature but younger wine drinking just as well.

You will notice that no values are attempted for "Prior" wines. Again, this does not mean that all such wines are valueless, but that the relevant values cannot be established by a rigid formula (as bottle to bottle variation becomes extreme in the last third of a wine's life).

The entry "N/R" means that the wine of that year has not been released as yet.

Alkoomi is a high quality Frankland River (Western Australia) producer of long-lived wines with admirably intense flavours. Winemaker: Michael Staniford.

ALKOOMI BLACKBUTT (BORDEAUX BLEND)

★★★★★

1994	6	2004	$58.00
1995	6	2005	$54.00
1996	6	2006	$50.00

ALKOOMI CABERNET SAUVIGNON

★★★★

before 1983		Prior	
1983	7	Now	$80.00
1984	6	Now	$64.00
1985	6	Now	$58.00
1986	6	Now	$54.00
1987	7	Now	$58.00
1988	6	Now	$47.00
1989	5	Now	$36.00
1990	6	2000	$40.00
1991	5	Now	$31.00
1992	5	Now	$29.00
1993	5	Now	$26.00
1994	6	2002	$29.00
1995	6	2005	$27.00
1996	6	2005	$25.00

ALKOOMI CHARDONNAY

★★★★

1989	6	Now	$50.00
1990	5	Now	$39.00
1991	7	Now	$50.00
1992	5	Now	$33.00
1993	6	Now	$37.00
1994	5	Now	$28.00
1995	7	2000	$37.00
1996	6	2000	$29.00
1997	6	2000	$27.00
1998	6	2002	$25.00

ALKOOMI RIESLING

★★★

before 1986		Prior	
1986	6	Now	$49.00
1987	5	Now	$38.00
1988	7	Now	$49.00
1989	5	Now	$32.00
1990	6	Now	$36.00
1991	6	Now	$33.00
1992	6	Now	$31.00

1993	7	Now	$33.00
1994	6	Now	$26.00
1995	5	Now	$20.00
1996	6	Now	$23.00
1997	7	2002	$24.00
1998	7	2006	$23.00

ALKOOMI SHIRAZ ★★★★

1994	5	2003	$29.00
1995	6	2007	$33.00
1996	5	2002	$25.00
1997	5	2003	$23.00

Allandale is a small Pokolbin area maker, producing a range of reliable wines. Winemakers: Bill Sneddon and Peter Orr.

ALLANDALE CABERNET SAUVIGNON ★★★

before 1987	Prior		
1987	7	Now	$49.00
1988	Not made		
1989	5	Prior	
1990	5	Prior	
1991	7	Now	$36.00
1992	6	Now	$28.00
1993	6	Now	$26.00
1994	6	2000	$24.00
1995	Not made		
1996	7	2002	$24.00

ALLANDALE CHARDONNAY ★★★★

before 1991	Prior		
1991	7	Now	$34.00
1992	5	Now	$22.00
1993	6	Now	$25.00
1994	6	Now	$23.00
1995	6	Now	$21.00
1996	7	2000	$23.00
1997	6	2001	$18.50

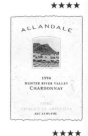

ALLANDALE MATTHEW SHIRAZ ★★★★

before 1987	Prior		
1987	6	Now	$39.00
1988	5	Prior	
1989	Not made		
1990	5	Now	$25.00
1991	7	Now	$33.00
1992	Not made		
1993	6	Now	$24.00
1994	6	2000	$22.00
1995	7	2002	$24.00
1996	7	2002	$22.00

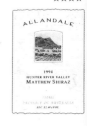

All Saints Estate is the label resulting from the amalgamation of St Leonards, whose white wines have always been remarkable achievements for the area, with Wahgunyah's (North East Victoria) oldest winery. St Leonards is listed seperately. Winemaker: Peter Brown.

ALL SAINTS ESTATE CABERNET SAUVIGNON

★★★★

before 1988		Prior	
1988	5	Now	$25.00
1989	Not made		
1990	6	Prior	
1991	6	Now	$24.00
1992	7	2000	$26.00
1993	6	2000	$20.00
1994	6	2001	$19.00
1995	5	2000	$14.50
1996	7	2003	$19.00

ALL SAINTS ESTATE CHARDONNAY

★★★

before 1992		Prior	
1992	5	Now	$19.50
1993	Not made		
1994	7	Now	$23.00
1995	6	2000	$18.50
1996	5	Now	$14.00
1997	5	Now	$13.00

ALL SAINTS ESTATE CHENIN BLANC

★★★

before 1992		Prior	
1992	6	Now	$19.50
1993	7	Now	$21.00
1994	6	Now	$17.00
1995	6	Now	$15.50
1996	6	2000	$14.50
1996	6	2001	$13.50
1997	6	2002	$12.50

ALL SAINTS ESTATE
LATE HARVEST SEMILLON (375ml)

★★★★

1993	7	2001	$24.00
1994	6	2002	$19.50
1995	5	2002	$15.00
1996	6	2003	$16.50
1997	6	2003	$15.50

ALL SAINTS MARSANNE ★★★

1992	5	Now	$21.00
1993	Not made		
1994	5	Now	$18.50
1995	5	2000	$17.00
1996	5	2001	$16.00
1997	6	2002	$17.50

ALL SAINTS MERLOT ★★★★

1994	4	Prior	
1995	6	2001	$19.00
1996	7	2003	$21.00

ALL SAINTS ESTATE SHIRAZ

★★★★

before 1990		Prior	
1990	6	Now	$26.00
1991	5	Now	$20.00
1992	7	2000	$26.00
1993	5	2000	$17.00
1994	6	2001	$19.00
1995	Not made		
1996	7	2003	$19.00

Amberley Estate is an impressive new Margaret River producer whose surprisingly large range includes some wines unusual for the area.
Winemakers: Eddie Price and Greg Tilbrook.

AMBERLEY ESTATE CABERNET/MERLOT ★★★★

before 1992		Prior	
1992	5	Now	$24.00
1993	6	Now	$27.00
1994	6	Now	$25.00
1995	6	2001	$23.00
1996	6	2003	$21.00

AMBERLEY ESTATE CHARDONNAY ★★★★

before 1993		Prior	
1993	6	Now	$33.00
1994	6	Now	$31.00
1995	5	Now	$23.00
1996	5	2000	$22.00
1997	6	2002	$24.00

AMBERLEY ESTATE CHENIN BLANC ★★★

before 1995		Prior	
1995	6	Now	$15.00
1996	7	Now	$16.50
1997	6	Now	$13.00

AMBERLEY ESTATE SAUVIGNON BLANC ★★★

before 1994		Prior	
1994	6	Now	$24.00
1995	5	Now	$18.50
1996	6	Now	$20.00
1997	5	Now	$15.50

AMBERLEY ESTATE SEMILLON ★★★★

before 1993		Prior	
1993	6	Now	$28.00
1994	5	Now	$21.00
1995	6	2001	$24.00
1996	6	2003	$22.00
1997	6	2003	$20.00

AMBERLEY ESTATE SEMILLON/SAUVIGNON BLANC ★★★

before 1994		Prior	
1994	6	Now	$18.00
1995	7	Now	$19.50
1996	6	Now	$15.50
1997	6	Now	$14.00

AMBERLEY ESTATE SHIRAZ ★★★★

1994	4	Now	$28.00
1995	7	2001	$46.00
1996	6	2003	$37.00

Andrew Garrett Wines are McLaren Vale makers now owned by Mildara Blass. Winemaker: Phillip Reschke.

ANDREW GARRETT CABERNET/MERLOT ★★★★

1989	7	Prior	
1990	7	Now	$30.00
1991	6	Now	$24.00
1992	5	Now	$18.50
1993	6	2000	$20.00
1994	5	2001	$16.00
1995	5	2001	$14.50
1996	6	2002	$16.50
1997	6	2002	$15.00

ANDREW GARRETT CHARDONNAY ★★★

before 1991		Prior	
1991	7	Now	$29.00
1992	4	Now	$15.50
1993	5	Now	$18.00
1994	5	Now	$16.50
1995	6	Now	$18.50
1996	6	Now	$17.00
1997	6	2000	$16.00
1998	6	2001	$14.50

ANDREW GARRETT SHIRAZ ★★★

1991	7	2000	$27.00
1992	5	Now	$17.50
1993	7	2000	$23.00
1994	6	2000	$18.00

1995	5	Now	$14.00
1996	7	2001	$18.00
1997	6	2002	$14.50

Angoves is a large, family owned Riverland company which produces some of our finest brandies as well as a range of graceful and reliable table wines.
Winemaker: Garry Wall.

ANGOVES CLASSIC RESERVE CABERNET SAUVIGNON ★★

before 1994	Prior		
1994	6	Now	$16.00
1995	5	Prior	
1996	5	Now	$11.50
1997	6	Now	$13.00

ANGOVES CLASSIC RESERVE CHARDONNAY ★★

before 1995	Prior		
1995	5	Now	$11.00
1996	6	Now	$12.50
1997	5	Now	$9.75
1998	6	Now	$10.50

ANGOVES CLASSIC RESERVE SHIRAZ ★★

before 1994	Prior		
1994	5	Now	$13.00
1995	6	Now	$14.50
1996	6	Now	$13.50
1997	6	Now	$12.50

ANGOVES MONDIALE RED ★★★

1995	5	Now	$14.00
1996	6	Now	$16.00
1997	6	2000	$14.50

ANGOVES SARNIA FARM CABERNET SAUVIGNON ★★★

1993	7	Now	$27.00
1994	6	Now	$21.00
1995	5	Now	$16.50
1996	6	Now	$18.50
1997	7	2002	$20.00

ANGOVES SARNIA FARM CHARDONNAY ★★★★

1993	6	Now	$26.00
1994	5	Now	$20.00
1995	4	Now	$15.00

1996	5	Now	$17.00
1997	6	Now	$19.00
1998	6	Now	$18.00

Annie's Lane is a Clare Valley vineyard owned by Mildara Blass. The fruit is vinified at the old Quelltaler winery, producing most agreeable and reasonably priced wines. Winemaker: David O'Leary

ANNIE'S LANE CABERNET/MERLOT ★★★

1995	5	2000	$13.50
1996	7	2001	$17.50
1997	6	2001	$14.00

ANNIE'S LANE CHARDONNAY ★★★

1996	5	Now	$12.00
1997	6	2000	$13.50
1998	6	2001	$12.50

ANNIE'S LANE RIESLING ★★★

1996	6	2000	$12.50
1997	7	2001	$13.50
1998	7	2002	$12.50

ANNIE'S LANE SEMILLON ★★★

1996	5	2000	$11.50
1997	6	2001	$12.50
1998	7	2002	$14.00

ANNIE'S LANE SHIRAZ ★★★

1995	5	2001	$13.50
1996	7	2002	$17.50
1997	6	2002	$14.00

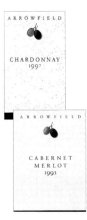

Arrowfield's 100 hectare vineyard is a substantial supplier to the Sydney wine market. Much of the fruit is from Cowra as well as from the home vineyards in the Upper Hunter. Winemaker: Don Buchanan.

ARROWFIELD CHARDONNAY ★★

before 1996		Prior	
1996	5	Now	$12.50
1997	6	Now	$14.00

ARROWFIELD CABERNET/MERLOT ★★

before 1995		Prior	
1995	6	Now	$15.00
1996	6	Now	$14.00
1997	6	2000	$13.00

ARROWFIELD COWRA CHARDONNAY ★★★

1996	5	Now	$14.50
1997	7	Now	$18.50
1998	6	Now	$15.00

ARROWFIELD COWRA MERLOT ★★★

1996	5	Now	$15.00
1997	6	Now	$17.00
1998	6	Now	$15.50

ARROWFIELD HUNTER VALLEY CHARDONNAY ★★★

1994	6	Now	$23.00
1995	6	Now	$21.00
1996	7	Now	$23.00
1997	5	Now	$15.00
1998	6	2000	$17.00

ARROWFIELD HUNTER VALLEY SEMILLON ★★★

1994	5	Now	$17.50
1995	7	Now	$23.00
1996	6	Now	$18.00
1997	6	Now	$17.00

ARROWFIELD SHOW RESERVE CABERNET SAUVIGNON ★★★

before 1991		Prior	
1991	5	Now	$34.00
1992	4	Prior	
1993	4	Now	$23.00
1994	4	Prior	
1995	6	2000	$30.00
1996	5	Now	$23.00
1997	6	Now	$25.00

ARROWFIELD SHOW RESERVE CHARDONNAY ★★★

before 1994		Prior	
1994	5	Now	$21.00
1995	6	Now	$23.00
1996	7	Now	$25.00
1997	7	2000	$23.00

ARROWFIELD SHOW RESERVE SHIRAZ ★★★

before 1993		Prior	
1993	6	Now	$29.00
1994	5	Prior	
1995	Not made		
1996	6	2000	$23.00
1997	Not made		

Ashton Hills is a 3.5 hectare vineyard in the Piccadilly region of the Adelaide Hills. The wines are very fine indeed. Winemaker: Stephen George.

ASHTON HILLS OBLIQUA (CABERNET/MERLOT) ★★★★

1988	5	Now	$47.00
1989	5	Now	$43.00
1990	6	Now	$48.00

1991	6	Now	$45.00
1992	6	Now	$41.00
1993	Not made		
1994	7	Now	$41.00
1995	Not made		
1996	6	Now	$30.00

ASHTON HILLS CHARDONNAY ★★★★

1988	5	Now	$47.00
1989	6	Now	$52.00
1990	6	Now	$48.00
1991	7	Now	$52.00
1992	5	Now	$34.00
1993	6	Now	$38.00
1994	Not made		
1995	6	Now	$33.00
1996	6	Now	$30.00

ASHTON HILLS PINOT NOIR ★★★★★

before 1994		Prior	
1994	6	Now	$48.00
1995	6	Now	$44.00
1996	6	Now	$41.00
1997	7	2000	$44.00

ASHTON HILLS RIESLING ★★★★

1987	5	Now	$41.00
1988	6	Now	$45.00
1989	6	Now	$42.00
1990	7	Now	$45.00
1991	7	Now	$42.00
1992	5	Now	$27.00
1993	6	Now	$31.00
1994	6	Now	$28.00
1995	6	Now	$26.00
1996	7	Now	$28.00
1997	7	Now	$26.00
1998	7	Now	$24.00

ASHTON HILLS SALMON BRUT

★★★★★

1992	6	Now	$36.00
1993	6	Now	$33.00
1994	6	Now	$31.00
1995	6	Now	$29.00

Ata Rangi is a small but high quality maker in New Zealand's Martinborough region producing some outstanding wines including the country's most sought-after Pinot Noir. Winemakers: Clive Paton and Oliver Masters.

ATA RANGI CELEBRE
(CABERNET/MERLOT/SYRAH)
★★★★

before 1991		Prior	
1991	7	Now	NZ$56.00
1992	4	Prior	

1993	5	Now	NZ$34.00
1994	5	Now	NZ$32.00
1995	6	Now	NZ$35.00
1996	6	Now	NZ$33.00
1997	7	2000	NZ$35.00
1998	7	2003	N/R

ATA RANGI CRAIGHALL CHARDONNAY   ★★★★

before 1994		Prior	
1994	6	Now	NZ$39.00
1995	6	Now	NZ$36.00
1996	7	Now	NZ$39.00
1997	7	2000	NZ$36.00
1998	7	2001	NZ$33.00

ATA RANGI PINOT NOIR   ★★★★★

before 1989		Prior	
1989	7	Now	NZ$88.00
1990	6	Prior	
1991	5	Prior	
1992	5	Now	NZ$50.00
1993	6	Now	NZ$56.00
1994	7	Now	NZ$60.00
1995	6	Now	NZ$48.00
1996	6	2000	NZ$44.00
1997	7	2000	NZ$48.00
1998	7	2002	NZ$44.00

Babich Wines are long established family operated New Zealand producers with a growing range of popular wines from grapes grown on many of the key viticultural regions. Winemaker: Neill Culley.

BABICH HAWKES BAY
SAUVIGNON BLANC   ★★★

before 1995		Prior	
1995	5	Now	NZ$15.00
1996	7	Now	NZ$19.50
1997	6	Now	NZ$15.50
1998	7	Now	NZ$16.50

BABICH IRONGATE CABERNET/MERLOT   ★★★★

1987	7	Now	NZ$52.00
1988	5	Prior	
1989	7	Now	NZ$44.00
1990	7	Now	NZ$41.00
1991	7	Now	NZ$38.00
1992	7	Now	NZ$35.00
1993	Not made		
1994	6	Now	NZ$26.00
1995	7	2000	NZ$28.00
1996	7	2000	NZ$26.00
1997	7	2002	N/R

BABICH IRONGATE CHARDONNAY ★★★★

1985	7	Now	NZ$82.00
1986	7	Now	NZ$76.00
1987	6	Prior	
1988	4	Prior	
1989	7	Now	NZ$60.00
1990	6	Now	NZ$48.00
1991	6	Now	NZ$45.00
1992	7	Now	NZ$48.00
1993	6	Now	NZ$38.00
1994	7	Now	NZ$41.00
1995	6	Now	NZ$33.00
1996	7	2000	NZ$35.00
1997	6	2000	NZ$28.00
1998	7	2002	NZ$30.00

BABICH MARA ESTATE CHARDONNAY ★★★

1992	6	Now	NZ$31.00
1993	5	Prior	
1994	7	Now	NZ$31.00
1995	6	Now	NZ$25.00
1996	6	Now	NZ$23.00
1997	6	Now	NZ$21.00
1998	6	2000	NZ$20.00

BABICH MARA ESTATE SYRAH
★★★

1994	6	Now	NZ$23.00
1995	7	Now	NZ$25.00
1996	6	Now	NZ$20.00
1997	6	2000	NZ$18.50
1998	7	2002	N/R

BABICH MARLBOROUGH
SAUVIGNON BLANC ★★★

before 1996		Prior	
1996	6	Now	NZ$14.50
1997	7	Now	NZ$15.50
1998	7	Now	NZ$14.50

Baileys, *now part of Mildara Blass, is the ultimate traditionalist Australian vineyard, situated at Taminick near Glenrowan, Victoria. It is renowned both for its long-living dry reds and its luscious fortified wines.*
Winemaker: Allen Hart.

BAILEYS 1920s BLOCK SHIRAZ
★★★★★

1991	6	2004	$36.00
1992	6	2007	$33.00
1993	6	2008	$31.00
1994	6	2008	$28.00
1995	7	2009	$31.00
1996	6	2008	$24.00
1997	7	2010	$26.00

BAILEYS CLASSIC SHIRAZ ★★★★

before 1973		Prior	
1973	6	Now	$105.00
1974	6	Now	$98.00
1975	7	Now	$105.00
1976	5	Now	$70.00
1977	7	Now	$90.00
1978	5	Now	$60.00
1979	7	Now	$78.00
1980	7	Now	$72.00
1981	5	Now	$48.00
1982	6	Now	$52.00
1983	5	Now	$41.00
1984	5	Now	$38.00
1985	7	Now	$49.00
1986	6	Now	$39.00
1987	6	Now	$36.00
1988	6	Now	$33.00
1989	5	Now	$26.00
1990	6	Now	$28.00
1991	5	Now	$22.00
1992	7	2002	$28.00
1993	6	Now	$22.00
1994	6	2000	$21.00
1995	7	2004	$22.00
1996	6	2004	$18.00
1997	7	2004	$19.50

BAILEYS VINTAGE PORT ★★★★

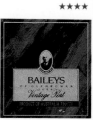

1972	3	Now	$33.00
1973	7	Now	$70.00
1974	7	Now	$66.00
1975	6	Now	$52.00
1976	5	Now	$40.00
1977	6	Now	$45.00
1978	7	2000	$48.00
1979	6	2000	$38.00
1980	7	2000	$41.00
1981	6	2000	$33.00
1982	5	2000	$25.00
1983	6	2010	$28.00
1984	7	2000	$30.00
1985	Not made		
1986	7	2000	$26.00
1987	6	2002	$20.00
1988	Not made		
1989	Not made		
1990	7	2010	$19.00

Baldivis Estate *is a small but growing operation in the South-West Coastal Plain of Western Australia. Winemaker: Marcus Ansems.*

BALDIVIS ESTATE CABERNET/MERLOT ★★★

1991	6	Prior	
1992	4	Now	$27.00
1993	5	2000	$31.00
1994	5	Now	$29.00
1995	6	2000	$32.00
1996	4	2001	$20.00

BALDIVIS ESTATE CHARDONNAY ★★★★

1992	6	Now	$40.00
1993	5	Now	$30.00
1994	5	Now	$28.00
1995	5	Now	$26.00
1996	6	Now	$29.00
1997	6	2000	$27.00

BALDIVIS ESTATE SAUVIGNON BLANC/SEMILLON ★★★

1992	5	Now	$25.00
1993	6	Now	$28.00
1994	5	Now	$21.00
1995	5	Now	$20.00
1996	4	Now	$15.00
1997	6	2000	$20.00

Balgownie Estate *is a once remarkable model vineyard near Bendigo, now owned by the Mildara Blass empire. Winemaker: Lindsay Ross.*

BALGOWNIE ESTATE CABERNET SAUVIGNON ★★★★

before 1976		Prior	
1976	7	Now	$125.00
1977	4	Prior	
1978	5	Now	$78.00
1979	3	Prior	
1980	7	Now	$94.00
1981	4	Now	$50.00
1982	5	Now	$58.00
1983	3	Prior	
1984	4	Now	$39.00
1985	6	Now	$54.00
1986	7	Now	$58.00
1987	6	Now	$47.00
1988	7	Now	$50.00
1989	6	Now	$40.00
1990	7	2000	$44.00
1991	Not made		
1992	7	2002	$37.00
1993	7	2003	$34.00
1994	6	2004	$27.00

13

1995	6	2005	$25.00
1996	6	2007	$23.00
1997	7	2008	$25.00

BALGOWNIE ESTATE SHIRAZ ★★★★

before 1980		Prior	
1980	5	Now	$66.00
1981	4	Now	$50.00
1982	4	Now	$46.00
1983	Not made		
1984	4	Now	$39.00
1985	5	Now	$46.00
1986	6	Now	$50.00
1987	6	Now	$47.00
1988	6	Now	$43.00
1989	7	Now	$47.00
1990	6	2000	$37.00
1991	Not made		
1992	Not made		
1993	6	2001	$29.00
1994	7	2002	$32.00
1995	6	2004	$25.00
1996	7	2006	$27.00
1997	7	2007	$25.00

Ballandean Estate *(formerly Sundown Valley Vineyards) is a well-established maker in Queensland's Granite Belt. Winemakers: Angelo Puglisi and Mark Ravenscroft.*

BALLANDEAN ESTATE SEMILLON/ SAUVIGNON BLANC ★★★

before 1997		Prior	
1997	6	Now	$13.50
1998	6	2000	$12.50

BALLANDEAN ESTATE SHIRAZ ★★★★

1989	7	Now	$41.00
1990	6	Prior	
1991	Not made		
1992	6	Now	$28.00
1993	5	Prior	
1994	6	Prior	
1995	7	2000	$26.00
1996	6	Now	$20.00
1997	7	2003	$22.00

BALLANDEAN ESTATE SYLVANER LATE HARVEST (375ml) ★★★★

1989	7	Now	$17.50
1990	6	Prior	
1991	7	2000	$15.00
1992	4	Prior	
1993	7	2000	$12.50
1994	6	2000	$10.00
Not made since 1994			

Balnaves of Coonawarra became winemakers rather than grapegrowers in 1990 although the vineyard was established in 1975. Winemaker: Peter Bissell.

BALNAVES CABERNET/MERLOT ★★★★

1990	7	2000	$44.00
1991	6	Now	$35.00
1992	Not made		
1993	4	Now	$20.00
1994	5	Now	$23.00
1995	Not made		
1996	6	2000	$24.00
1997	5	2000	N/R
1998	7	2002	N/R

BALNAVES CABERNET SAUVIGNON ★★★★

1990	7	2000	$52.00
1991	7	2000	$49.00
1992	Not made		
1993	4	Now	$24.00
1994	5	Now	$27.00
1995	5	Now	$25.00
1996	6	2002	$28.00
1997	6	2002	N/R
1998	7	2006	N/R

BALNAVES CHARDONNAY

before 1993	Prior		★★★
1993	4	Now	$21.00
1994	5	Now	$25.00
1995	5	Now	$23.00
1996	5	Now	$21.00
1997	6	Now	$23.00
1998	6	2001	$22.00

Bannockburn is a purist Geelong area producer with a low-yielding vineyard whose fine fruit is annually crafted into admirable wines. Winemaker: Gary Farr.

BANNOCKBURN CABERNET ★★★★
SAUVIGNON/MERLOT

before 1984	Prior		
1984	5	Now	$64.00
1985	5	Now	$60.00
1986	5	Now	$56.00
1987	6	Now	$62.00
1988	6	Now	$56.00
1989	4	Now	$35.00
1990	5	Now	$41.00
1991	5	2000	$38.00

15

1992	5	2001	$35.00
1993	5	2002	$32.00
1994	6	2003	$36.00
1995	7	2005	$39.00

BANNOCKBURN CHARDONNAY ★★★★★

before 1986	Prior	
1986	5	Now	$86.00
1987	5	Now	$78.00
1988	6	Now	$88.00
1989	6	Now	$82.00
1990	5	Now	$62.00
1991	5	Now	$58.00
1992	7	Now	$76.00
1993	7	Now	$70.00
1994	7	2000	$64.00
1995	7	2001	$60.00
1996	6	2000	$47.00
1997	7	2005	$50.00

BANNOCKBURN PINOT NOIR ★★★★★

before 1986	Prior	
1986	5	Now	$86.00
1987	5	2000	$80.00
1988	6	Now	$88.00
1989	6	Now	$82.00
1990	6	Now	$76.00
1991	5	Now	$58.00
1992	7	Now	$76.00
1993	6	2000	$60.00
1994	6	2001	$56.00
1995	7	2002	$60.00
1996	6	2003	$48.00
1997	7	2005	$52.00

BANNOCKBURN SAUVIGNON BLANC ★★★★

before 1990	Prior	
1990	6	Now	$38.00
1991	6	Now	$35.00
1992	6	Now	$33.00
1993	5	Now	$25.00
1994	5	Now	$23.00
1995	6	Now	$26.00
1996	6	Now	$24.00
1997	7	Now	$26.00

BANNOCKBURN SHIRAZ ★★★★

before 1986	Prior	
1986	5	Now	$62.00
1987	6	Now	$68.00

1988	7	2000	$74.00
1989	7	Now	$68.00
1990	6	Now	$54.00
1991	6	Now	$50.00
1992	7	2000	$54.00
1993	7	2001	$50.00
1994	7	2002	$47.00
1995	7	2003	$43.00
1996	6	2004	$34.00
1997	7	2006	$37.00

Barossa Valley Estate *is an independent co-operative of Barossa Valley grapegrowers, with some distribution links with BRL Hardy. Winemaker: Natasha Mooney.*

BAROSSA VALLEY ESTATE E&E BLACK PEPPER SHIRAZ ★★★★★

1988	7	2000	$86.00
1989	6	2000	$68.00
1990	6	2010	$62.00
1991	7	2010	$68.00
1992	7	2015	$62.00
1993	5	2005	$41.00
1994	6	2015	$46.00
1995	6	2015	$43.00

BAROSSA VALLEY ESTATE E&E SPARKLING SHIRAZ ★★★★

1990	6	Now	$47.00
1991	7	Now	$50.00
1992	7	Now	$47.00
1993	5	Now	$31.00
1994	7	Now	$40.00
1995	6	2000	$32.00

BAROSSA VALLEY ESTATE EBENEZER CABERNET/ MALBEC/MERLOT ★★★

1989	7	Now	$45.00
1990	Not made		
1991	6	Now	$33.00
1992	7	2000	$35.00
1993	5	Now	$23.00
1994	6	2000	$26.00
1995	6	2000	$24.00

BAROSSA VALLEY ESTATE EBENEZER CHARDONNAY ★★★

1992	7	Now	$37.00
1993	6	Now	$29.00
1994	7	Now	$32.00

1995	7	Now	$29.00
1996	7	Now	$27.00
1997	7	Now	$25.00

BAROSSA VALLEY ESTATE EBENEZER SHIRAZ

★★★★

1991	7	Now	$36.00
1992	7	Now	$33.00
1993	6	Now	$26.00
1994	6	2004	$24.00
1995	7	2005	$26.00

BAROSSA VALLEY ESTATE MOCULTA CABERNET/MERLOT

★★★

before 1989		Prior	
1989	7	Now	$33.00
1990	6	Now	$26.00
1991	7	Now	$28.00
1992	6	Prior	
1993	6	Prior	
1994	5	Prior	
1995	6	Now	$17.50
1996	7	2000	$19.00
1997	6	Now	$15.00

BAROSSA VALLEY ESTATE MOCULTA CHARDONNAY ★★★

before 1993		Prior	
1993	6	Now	$24.00
1994	7	Now	$25.00
1995	7	Now	$24.00
1996	7	Now	$22.00
1997	7	Now	$20.00

BAROSSA VALLEY ESTATE MOCULTA SEMILLON/SAUVIGNON BLANC

★★

before 1995		Prior	
1995	5	Now	$12.50
1996	7	Now	-$16.00

BAROSSA VALLEY ESTATE MOCULTA SHIRAZ ★★

1985	7	Now	$46.00
1986	5	Now	$30.00
1987	6	Now	$34.00
1988	5	Now	$26.00
1989	6	Now	$29.00
1990	7	Now	$31.00
1991	7	Now	$29.00
1992	6	Now	$23.00
1993	6	Now	$21.00
1994	5	Now	$16.50
1995	6	Now	$18.00
1996	7	2000	$19.50
1997	6	Now	$15.50

Barry, Brian - see Jud's Hill

Barry, Jim - see Jim Barry Wines.

Barwang is the name of McWilliam's newest vineyard, in the Hilltops area of the Great Dividing Range near Young in NSW. Winemaker: Jim Brayne.

BARWANG CABERNET SAUVIGNON   ★★★★

1990	6	Now	$28.00
1991	6	Now	$25.00
1992	6	Now	$24.00
1993	6	2000	$22.00
1994	6	2004	$20.00
1995	5	2002	$15.50
1996	6	2006	$17.50
1997	6	2006	$16.00

BARWANG CHARDONNAY ★★★

1990	5	Now	$25.00
1991	5	Now	$23.00
1992	6	Now	$26.00
1993	5	Now	$20.00
1994	5	Now	$18.50
1995	5	Now	$17.00
1996	6	2000	$19.00
1997	6	2001	$17.50

BARWANG SHIRAZ   ★★★★

1990	6	Now	$28.00
1991	6	Now	$25.00
1992	6	2000	$24.00
1993	6	2000	$22.00
1994	6	2002	$20.00
1995	5	2000	$15.50
1996	6	2004	$17.50
1997	6	2004	$16.00

Basedows are long established Barossa makers whose wines over recent years are among the valley's best, in particular the Chardonnay and the heavily oaked Semillon. Winemaker: Craig Starsborough.

BASEDOW BAROSSA SHIRAZ   ★★★★

1970	7	Now	$100.00
1971	7	Now	$96.00
1972	6	Now	$76.00
1973		Prior	
1979	Not made		
1980	5	Now	$50.00
1981	6	Now	$56.00
1982	7	Prior	
1983	4	Prior	
1984	6	Now	$45.00
1985	5	Prior	

1986	6	Now	$38.00
1987	6	Now	$35.00
1988	6	Now	$33.00
1989	7	Now	$35.00
1990	7	Now	$33.00
1991	7	2003	$30.00
1992	5	Now	$20.00
1993	7	2003	$26.00
1994	7	2010	$24.00
1995	7	2010	$22.00

BASEDOW CHARDONNAY ★★★★

1984	5	Prior	
1985	7	2000	$47.00
1986	5	Now	$31.00
1987	7	2000	$40.00
1988	6	Prior	
1989	7	2003	$35.00
1990	6	Now	$27.00
1991	6	Now	$25.00
1992	6	Prior	
1993	7	2005	$25.00
1994	7	2010	$23.00
1995	7	2010	$22.00

BASEDOW WHITE BURGUNDY (SEMILLON) ★★★★

1985	7	2000	$36.00
1986	5	Now	$24.00
1987	7	Prior	
1988	7	2002	$29.00
1989	6	Now	$23.00
1990	6	Now	$21.00
1991	7	2005	$23.00
1992	6	Now	$18.00
1993	5	Now	$14.00
1994	5	Now	$13.00
1995	7	2010	$16.50
1996	7	2005	$15.50

Bass Phillip in Gippsland's Leongatha region produces a magnificent Pinot Noir. Winemaker: Phillip Jones.

BASS PHILLIP PINOT NOIR (PREMIUM) ★★★★★

1984	6	Now	$130.00
1985	5	Now	$100.00
1986	6	Now	$110.00
1987	6	Now	$100.00
1988	6	Now	$96.00
1989	7	Now	$100.00
1990	5	Now	$68.00

1991	7	Now	$88.00
1992	7	Now	$82.00
1993	6	Now	$64.00
1994	7	Now	$70.00
1995	7	2000	$64.00
1996	7	2002	$60.00

Best's at Great Western (Victoria) have produced consistently beguiling wines for many decades. Winemaker: Viv Thomson.

BEST'S GREAT WESTERN CABERNET SAUVIGNON ★★★★

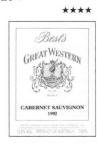

1987	4	Prior	
1988	7	2000	$52.00
1989	5	Prior	
1990	6	Now	$39.00
1991	7	2000	$42.00
1992	6	Now	$34.00
1993	6	Now	$31.00
1994	7	Now	$34.00
1995	6	2000	$27.00
1996	6	2006	$25.00

BEST'S GREAT WESTERN CHARDONNAY ★★★★

before 1984		Prior	
1984	7	Now	$80.00
1985	6	Now	$62.00
1986	6	Now	$58.00
1987	6	Now	$54.00
1988	6	Now	$50.00
1989	7	Now	$54.00
1990	6	Now	$43.00
1991	5	Now	$33.00
1992	5	Now	$30.00
1993	5	Now	$28.00
1994	5	Now	$26.00
1995	6	2000	$29.00
1996	7	2004	$31.00
1997	6	2004	$25.00

BEST'S GREAT WESTERN PINOT MEUNIER ★★★★

before 1987		Prior	
1987	6	Now	$56.00
1988	6	Now	$52.00
1989	5	Prior	
1990	6	Now	$45.00
1991	6	Now	$41.00
1992	6	Now	$38.00
1993	5	Now	$29.00

1994	7	2002	$38.00
1995	6	2004	$30.00
1996	6	2002	$28.00

BESTS GREAT WESTERN PINOT NOIR ★★★★

1991	5	Now	$30.00
1992	7	Now	$39.00
1993	5	Now	$26.00
1994	5	Now	$24.00
1995	6	2000	$26.00

BEST'S GREAT WESTERN RIESLING ★★★

before 1982		Prior	
1982	6	Now	$45.00
1983	5	Prior	
1984	5	Now	$32.00
1985	7	Now	$42.00
1986	5	Prior	
1987	6	Now	$30.00
1988	7	Now	$33.00
1989	4	Prior	
1990	7	Now	$28.00
1991	6	Now	$22.00
1992	6	Now	$21.00
1993	5	Prior	
1994	6	Now	$18.00
1995	7	2000	$19.00
1996	6	2001	$15.00
1997	6	2002	$14.00

BEST'S GREAT WESTERN SHIRAZ ★★★★★

1976	7	Now	$135.00
1977	6	Now	$105.00
1978	6	Now	$100.00
1979	5	Prior	
1980	6	Now	$86.00
1981	5	Now	$66.00
1982	5	Prior	
1983	5	Now	$56.00
1984	7	Now	$74.00
1985	6	Now	$58.00
1986	5	Now	$45.00
1987	7	2004	$58.00
1988	7	2008	$54.00
1989	5	2000	$36.00
1990	6	2004	$40.00
1991	6	2002	$37.00
1992	7	2006	$40.00
1993	6	2006	$31.00
1994	6	2008	$29.00
1995	6	2006	$27.00

***Bethany Wines** is a small family-run winery at Bethany in the Barossa Valley, where the owners' family have been grapegrowers since last century.*
Winemaker: Paul Bailey.

BETHANY CABERNET/MERLOT ★★★

1988	7	Now	$47.00
1989	7	Now	$44.00
1990	6	Now	$35.00
1991	7	Now	$37.00
1992	7	Now	$35.00
1993	6	Now	$27.00
1994	7	Now	$30.00
1995	6	Now	$23.00
1996	7	2006	$25.00
1997	5	2002	$17.00

BETHANY CHARDONNAY ★★★

before 1989		Prior	
1989	7	Now	$36.00
1990	7	Now	$33.00
1991	7	Now	$31.00
1992	7	Now	$29.00
1993	7	Now	$26.00
1994	6	Now	$21.00
1995	6	Now	$19.50
1996	7	Now	$21.00
1997	7	Now	$19.50
1998	6	2002	$15.50

BETHANY GRENACHE PRESSINGS ★★★

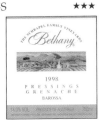

1991	7	Now	$29.00
1992	7	Now	$27.00
1993	6	Now	$21.00
1994	7	Now	$23.00
1995	6	Now	$18.50
1996	7	Now	$20.00
1997	6	2000	$15.50
1998	6	2003	$14.50

BETHANY RESERVE RIESLING ★★★

before 1991		Prior	
1991	6	Now	$21.00
1992	6	Now	$19.50
1993	7	Now	$21.00
1994	6	Now	$17.00
1994	7	Now	$18.00
1995	6	Now	$14.50
1996	7	Now	$15.50
1997	6	2000	$12.50
1998	7	2004	$13.50

BETHANY SELECT LATE HARVEST RIESLING (CORDON PRUNED)

★★★★

1985	5	Now	$35.00
1986	7	Now	$46.00
1987	5	Prior	
1988	5	Now	$28.00
1989	6	Now	$31.00
1990	6	Now	$29.00
1991	6	Now	$27.00
1992	6	Now	$25.00
1993	6	Now	$23.00
1994	6	Now	$21.00
1995	7	Now	$23.00
1996	7	Now	$21.00
1997	7	2002	$19.50
1998	6	2001	$15.50

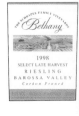

BETHANY SEMILLON

★★★★

1989	7	Now	$34.00
1990	6	Now	$27.00
1991	7	Now	$29.00
1992	6	Now	$23.00
1993	7	Now	$25.00
1994	6	Now	$20.00
1995	6	Now	$18.50
1996	5	Now	$14.50
1997	7	2002	$18.50
1998	7	2003	$17.50

BETHANY SHIRAZ

★★★★

1981	4	Prior	
1982	7	Now	$84.00
1983	5	Now	$56.00
1984	6	Now	$62.00
1985	3	Prior	
1986	6	Now	$52.00
1987	6	Now	$49.00
1988	7	Now	$52.00
1989	6	Now	$42.00
1990	6	Now	$39.00
1991	5	Now	$30.00
1992	7	Now	$39.00
1993	6	Now	$31.00
1994	7	Now	$33.00
1995	5	2000	$22.00
1996	6	2008	$24.00
1997	6	2005	$23.00

BETHANY "THE MANSE" ★★★

1994	5	Now	$15.00
1995	6	Now	$16.50
1996	6	Now	$15.50
1997	6	Now	$14.00
1998	5	Now	$11.00

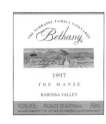

Bindi Winegrowers are new makers in the Gisborne area of the Macedon Ranges, specialising in impressive examples of the Burgundian varieties.
Winemakers: Stuart Anderson and Michael Dhillon.

BINDI CHARDONNAY ★★★★

1991	6	Now	$68.00
1992	4	Now	$42.00
1993	4	Now	$39.00
1994	6	2001	$54.00
1995	6	2001	$50.00
1996	4	2001	$31.00
1997	6	2003	$43.00
1998	6	2003	$40.00

BINDI PINOT NOIR ★★★★★

1992	4	Now	$39.00
1993	5	2000	$46.00
1994	6	2002	$50.00
1995	6	2002	$47.00
1996	6	2004	$43.00
1997	6	2005	$40.00
1998	6	2006	$37.00

Blackjack Wines in Central Victoria's Harcourt area are red wine specialists.
Winemakers: Ian McKenzie and Ken Pollock.

BLACKJACK CABERNET/MERLOT ★★★★★

1993	6	Now	$30.00
1994	7	2000	$33.00
1995	4	2000	$17.50
1996	6	2002	$24.00
1997	6	2002	$22.00

BLACKJACK SHIRAZ ★★★★

1993	5	Now	$25.00
1994	6	2000	$28.00
1995	6	2001	$26.00
1996	6	2001	$24.00
1997	6	2003	$22.00

Blass - see Wolf Blass.

Bleasdale's vineyard at Langhorne Creek in South Australia produces a large range of honest, dependable and inexpensive wines. Winemaker: Michael Potts.

BLEASDALE CABERNET SAUVIGNON ★★★

	before 1990	Prior	
1990	6	Now	$30.00
1991	5	Now	$23.00
1992	7	Now	$30.00
1993	6	Now	$24.00
1994	5	Now	$18.50
1995	5	Now	$17.00
1996	6	2000	$19.00
1997	6	2001	$17.50
1998	6	2002	$16.50

BLEASDALE MALBEC ★★

1990	6	Now	$27.00
1991	4	Prior	
1992	6	Now	$23.00
1993	Not made		
1994	6	Now	$19.50
1995	6	Now	$18.00
1996	5	Now	$14.00
1997	6	2000	$15.50
1998	7	2001	$17.00

BLEASDALE SHIRAZ ★★★

	before 1990	Prior	
1990	6	Now	$30.00
1991	5	Now	$23.00
1992	6	Now	$26.00
1993	6	Now	$24.00
1994	5	Now	$18.50
1995	5	Now	$17.00
1996	6	2000	$19.00
1997	7	2001	$20.00
1998	6	2002	$16.50

Blue Pyrenees (formerly Chateau Remy) is a French owned producer in the Avoca region of Victoria. Well marketed and promoted, the wines have a loyal and dedicated following. Winemaker: Kim Hart.

BLUE PYRENEES ESTATE CHARDONNAY ★★★★

1992	6	Prior	
1993	7	Now	$33.00
1994	6	Now	$26.00
1995	6	2000	$24.00
1996	6	2001	$22.00
1997	7	2002	$24.00

BLUE PYRENEES ESTATE RED (CAB.SAUV/MERLOT CAB.FRANC/SHIRAZ) ★★★★

before 1988		Prior	
1988	7	Now	$58.00
1989	5	Now	$39.00
1990	7	Now	$50.00
1991	6	Now	$40.00
1992	7	2000	$43.00
1993	6	2001	$34.00
1994	7	2004	$37.00
1995	7	2003	$34.00
1996	7	2006	$32.00

Botobolar is a Mudgee vineyard whose organically grown wines are powerful and individual.
Winemaker: Kevin Karstrom.

BOTOBOLAR CABERNET SAUVIGNON ★★★

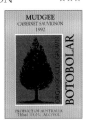

before 1982		Not made	
1982	7	Now	$60.00
1983	Not made		
1984	7	Now	$50.00
1985	7	Now	$47.00
1986	6	Now	$37.00
1987	7	Now	$40.00
1988	7	Now	$37.00
1989	Not made		
1990	5	Now	$23.00
1991	7	Now	$30.00
1992	6	Now	$23.00
1993	Not made		
1994	7	2000	$23.00
1995	Not made		
1996	Not made		
1997	7	2002	$18.50
1998	Not made		

BOTOBOLAR CHARDONNAY ★★

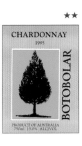

before 1988		Prior	
1988	7	Now	$40.00
1989	7	Now	$37.00
1990	7	Now	$34.00
1991	7	Now	$31.00
1992	6	Now	$25.00
1993	7	Now	$27.00
1994	5	Now	$18.00
1995	4	Now	$13.00
1996	5	Now	$15.00
1997	7	Now	$20.00
1998	7	2001	N/R

BOTOBOLAR MARSANNE ★★★

1995	5	Now	$19.50
1996	5	Now	$18.00
1997	6	2000	$20.00
1998	Not made		

BOTOBOLAR SHIRAZ ★★★

before 1985	Prior		
1985	6	Now	$43.00
1986	5	Now	$33.00
1987	5	Now	$30.00
1988	5	Now	$28.00
1989	7	Now	$37.00
1990	6	Now	$29.00
1991	6	Now	$27.00
1992	7	Now	$29.00
1993	Not made		
1994	6	Now	$21.00
1995	5	Now	$16.50
1996	6	2000	$18.50

Bowen Estate *is one of Coonawarra's smaller vineyards but is making some of the area's best wines.*
Winemaker: Doug Bowen.

BOWEN ESTATE CABERNET SAUVIGNON ★★★★

before 1986	Prior		
1986	6	Now	$52.00
1987	6	Now	$49.00
1988	6	Now	$45.00
1989	6	Now	$42.00
1990	7	Now	$45.00
1991	7	2000	$42.00
1992	7	2001	$39.00
1993	7	2002	$36.00
1994	7	2003	$33.00
1995	6	2002	$26.00
1996	7	2009	$28.00

BOWEN ESTATE CABERNET SAUVIGNON/MERLOT/CABERNET FRANC ★★★★

1990	7	Now	$40.00
1991	6	Now	$32.00
1992	6	2000	$29.00
1993	7	2001	$32.00
1994	7	2003	$29.00
1995	6	2002	$23.00
1996	7	2004	$25.00

BOWEN ESTATE CHARDONNAY ★★★★

before 1993		Prior	
1993	6	Now	$29.00
1994	6	Now	$27.00
1995	5	Now	$21.00
1996	6	Now	$23.00
1997	6	2000	$21.00

Brajkovich is the second label of New Zealand's exemplary Kumeu River Vineyard. Unlike the latter, some of the grapes are sourced from other regions.
Winemaker: Michael Brajkovich MW.

BRAJKOVICH CHARDONNAY ★★★

before 1993		Prior	
1993	7	Now	NZ$22.00
1994	7	Now	NZ$21.00
1995	6	Now	NZ$16.50
1996	7	Now	NZ$18.00

BRAJKOVICH CABERNET FRANC ★★★

before 1993		Prior	
1993	6	Now	NZ$18.00
1994	7	Now	NZ$19.50
1995	5	Now	NZ$12.50
1996	7	Now	NZ$16.50

BRAJKOVICH MERLOT ★★★

before 1991		Prior	
1991	7	Now	NZ$24.00
1992	5	Now	NZ$16.00
1993	6	Now	NZ$17.50
1994	6	Now	NZ$16.50
1995	7	Now	NZ$17.50
1996	7	Now	NZ$16.50

BRAJKOVICH SAUVIGNON ★★★

before 1993		Prior	
1993	7	Now	NZ$18.00
1994	6	Now	NZ$14.00
1995	6	Now	NZ$13.00
1996	Not made		

Brands Laira vineyard has been producing respected and sought-after wines at Coonawarra since 1965. They are part of the McWilliams organisation.
Winemakers: Jim Brayne and Jim Brand.

BRANDS LAIRA CABERNET SAUVIGNON ★★★

1970	5	Now	$110.00
1971	6	Now	$120.00
1972	5	Now	$96.00
1973	5	Now	$88.00

1974	7	Now	$110.00
1975	6	Now	$90.00
1976	6	Now	$84.00
1977	6	Now	$78.00
1978	6	Now	$72.00
1979	7	Now	$78.00
1980	5	Now	$52.00
1981	7	Now	$66.00
1982	7	Now	$62.00
1983	5	Now	$41.00
1984	7	Now	$52.00
1985	6	Now	$42.00
1986	6	Now	$39.00
1987	7	Now	$42.00
1988	5	Now	$28.00
1989	Not made		
1990	6	2000	$28.00
1991	5	2000	$22.00
1992	6	2002	$24.00
1993	5	2003	$19.00
1994	6	2003	$21.00
1995	6	2004	$19.50
1996	6	2006	$18.00
1997	6	2006	N/R

BRANDS LAIRA CABERNET/MERLOT ★★★★

1984	6	Now	$47.00
1985	6	Now	$43.00
1986	6	Now	$40.00
1987	7	Now	$43.00
1988	5	Now	$28.00
1989	Not made		
1990	6	Now	$29.00
1991	5	Now	$22.00
1992	6	2000	$25.00
1993	5	2002	$19.50
1994	6	2004	$21.00
1995	5	2005	$16.50
1996	6	2006	$18.50
1997	6	2006	N/R

BRANDS LAIRA CHARDONNAY ★★★

1986	6	Now	$40.00
1987	5	Now	$31.00
1988	5	Now	$29.00
1989	5	Now	$26.00
1990	6	Now	$29.00
1991	5	Now	$23.00
1992	6	Now	$25.00

1993	5	Now	$19.50
1994	6	Now	$21.00
1995	5	Now	$16.50
1996	6	2000	$18.50
1997	6	2001	$17.00

BRANDS LAIRA SHIRAZ ★★★★

1974	6	Now	$82.00
1975	5	Now	$62.00
1976	6	Now	$70.00
1977	7	Now	$76.00
1978	7	Now	$70.00
1979	6	Now	$56.00
1980	5	Now	$43.00
1981	6	Now	$48.00
1982	7	Now	$52.00
1983	5	Now	$34.00
1984	7	Now	$44.00
1985	5	Now	$29.00
1986	6	Now	$32.00
1987	5	Now	$25.00
1988	5	Now	$23.00
1989	Not made		
1990	6	2000	$24.00
1991	6	2000	$22.00
1992	6	2002	$20.00
1993	5	2001	$15.50
1994	6	2003	$17.50
1995	6	2005	$16.00
1996	7	2006	$17.00
1997	6	2007	N/R

Briar Ridge *are Mount View (Hunter Valley) makers whose vineyard was once known as the Robson Vineyard. Their Semillon is particularly worthy of respectful attention. Winemakers: Neil McGuigan and Karl Stockhausen.*

BRIAR RIDGE CHARDONNAY ★★★

before 1993	Prior		
1993	5	Now	$22.00
1994	6	Now	$24.00
1995	6	Now	$22.00
1996	6	Now	$20.00
1997	5	2000	$16.00
1998	6	2001	$18.00

BRIAR RIDGE STOCKHAUSEN
HERMITAGE ★★★★

1991	5	Prior	
1992	5	Now	$28.00
1993	6	Now	$31.00
1994	6	Now	$29.00

1995	7	2003	$31.00
1996	7	2001	$29.00
1997	7	2001	$27.00

BRIAR RIDGE STOCKHAUSEN SEMILLON ★★★★

1992	5	Now	$27.00
1993	6	Now	$30.00
1994	6	Now	$27.00
1995	6	Now	$25.00
1996	7	2001	$27.00
1997	6	2003	$22.00
1998	7	2004	$23.00

Bridgewater Mill is the second label of Petaluma, using fruit from Clare, Coonawarra and McLaren Vale. Winemaker: Brian Croser.

BRIDGEWATER MILL CHARDONNAY ★★★★

before 1990		Prior	
1990	5	Now	$29.00
1991	4	Now	$21.00
1992	6	Now	$29.00
1993	5	Now	$23.00
1994	4	Now	$17.00
1995	5	Now	$19.50
1996	5	Now	$18.00
1997	6	2000	$20.00

BRIDGEWATER MILL MILLSTONE SHIRAZ ★★★★

1989	4	Now	$29.00
1990	6	Now	$41.00
1991	5	Now	$31.00
1992	6	2000	$35.00
1993	4	Now	$21.00
1994	5	Now	$25.00
1995	5	2000	$23.00
1996	5	2001	$21.00
1997	5	2005	$20.00

BRIDGEWATER MILL SAUVIGNON BLANC ★★★★

before 1994		Prior	
1994	7	Now	$26.00
1995	5	Now	$17.00
1996	5	Now	$16.00
1997	6	Now	$17.50
1998	6	Now	$16.50

Brokenwood is a small Pokolbin vineyard producing wines
of very fine quality and exemplary style.
Winemakers: Iain Riggs and Dan Dineen.

BROKENWOOD CABERNET SAUVIGNON   ★★★★

before 1986		Prior	
1986	6	Now	$64.00
1987	4	Now	$39.00
1988	4	Now	$37.00
1989	5	Now	$42.00
1990	5	Now	$39.00
1991	6	Now	$44.00
1992	4	Now	$27.00
1993	6	Now	$37.00
1994	5	Now	$29.00
1995	4	Now	$21.00
1996	6	Now	$30.00

BROKENWOOD CHARDONNAY   ★★★★

before 1987		Prior	
1987	6	Now	$47.00
1988	5	Now	$36.00
1989	5	Now	$33.00
1990	4	Now	$25.00
1991	3	Now	$17.00
1992	6	Now	$32.00
1993	5	Now	$24.00
1994	5	Now	$23.00
1995	6	Now	$25.00
1996	6	Now	$23.00
1997	6	Now	$22.00

BROKENWOOD HERMITAGE (GRAVEYARD VINEYARD)   ★★★★★

before 1983		Prior	
1983	6	Now	$145.00
1984	3	Now	$68.00
1985	5	Now	$105.00
1986	7	Now	$135.00
1987	4	Now	$72.00
1988	5	Now	$84.00
1989	6	Now	$94.00
1990	5	Now	$72.00
1991	7	Now	$94.00
1992	Not made		
1993	4	Now	$46.00
1994	7	2002	$74.00
1995	5	2002	$49.00
1996	7	2004	$64.00

BROKENWOOD SEMILLON ★★★★

1983	6	Now	$50.00
1984	4	Prior	
1985	7	Now	$50.00
1986	6	Now	$40.00
1987	5	Now	$31.00
1988	4	Now	$23.00
1989	4	Now	$21.00
1990	5	Now	$24.00
1991	7	Now	$32.00
1992	5	Now	$21.00
1993	6	Now	$23.00
1994	6	Now	$21.00
1995	6	2000	$20.00
1996	7	2001	$21.00
1997	5	2000	$14.00

Brookland Valley is a Margaret River maker in an idyllic setting (and a very fine winery restaurant).
Winemaker: Malcolm.Jones.

BROOKLAND VALLEY CHARDONNAY ★★★★★

1990	7	Now	$50.00
1991	6	Now	$40.00
1992	7	Now	$44.00
1993	6	Now	$35.00
1994	7	Now	$37.00
1995	7	2000	$35.00
1996	7	2000	$32.00
1997	7	2002	$30.00

BROOKLAND VALLEY
CABERNET/MERLOT ★★★★

1990	6	Now	$38.00
1991	7	Now	$41.00
1992	7	Now	$38.00
1993	7	2000	$36.00
1994	7	2000	$33.00
1995	7	2002	$30.00
1996	7	2000	$28.00

BROOKLAND VALLEY
MERLOT ★★★★

1995	7	Now	$32.00
1996	7	Now	$30.00
1997	7	2001	$28.00

Brown Brothers is a medium size family owned and operated company with substantial holdings in North East Victoria and a substantial reputation, both here and overseas. Winemaker: Terry Barnett.

BROWN BROS CHARDONNAY ★★★

before 1992		Prior	
1992	6	Now	$27.00
1993	5	Now	$21.00
1994	6	Now	$23.00
1995	5	Now	$18.00
1996	5	Now	$16.50
1997	6	2001	$18.50

BROWN BROS NOBLE RIESLING ★★★★★

before 1984		Prior	
1984	5	Now	$82.00
1985	6	Now	$92.00
1986	Not made		
1987	6	Now	$78.00
1988	5	Prior	
1989	Not made		
1990	Not made		
1991	Not made		
1992	6	2001	$54.00
1993	5	2000	$41.00
1994	7	2004	$54.00
1995	Not made		
1996	7	2006	$46.00

BROWN BROS MILAWA RIESLING ★★★

before 1990		Prior	
1990	6	Now	$25.00
1991	6	Prior	
1992	6	Now	$22.00
1993	5	Now	$17.00
1994	6	2000	$19.00
1995	5	Now	$14.50
1996	6	2001	$16.00
1997	6	2002	$15.00

BROWN BROS SHIRAZ ★★★

before 1990		Prior	
1990	6	Now	$32.00
1991	5	Now	$25.00
1992	5	Now	$23.00
1993	5	2000	$21.00
1994	6	2002	$23.00
1995	4	Now	$14.50
1996	6	2003	$20.00

Bullers Calliope Wines are long established Rutherglen producers whose range of wines includes some magnificent fortifieds. Winemakers: Andrew and Richard Buller.

BULLERS BEVERFORD CHARDONNAY ★★★

1992	5	Prior	
1993	Not made		
1994	4	Now	$13.50
1995	4	Now	$12.50
1996	5	2000	$14.50
1997	6	2001	$16.00

BULLERS BEVERFORD
WOODED SEMILLON ★★★

before 1994	Prior	
1994	6	Now	$14.50
1995	6	Now	$13.50
1996	6	Now	$12.50

BULLERS CALLIOPE SHIRAZ ★★★★

1990	5	Prior	
1991	7	2000	$41.00
1992	5	Now	$27.00
1993	Not made		
1994	6	2003	$27.00
1995	6	2003	$25.00

BULLERS SHIRAZ/MONDEUSE ★★★

1991	7	2000	$30.00
1992	5	Now	$20.00
1993	4	Prior	
1994	5	2000	$17.00
1995	5	2001	$16.00
1996	6	2005	$18.00

Buring - see Leo Buring.

Campbells are Rutherglen producers who have moved with the times and make some fine white wines as well as the traditionally expected North East Victorian fortifieds. Winemaker: Colin Campbell.

CAMPBELLS BOBBIE BURNS
SHIRAZ ★★★★

before 1985	Prior	
1985	6	Now	$52.00
1986	7	Now	$56.00
1987	5	Prior	
1988	5	Now	$35.00
1989	4	Prior	
1990	5	Now	$30.00

1991	5	Now	$28.00
1992	7	2000	$36.00
1993	7	2002	$33.00
1994	6	2001	$26.00
1995	6	2002	$24.00
1996	7	2003	$26.00
1997	7	2005	$24.00

CAMPBELLS CHARDONNAY ★★★

before 1991	Prior	
1991	5	Now	$21.00
1992	6	Now	$23.00
1993	6	Now	$22.00
1994	5	Now	$17.00
1995	5	Now	$15.50
1996	6	Now	$17.00
1997	5	2000	$13.50
1998	5	2000	$12.50

CAMPBELLS PEDRO XIMENEZ ★★★★

before 1988	Prior	
1988	5	Now	$30.00
1989	5	Now	$28.00
1990	5	Now	$25.00
1991	5	Now	$24.00
1992	7	Now	$31.00
1993	5	2001	$20.00

CAMPBELLS RIESLING ★★★

before 1990	Prior	
1990	5	Now	$24.00
1991	5	Now	$22.00
1992	7	Now	$28.00
1993	5	Now	$19.00
1994	6	Now	$21.00
1995	7	Now	$23.00
1996	No data		
1997	5	2000	$14.00
1998	6	2005	$15.50

CAMPBELLS RUTHERGLEN SHIRAZ ★★★★

1986	6	Now	$36.00
1987	5	Prior	
1988	5	Prior	
1989	Not made		
1990	7	2000	$31.00
1991	6	2001	$24.00
1992	7	2002	$26.00
1993	6	2003	$21.00
1994	7	2004	$22.00

CAMPBELLS "THE BARKLY" DURIF

★★★★

1984	4	Prior	
1985	Not made		
1986	4	Now	$58.00
1987	5	Prior	
1988	5	Now	$62.00
1989	3	Prior	
1990	6	Now	$64.00
1991	5	2000	$50.00
1992	7	2002	$64.00
1993	6	2000	$50.00
1994	5	2001	$39.00
1995	6	2005	$44.00
1996	7	2008	$48.00

Capel Vale is an extremely fine maker near Bunbury in Western Australia. Their wines are of considerable beauty. Winemakers: Robert Bowen and Krister Jonsson.

CAPEL VALE BAUDIN (MERLOT/CABERNET) ★★★★

1985	6	Now	$41.00
1986	7	Now	$45.00
1987	7	Now	$41.00
1988	5	Now	$27.00
1989	7	Now	$35.00
1990	5	Now	$23.00
1991	7	Now	$30.00
1992	6	Now	$24.00
1993	6	Now	$22.00

CAPEL VALE CABERNET SAUVIGNON

★★★★

before 1983		Prior	
1983	5	Now	$58.00
1984	5	Prior	
1985	5	Now	$49.00
1986	6	Now	$54.00
1987	6	Now	$50.00
1988	7	Now	$54.00
1989	7	Now	$50.00
1990	5	Now	$33.00
1991	6	Now	$37.00
1992	6	Now	$34.00
1993	7	Now	$37.00
1994	6	Now	$29.00
1995	6	2001	$27.00
1996	5	2001	$21.00

CAPEL VALE CHARDONNAY

★★★★★

before 1985		Prior	
1985	6	Now	$54.00
1986	6	Now	$50.00
1987	7	Now	$54.00

1988	5	Now	$35.00
1989	6	Now	$39.00
1990	5	Now	$30.00
1991	5	Now	$28.00
1992	7	Now	$36.00
1993	6	Now	$29.00
1994	7	Now	$31.00
1995	7	2001	$29.00
1996	6	2002	$23.00

CAPEL VALE MERLOT ★★★★

1992	5	Now	$26.00
1993	6	Now	$29.00
1994	6	Now	$27.00
1995	7	2001	$29.00
1996	6	2004	$23.00

CAPEL VALE RIESLING ★★★★

before 1985		Prior	
1985	5	Now	$37.00
1986	7	Now	$48.00
1987	5	Now	$32.00
1988	7	Now	$41.00
1989	7	Now	$38.00
1990	5	Now	$25.00
1991	6	Now	$28.00
1992	7	Now	$30.00
1993	6	Now	$24.00
1994	5	Now	$18.50
1995	6	Now	$20.00
1996	7	2000	$22.00
1997	5	Now	$15.00

CAPEL•VALE
1990
WESTERN AUSTRALIA
RHINE RIESLING

CAPEL VALE SAUVIGNON BLANC/SEMILLON
★★★★

before 1993		Prior	
1993	7	Now	$26.00
1994	6	Now	$20.00
1995	7	Now	$22.00
1996	6	Now	$17.50
1997	5	Now	$13.50

CAPEL•VALE
SAUVIGNON BLANC
SEMILLON

CAPEL VALE SHIRAZ ★★★★

before 1983		Prior	
1983	6	Now	$64.00
1984	5	Prior	
1985	5	Prior	
1986	6	Now	$50.00
1987	6	Now	$47.00
1988	7	Now	$50.00
1989	6	Now	$40.00
1990	5	Now	$31.00

CAPEL•VALE
SHIRAZ

1991	6	Now	$34.00
1992	6	Now	$32.00
1993	7	2005	$34.00
1994	6	Now	$27.00
1995	6	Now	$25.00
1996	6	Now	$23.00

Cape Clairault is yet another maker whose product attests to the extreme quality of Margaret River as a wine area. Winemaker: Ian Lewis.

CAPE CLAIRAULT "THE CLAIRAULT" (CABERNET SAUVIGNON/FRANC) ★★★★

before 1986	Prior		
1986	6	Now	$58.00
1987	6	2000	$54.00
1988	6	Now	$50.00
1989	6	Now	$47.00
1990	7	2002	$50.00
1991	7	2004	$47.00
1992	Not made		
1993	6	2003	$34.00
1994	7	2005	$37.00
1995	7	2005	$34.00

CAPE CLAIRAULT SAUVIGNON BLANC ★★★★

before 1995	Prior		
1995	6	Now	$18.50
1996	7	2000	$20.00
1997	7	2001	$18.50

CAPE CLAIRAULT SEMILLON/SAUVIGNON BLANC ★★★

before 1994	Prior		
1994	6	Now	$19.50
1995	6	2000	$18.00
1996	7	2001	$19.50
1997	7	2002	$18.00

Cape Mentelle is a very fine Margaret River producer of deep, powerful and well-balanced wines. Winemaker: John Durham.

CAPE MENTELLE CABERNET SAUVIGNON ★★★★★

1977	4	Now	$130.00
1978	6	Now	$185.00
1979	5	Now	$140.00
1980	4	Now	$105.00
1981	5	Now	$120.00

1982	6	Now	$135.00
1983	6	Now	$125.00
1984	4	Now	$78.00
1985	5	Now	$90.00
1986	6	Now	$100.00
1987	4	Now	$62.00
1988	6	Now	$86.00
1989	4	Now	$52.00
1990	6	Now	$72.00
1991	6	Now	$68.00
1992	5	Now	$52.00
1993	6	2002	$58.00
1994	7	2001	$62.00
1995	6	2003	$50.00
1996	7	2004	$54.00
1997	6	2005	$43.00

CAPE MENTELLE CABERNET/MERLOT ★★★★

1990	3	Prior	
1991	4	Now	$28.00
1992	5	Now	$32.00
1993	6	Now	$36.00
1994	5	Now	$28.00
1995	6	Now	$31.00
1996	6	Now	$29.00
1997	6	2000	$26.00

CAPE MENTELLE CHARDONNAY ★★★★★

before 1993		Prior	
1993	6	Now	$40.00
1994	6	Now	$37.00
1995	6	Now	$34.00
1996	5	Now	$27.00
1997	7	Now	$35.00

CAPE MENTELLE
CHARDONNAY 1992

CAPE MENTELLE SEMILLON
/SAUVIGNON BLANC ★★★★

before 1989		Prior	
1989	6	Now	$34.00
1990	6	Now	$31.00
1991	6	Now	$29.00
1992	6	Now	$27.00
1993	7	Now	$29.00
1994	6	Now	$23.00
1995	6	Now	$21.00
1996	6	Now	$20.00
1997	6	Now	$18.50

CAPE MENTELLE
SEMILLON SAUVIGNON BLANC 1992

CAPE MENTELLE SHIRAZ

★★★★

1983	5	Now	$62.00
1984	4	Prior	
1985	5	Now	$52.00
1986	5	Now	$49.00
1987	4	Prior	
1988	5	Now	$42.00
1989	5	Now	$39.00
1990	5	Now	$36.00
1991	6	Now	$40.00
1992	4	Now	$25.00
1993	6	Now	$34.00
1994	5	Now	$26.00
1995	6	2000	$29.00
1996	5	2000	$23.00
1997	7	2001	$30.00

CAPE MENTELLE ZINFANDEL

★★★★

1980	4	Now	$50.00
1981	6	Now	$70.00
1982	6	Now	$66.00
1983	5	Now	$50.00
1984	4	Prior	
1985	4	Prior	
1986	4	Prior	
1987	5	Now	$37.00
1988	7	Now	$48.00
1989	5	Now	$32.00
1990	5	Now	$29.00
1991	6	Now	$33.00
1992	7	Now	$35.00
1993	5	Now	$23.00
1994	4	Now	$17.50
1995	7	Now	$28.00
1996	6	Now	$22.00

***Cassegrain Vineyards** are innovative and painstaking makers in the Hastings Valley area near Port Macquarie in northern New South Wales. Winemaker: David Barker.*

CASSEGRAIN CHARDONNAY

★★★★

before 1991		Prior	
1991	7	Now	$29.00
1992	6	Now	$23.00
1993	7	Now	$25.00
1994	6	Now	$19.50
1995	7	Now	$21.00
1996	5	Now	$14.00
1997	7	Now	$18.50

CASSEGRAIN CHAMBOURCIN ★★★

1987	6	Now	$35.00
1988	5	Now	$27.00
1989	5	Now	$25.00
1990	6	Now	$27.00
1991	6	Now	$25.00
1992	6	Now	$23.00
1993	6	Now	$22.00
1994	6	Now	$20.00
1995	6	Now	$18.50
1996	6	Now	$17.50
1997	7	Now	$18.50

CASSEGRAIN FROMENTEAU CHARDONNAY ★★★★★

before 1987		Prior	
1987	5	Now	$43.00
1988	Not made		
1989	7	Now	$52.00
1990	5	Prior	
1991	7	Now	$45.00
1992	5	Now	$29.00
1993	6	Now	$33.00
1994	Not made		
1995	6	Now	$28.00
1996	6	2000	$26.00
1997	6	2001	$24.00

CASSEGRAIN PINOT NOIR ★★★★

1991	6	Now	$22.00
1992	5	Now	$17.00
1993	6	Now	$19.00
1994	6	Now	$17.50

Not made since 1994.

CASSEGRAIN SEMILLON ★★★

1985	7	Now	$52.00
1986	6	Now	$41.00
1987	Not made		
1988	5	Now	$29.00
1989	7	Now	$38.00
1990	Not made		
1991	6	Now	$28.00
1992	6	Now	$26.00
1993	5	Now	$20.00
1994	5	Now	$18.50
1995	6	2002	$20.00
1996	5	2004	$15.50
1997	6	2005	$17.50
1998	6	2006	$16.00

43

Castle Rock Estate *is a Mount Barker region vineyard.*
Their Rhine Riesling is a wine of considerable beauty.
Winemaker: Michael Staniford.

CASTLE ROCK CABERNET SAUVIGNON ★★★

before 1990	Prior		
1990	6	Now	$34.00
1991	5	Now	$26.00
1992	6	2001	$29.00
1993	4	Now	$18.00
1994	5	2001	$21.00
1995	Not made		
1996	7	2002	$25.00

CASTLE ROCK CHARDONNAY ★★★

before 1994	Prior		
1994	5	Now	$20.00
1995	Not made		
1996	5	Now	$17.00
1997	7	2000	$22.00

CASTLE ROCK PINOT NOIR ★★★

1992	5	Prior	
1993	6	Now	$28.00
1994	Not made		
1995	Not made		
1996	7	Now	$26.00
1997	Not made		
1998	7	2001	$22.00

CASTLE ROCK RIESLING ★★★★★

before 1993	Prior		
1993	5	Now	$20.00
1994	6	Now	$23.00
1995	Not made		
1996	7	Now	$23.00
1997	6	2000	$18.00
1998	6	2002	$17.00

Cathcart Ridge Estate *is a small Grampians (Great Western*
district) vineyard producing a blockbuster of a Cabernet and a
very fine Merlot. Winemaker: David Farnhill.

CATHCART RIDGE CABERNET SAUVIGNON ★★★★

1994	3	2005	$70.00
1995	5	2007	$105.00
1996	6	2008	$120.00

CATHCART RIDGE CABERNET/MERLOT ★★★★

1985	4	Now	$47.00
1986	5	Now	$54.00
1987	5	Now	$50.00

1988	7	Now	$66.00
1989	6	Now	$52.00
1990	7	Now	$56.00
1991	6	Now	$44.00
1992	7	Now	$48.00
1993	Not made		
1994	6	2000	$35.00

CATHCART RIDGE CHARDONNAY ★★★

1987	5	Now	$38.00
1988	5	Now	$36.00
1989	6	Now	$40.00
1990	6	Now	$37.00
1991	6	Now	$34.00
1992	5	Now	$26.00
1993	6	Now	$29.00
1994	7	Now	$31.00
1995	7	Now	$29.00
1996	6	Now	$23.00

CATHCART RIDGE MERLOT ★★★★★

1994	6	2000	$49.00
1995	6	2002	$46.00
1996	7	2005	$49.00

CATHCART RIDGE SHIRAZ ★★★★

1985	7	Now	$44.00
1986	6	Now	$35.00
1987	6	Now	$32.00
1988	6	Now	$30.00
1989	5	Now	$23.00
1990	6	Now	$26.00
1991	6	Now	$24.00
1992	Not made		
1993	7	Now	$24.00
1994	6	Now	$19.00

Chain of Ponds *is the label under which a growing range of wines is released made from fruit from the Gumeracha Vineyard in the Adelaide Hills. Winemaker: Caj Amadio.*

CHAIN OF PONDS CABERNET SAUVIGNON "AMADEUS" ★★★★

1993	7	Now	$42.00
1994	6	2000	$33.00
1995	Not made		
1996	7	2002	$33.00
1997	6	2003	$26.00

CHAIN OF PONDS CHARDONNAY ★★★★

1993	6	Now	$42.00
1994	7	Now	$45.00
1995	6	Now	$36.00
1996	7	2000	$39.00
1997	7	2004	$36.00
1998	7	2003	$33.00

CHAIN OF PONDS RIESLING ★★★

1994	7	Now	$24.00
1995	Not made		
1996	7	Now	$20.00
1997	7	Now	$19.00
1998	7	2000	$18.00

CHAIN OF PONDS SEMILLON ★★★★★

1993	6	Now	$28.00
1994	7	Now	$30.00
1995	6	Now	$24.00
1996	6	2000	$22.00
1997	7	2004	$24.00
1998	7	2005	$22.00

Charles Melton Wines is a very small Barossa Valley producer with a range of wines which have excited an intensely loyal following. No ratings have been received from the maker. Winemakers: Charles Melton and Jo Ahearne.

CHARLES MELTON CABERNET SAUVIGNON ★★★★

CHARLES MELTON NINE POPES (SHIRAZ/GRENACHE/MOURVERDRE) ★★★★★

Chateau Francois is a small Pokolbin maker of hobbyist size but perfectionist aspirations. Winemaker: Don Francois.

CHATEAU FRANCOIS CHARDONNAY ★★★

before 1985	Prior		
1985	6	Now	$23.00
1986	6	Now	$21.00
1987	6	Now	$20.00
1988	5	Now	$15.50
1989	7	Now	$20.00
1990	Not made		
1991	4	Now	$9.75
1992	6	Now	$13.50
1993	5	Now	$10.50
Not made since 1993			

CHATEAU FRANCOIS SHIRAZ/PINOT NOIR ★★★

before 1978		Prior	
1978	5	Now	$34.00
1979	7	Now	$44.00
1980	6	Now	$35.00
1981	Not made		
1982	7	Now	$35.00
1983	3	Prior	
1984	5	Now	$21.00
1985	6	Now	$24.00
1986	6	Now	$22.00
1987	6	Now	$20.00
1988	4	Prior	
1989	6	Now	$17.50
1990	7	Now	$19.00
1991	6	Now	$15.00
1992	5	Now	$11.50
1993	6	Now	$13.00
1994	5	Now	$10.00
1995	6	Now	$11.00
1996	6	2000	N/R
1997	7	2001	N/R
1998	7	202	N/R

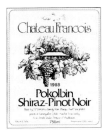

CHATEAU FRANCOIS SEMILLON ★★★★

before 1985		Prior	
1985	5	Now	$18.00
1986	6	Now	$20.00
1987	7	Now	$22.00
1988	6	Now	$17.50
1989	6	Now	$16.00
1990	6	Now	$15.00
1991	6	Now	$13.50
1992	7	Now	$15.00
1993	7	Now	$13.50
1994	7	Now	$12.50
1995	7	Now	$11.50
1996	7	2000	N/R
1997	6	2001	N/R
1998	7	2002	N/R

Chateau Reynella is an historic McLaren Vale maker now owned and operated by BRL Hardy. The label has now been deleted. Winemaker: David O'Leary.

CHATEAU REYNELLA BASKET PRESSED
CABERNET/MERLOT ★★★★

before 1986		Prior	
1986	7	Now	$44.00
1987	6	Now	$35.00

1988	6	Now	$32.00
1989	5	1984	$25.00
1990	7	2000	$32.00
1991	7	2000	$30.00
1992	6	2003	$23.00
1993	7	2004	$25.00
1994	7	2005	$24.00
1995	5	2001	$15.50

No longer made.

CHATEAU REYNELLA BASKET PRESSED
CABERNET SAUVIGNON ★★★★

before 1982		Prior	
1982	7	Now	$56.00
1983	6	Now	$44.00
1984	6	Now	$41.00
1985	7	2000	$44.00
1986	7	2000	$41.00
1987	6	Now	$33.00
1988	6	2000	$30.00
1989	5	Now	$23.00
1990	6	2000	$26.00
1991	7	2006	$28.00
1992	6	2007	$22.00
1993	5	2002	$17.00
1994	7	2006	$22.00

No longer made.

CHATEAU REYNELLA BASKET PRESSED
SHIRAZ ★★★

1989	7	Now	$30.00
1990	6	Now	$23.00
1991	7	2000	$25.00
1992	6	2000	$20.00
1993	6	2006	$18.50
1994	7	2008	$20.00

No longer made.

CHATEAU REYNELLA CHARDONNAY ★★★

1989	6	Now	$24.00
1990	6	Now	$22.00
1991	5	Now	$17.00
1992	6	Now	$19.00
1993	5	Now	$14.50
1994	5	Now	$13.50

No longer made.

CHATEAU REYNELLA VINTAGE
PORT ★★★★

1966	4	Now	$68.00
1967	7	Now	$110.00
1968	3	Now	$44.00

1969	Not made		
1970	6	2000	$74.00
1971	6	Now	$70.00
1972	6	2000	$64.00
1973	Not made		
1974	4	Now	$37.00
1975	7	2000	$60.00
1976	6	2000	$47.00
1977	7	2000	$50.00
1978	6	2000	$41.00
1979	7	2005	$44.00
1980	6	2000	$35.00
1981	7	2000	$37.00
1982	7	Now	$35.00
1983	6	Now	$27.00
1984	Not made		
1985	Not made		
1986	Not made		
1987	7	2012	$23.00
1988	6	2005	$19.00

No longer made.

Chateau Tahbilk *has been producing wine in the Goulburn Valley since the mid 19th century. The historic vineyard and beautiful winery are still family owned and operated. Winemaker: Alister Purbrick.*

CHATEAU TAHBILK CABERNET SAUVIGNON

★★★★

before 1962	Prior		
1962	7	2000	$350.00
1963	5	Prior	
1964	7	2000	$300.00
1965	6	Now	$240.00
1966	6	Now	$220.00
1967	5	Now	$170.00
1968	7	2000	$220.00
1969	4	Prior	
1970	4	Prior	
1971	7	2005	$175.00
1972	5	Prior	
1973	4	Prior	
1974	4	Now	$80.00
1975	3	Prior	
1976	6	2005	$100.00
1977	5	2000	$80.00
1978	6	2005	$88.00
1979	6	2005	$82.00
1980	6	Now	$76.00
1981	7	2005	$82.00
1982	6	2000	$64.00

1983	6	2005	$60.00
1984	6	2005	$56.00
1985	6	2005	$50.00
1986	7	2005	$56.00
1987	5	2000	$37.00
1988	5	2005	$34.00
1989	4	Now	$25.00
1990	6	2005	$35.00
1991	7	2010	$38.00
1992	6	2005	$30.00
1993	5	2005	$23.00
1994	5	2010	$21.00
1995	6	2013	$24.00
1996	6	2010	$22.00
1997	7	2015	$24.00
1998	7	2015	N/R

CHATEAU TAHBILK CHARDONNAY ★★★

before 1992		Prior	
1992	6	Now	$23.00
1993	6	2000	$21.00
1994	6	2000	$20.00
1995	6	2003	$18.50
1996	6	2003	$17.00
1997	6	2005	$15.50

CHATEAU TAHBILK MARSANNE ★★★★

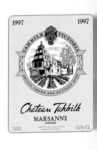

before 1976		Prior	
1976	6	Now	$74.00
1977	5	Prior	
1978	5	Prior	
1979	7	Now	$68.00
1980	6	Now	$54.00
1981	6	Prior	
1982	6	Now	$47.00
1983	4	Prior	
1984	6	Now	$40.00
1985	5	Now	$31.00
1986	5	Now	$28.00
1987	7	2000	$37.00
1988	6	Now	$29.00
1989	7	2002	$32.00
1990	6	2005	$25.00
1991	6	2000	$23.00
1992	7	2005	$25.00
1993	6	2005	$20.00
1994	6	2005	$18.50

1995	6	2005	$17.00
1996	6	2003	$16.00
1997	6	2005	$14.50
1998	6	2007	$13.50

CHATEAU TAHBILK RESERVE CABERNET
(SHIRAZ IN '71, '72 AND '74)   ★★★★★

1970	5	Prior	
1971	7	2005	$300.00
1972	6	Now	$240.00
1973	5	Now	$180.00
1974	7	2000	$240.00
1975	5	Now	$155.00
1976	6	2005	$175.00
1977	5	Prior	
1978	5	2000	$125.00
1979	6	2000	$140.00
1980	6	2000	$125.00
1981	7	2005	$140.00
1982	7	2005	$125.00
1983	7	2005	$120.00
1984	7	2005	$110.00
1985	6	2005	$88.00
1986	6	2005	$80.00
1987	Not made		
1988	Not made		
1989	Not made		
1990	Not made		
1991	7	2010	$64.00
1992	6	2005	$50.00

CHATEAU TAHBILK RIESLING   ★★★★

before 1980	Prior		
1980	6	Now	$56.00
1981	4	Prior	
1982	6	Now	$48.00
1983	4	Prior	
1984	5	Prior	
1985	Not made		
1986	Not made		
1987	6	Now	$33.00
1988	Not made		
1989	6	Now	$28.00
1990	7	Now	$30.00
1991	5	Now	$20.00
1992	6	Now	$22.00
1993	5	Now	$17.00
1994	7	2005	$22.00

1995	6	2005	$17.50
1996	6	2005	$16.50
1997	6	2006	$15.00
1998	6	2005	$14.00

CHATEAU TAHBILK SHIRAZ ★★★★

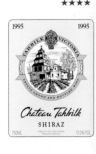

1961	6	Now	$330.00
1962	7	Now	$360.00
1963	5	Prior	
1964	5	Prior	
1965	6	Now	$245.00
1966	6	Now	$225.00
1967	6	Now	$210.00
1968	7	Now	$225.00
1969	4	Prior	
1970	4	Prior	
1971	7	Now	$180.00
1972	5	Prior	
1973	4	Prior	
1974	4	Prior	
1975	2	Prior	
1976	6	2005	$100.00
1977	5	Prior	
1978	5	2000	$74.00
1979	6	2000	$82.00
1980	6	2000	$76.00
1981	7	2005	$82.00
1982	6	2000	$66.00
1983	Not made		
1984	6	2005	$56.00
1985	5	2000	$44.00
1986	7	2005	$56.00
1987	5	2000	$37.00
1988	6	2000	$42.00
1989	4	Now	$25.00
1990	5	2000	$30.00
1991	7	2010	$38.00
1992	5	2000	$25.00
1993	5	2005	$23.00
1994	6	2005	$26.00
1995	6	2010	$24.00
1996	6	2010	$22.00
1997	7	2015	$24.00
1998	7	2015	N/R

CHATEAU TAHBILK
SHIRAZ 1860 VINES ★★★★★

1979	5	Now	$210.00
1980	Not made		
1981	6	2005	$215.00
1982	6	2005	$200.00

1983	Not made		
1984	7	2010	$200.00
1985	6	2005	$160.00
1986	7	2010	$170.00
1987	6	Now	$135.00
1988	6	2000	$125.00
1989	5	Now	$98.00
1990	6	2000	$105.00
1991	7	2005	$115.00
1992	7	2010	$105.00
1993	6	2003	$86.00

Chateau Xanadu is a Margaret River winery whose wines show markedly generous fruit. Winemaker: Jurg Muggli.

CHATEAU XANADU CABERNET SAUVIGNON ★★★

before 1989	Prior		
1989	5	Now	$52.00
1990	6	Now	$58.00
1991	6	2005	$54.00
1992	6	2003	$50.00
1993	5	2003	$38.00
1994	7	2005	$50.00
1995	7	2010	$46.00
1996	7	2007	$43.00
1997	6	2010	$34.00

CHATEAU XANADU
CABERNET SAUVIGNON RESERVE ★★★★★

1989	5	Now	$82.00
1990	6	Now	$90.00
1991	7	2010	$98.00
1992	6	2008	$78.00
1993	5	2003	$60.00
1994	6	2010	$66.00
1995	7	2015	$72.00
1996	7	2015	$66.00
1997	7	2015	N/A

CHATEAU XANADU CHARDONNAY ★★★★

before 1991	Prior		
1991	6	Now	$48.00
1992	6	Now	$45.00
1993	6	2000	$41.00
1994	6	2005	$38.00
1995	4	Now	$23.00
1996	6	2005	$33.00
1997	7	2005	$35.00

CHATEAU XANADU SEMILLON ★★★

before 1989		Prior	
1989	5	Now	$47.00
1990	5	Now	$43.00
1991	6	Now	$48.00
1992	6	Now	$44.00
1993	5	Now	$34.00
1994	6	2002	$38.00
1995	6	2000	$35.00
1996	7	2005	$38.00
1997	7	2005	$35.00

Chatsfield Wines' Mount Barker fruit produces three
greatly respected white wines and, unusually for the area, a
fine Shiraz. Winemaker: Gavin Berry.

CHATSFIELD CHARDONNAY ★★★★

before 1995		Prior	
1995	5	2000	$18.50
1996	6	2000	$21.00
1997	7	2005	$22.00

CHATSFIELD GEWURZTRAMINER ★★★

before 1990		Prior	
1990	6	2000	$27.00
1991	Not made		
1992	5	Prior	
1993	5	2000	$18.00
1994	6	2003	$20.00
1995	6	2003	$18.50
1996	6	2003	$17.00
1997	6	2005	$16.00
1998	7	2008	$17.00

CHATSFIELD MERIDIAN (CABERNET FRANC) ★★★

before 1995		Prior	
1995	6	Now	$16.50
1996	7	2002	$18.00
1997	6	2002	$14.00
1998	7	2005	$15.50

CHATSFIELD RIESLING ★★★

before 1990		Prior	
1990	6	2000	$28.00
1991	Not made		
1992	5	Prior	
1993	5	2000	$18.50
1994	6	2003	$20.00
1995	6	2003	$19.00
1996	6	2005	$17.50
1997	6	2005	$16.00
1998	6	2008	$15.00

CHATSFIELD SHIRAZ

★★★★

before 1990		Prior	
1990	7	2000	$32.00
1991	7	2000	$30.00
1992	7	2002	$28.00
1993	6	2002	$22.00
1994	7	2005	$24.00
1995	6	2005	$19.00
1996	6	2005	$17.50

Clarendon Hills *is a McLaren Vale maker with a range of blockbusting wines, including some very fine but massive Shiraz. The dollar values printed below are not misprints, but are based on the current prices given to me by the owner/winemaker. Winemaker: Roman Bratasiuk.*

CLARENDON HILLS ASTRALIS SHIRAZ ★★★★★

1994	7	2016	$220.00
1995	7	2020	$200.00
1996	7	2018	$185.00
1997	7	2020	$170.00
1998	7	2018	N/R

CLARENDON HILLS BLEWITT SPRINGS OLD VINE
GRENACHE ★★★★

1991	7	2000	$100.00
1992	7	2003	$96.00
1993	6	2000	$76.00
1994	7	2002	$82.00
1995	7	2005	$76.00
1996	7	2002	$70.00
1997	7	2002	$66.00

CLARENDON HILLS CABERNET SAUVIGNON

★★★★

1991	7	2000	$170.00
1992	7	2000	$155.00
1993	7	2005	$145.00
1994	Not made		
1995	7	2010	$120.00
1995	Not made		
1996	Not made		
1997	7	2010	$100.00
1998	7	2015	N/R

CLARENDON HILLS KANGARILLA
CHARDONNAY ★★★★

1996	6	2002	$56.00
1997	7	2003	$62.00
1998	7	2005	$56.00

CLARENDON HILLS MERLOT ★★★★

1990	5	Now	$130.00
1991	6	Now	$140.00
1992	7	2005	$155.00
1993	6	2000	$120.00
1994	7	2005	$130.00
1995	7	2002	$120.00
1996	7	2003	$110.00
1997	7	2005	$105.00
1998	7	2006	N/R

CLARENDON HILLS OLD VINES GRENACHE ★★★

1991	7	Now	$28.00
1992	7	Now	$25.00
1993	6	Now	$20.00
1994	7	Now	$22.00
1995	7	2000	$20.00

Cleveland Estate is a small maker in Victoria's Macedon region. The wines are reliable and sometimes very good indeed. Winemaker: Keith Brien.

CLEVELAND ESTATE BRUT MACEDON ★★★★

1991	6	Now	$54.00
1992	6	Now	$50.00
1993	6	Now	$46.00
1994	6	Now	$43.00
1995	6	2000	$39.00
1996	6	2001	$37.00
1997	6	2002	N/R
1998	6	2003	N/R

CLEVELAND ESTATE CABERNET SAUVIGNON "MINUS FIVE" ★★★★

1988	5	Now	$45.00
1989	6	Now	$50.00
1990	5	Now	$39.00
1991	7	2000	$50.00
1992	6	2002	$40.00
1993	6	2003	$37.00
1994	Not made		
1995	6	2003	$32.00
1996	Not made		
1997	7	2005	$32.00
1998	7	2010	N/R

CLEVELAND ESTATE CHARDONNAY ★★★★

1988	4	Now	$41.00
1989	5	Now	$48.00
1990	5	Now	$44.00
1991	6	Now	$49.00
1992	6	Now	$45.00

1993	6	2002	$42.00
1994	7	2000	$45.00
1995	6	2000	$36.00
1996	6	2003	$33.00
1997	7	2004	$36.00
1998	6	2002	$28.00

CLEVELAND ESTATE PINOT NOIR ★★★★

1989	6	Now	$56.00
1990	6	Now	$52.00
1991	6	2001	$48.00
1992	6	2002	$44.00
1993	5	Now	$34.00
1994	7	2005	$44.00
1995	5	2000	$29.00
1996	6	2002	$32.00
1997	7	2006	$35.00
1998	7	2007	N/R

Clonakilla is a Canberra district maker who predates the Doonkuna Estate as Murrumbateman's longest established maker. Winemaker: Tim Kirk.

CLONAKILLA CABERNET/MERLOT ★★★

before 1987	Prior		
1987	4	Now	$36.00
1988	6	Now	$50.00
1989	Not made		
1990	3	2001	$21.00
1991	4	Now	$26.00
1992	6	Now	$37.00
1993	5	Now	$28.00
1994	6	2004	$32.00
1995	5	2002	$24.00
1996	5	2004	$22.00
1997	6	2006	$25.00
1998	7	2008	N/R

CLONAKILLA RIESLING ★★★★

1986	6	Now	$49.00
1987	5	Now	$38.00
1988	6	2001	$42.00
1989	2	Prior	
1990	4	Now	$24.00
1991	5	2003	$28.00
1992	5	2000	$26.00
1993	7	2004	$33.00
1994	6	2004	$26.00
1995	6	2005	$24.00
1996	6	2004	$23.00
1997	7	2007	$24.00
1998	6	2006	$19.50

CLONAKILLA SEMILLON/ SAUVIGNON BLANC ★★★

before 1995		Prior	
1995	6	Now	$21.00
1996	5	Now	$16.50
1997	5	Now	$15.50
1998	6	Now	$17.00

CLONAKILLA SHIRAZ/ VIOGNER ★★★★

1990	3	Now	$32.00
1991	4	Now	$39.00
1992	5	Now	$45.00
1993	5	2001	$42.00
1994	7	2006	$54.00
1995	6	2003	$43.00
1996	5	2001	$33.00
1997	7	2007	$43.00
1998	7	2009	N/R

Cloudy Bay is the notably successful New Zealand arm of Cape Mentelle. The wines are very good indeed, the Sauvignon Blanc in particular being internationally renowned. Winemaker: Kevin Judd.

CLOUDY BAY CABERNET/MERLOT ★★★★

before 1991		Prior	
1991	6	Now	NZ$39.00
1992	Not made		
1993	Not made		
1994	6	Now	NZ$31.00
1995	Not made		
1996	6	2001	NZ$27.00
Not made since 1996			

CLOUDY BAY CHARDONNAY ★★★★★

before 1992		Prior	
1992	6	Now	NZ$49.00
1993	5	Now	NZ$38.00
1994	6	Now	NZ$42.00
1995	5	2000	NZ$32.00
1996	6	2002	NZ$36.00
1997	6	2003	NZ$33.00

CLOUDY BAY PINOT NOIR ★★★★

1994	4	Now	$34.00
1995	Not made		
1996	5	Now	$37.00
1997	5	2000	$34.00

CLOUDY BAY SAUVIGNON BLANC ★★★★★

before 1996		Prior	
1996	6	Now	NZ$26.00
1997	6	Now	NZ$24.00
1998	5	Now	NZ$18.50

Clover Hill is a very fine sparkling wine crafted by Taltarni (qv) from premium Tasmanian grapes. Winemaker: Chris Markell.

CLOVER HILL METHODE CHAMPENOISE ★★★★★

1991	6	Now	$47.00
1992	6	Now	$44.00
1993	6	Now	$40.00
1994	6	Now	$37.00
1995	6	Now	$34.00
1996	5	2000	$26.00
1997	5	2001	N/R
1998	6	2002	N/R

Clyde Park began as a very small Geelong area vineyard, but has now been considerably extended. The sensitively made wines are of very good quality. Winemaker: Roland Cavell.

CLYDE PARK CHARDONNAY ★★★★

1983	4	Now	$50.00
1984	5	Now	$58.00
1985	6	Now	$64.00
1986	6	Now	$58.00
1987	7	2000	$64.00
1988	6	Now	$50.00
1989	6	Now	$47.00
1990	7	Now	$50.00
1991	7	2000	$47.00
1992	6	Now	$37.00
1993	7	2000	$40.00
1994	7	Now	$37.00
1995	6	Now	$29.00
1996	6	2000	$27.00
1997	5	2001	$21.00

CLYDE PARK RESERVE PINOT ★★★★

1989	5	Now	$40.00
1990	6	Now	$44.00
1991	6	Now	$41.00
1992	7	Now	$44.00
1993	6	Now	$35.00
1994	6	Now	$32.00
1995	6	2000	$30.00
1996	Not made		
1997	6	2002	$26.00
1998	6	2003	N/R

59

Cockfighter's Ghost is a 12 hectare vineyard at Broke in the Hunter Valley owned and operated by Harbridge Fine Wines.
Winemaker: Various contract makers.

COCKFIGHTER'S GHOST
CHARDONNAY ★★★

1996	5	Now	$16.50
1997	6	Now	$18.00
1998	7	2000	$19.50

COCKFIGHTER'S GHOST
PINOT NOIR ★★★★

1995	5	Now	$21.00
1996	7	Now	$27.00
1997	6	2000	$22.00

COCKFIGHTER'S GHOST
SEMILLON ★★★

1995	5	2000	$16.00
1996	5	2000	$15.00
1997	7	2002	$19.50

COCKFIGHTER'S GHOST
SHIRAZ ★★★★

1995	5	Now	$20.00
1996	6	2000	$22.00
1997	7	2002	$24.00

Coldstream Hills, *now owned by Southcorp, is a leading Yarra Valley vineyard and winery founded by Australia's leading wine writer, James Halliday.*
Winemaker: James Halliday.

COLDSTREAM BRIARSTON HILLS
CABERNET/MERLOT ★★★★★

1988	7	Now	$56.00
1989	4	Now	$29.00
1990	6	Now	$41.00
1991	7	2000	$44.00
1992	7	2002	$41.00
1993	5	Now	$27.00
1994	6	2003	$30.00
1995	5	2002	$23.00
1996	5	2003	$21.00

COLDSTREAM HILLS RESERVE CABERNET
SAUVIGNON ★★★★★

1985	5	Now	$68.00
1986	6	Now	$76.00
1987	5	Now	$58.00
1988	7	2000	$76.00
1989	4	Now	$40.00

1990	6	2000	$56.00
1991	7	2005	$60.00
1992	7	2010	$56.00
1993	6	2003	$45.00
1994	6	2004	$41.00
1995	6	2005	$38.00
1996	Not made		

COLDSTREAM HILLS RESERVE CHARDONNAY

★★★★★

1986	6	Now	$88.00
1987	5	Now	$68.00
1988	7	Now	$88.00
1989	3	Prior	
1990	5	Now	$54.00
1991	7	Now	$70.00
1992	7	Now	$66.00
1993	7	2002	$60.00
1994	7	2000	$56.00
1995	5	2002	$37.00
1996	6	2004	$41.00
1997	6	2003	$38.00

COLDSTREAM HILLS RESERVE PINOT NOIR ★★★★★

before 1987	Prior		
1987	6	Now	$92.00
1988	7	Now	$100.00
1989	4	Prior	
1990	3	Prior	
1991	7	Now	$80.00
1992	7	2002	$74.00
1993	4	Now	$39.00
1994	7	2001	$62.00
1995	5	2000	$42.00
1996	7	2002	$54.00
1997	7	2004	$50.00

COLDSTREAM HILLS SAUVIGNON BLANC
(SEMILLON/ until 1997)

★★★★

1985	3	Now	$34.00
1986	5	Now	$52.00
1987	6	Now	$58.00
1988	5	Now	$45.00
1989	4	Now	$33.00
1990	6	Now	$46.00
1991	6	Now	$43.00
1992	7	2000	$46.00
1993	Not made		
1994	7	2000	$40.00
1995	5	Now	$26.00
1996	6	2000	$29.00
1997	6	Now	$27.00

Collards are Henderson (New Zealand) based winemakers whose fruit, however, comes from a selection of the country's premium areas. The outstanding wines in their stable are undoubtedly the Chardonnays and Sauvignon Blancs. Winemaker: Bruce Collard.

COLLARDS CABERNET SAUVIGNON ★★★★

1990	6	Now	NZ$29.00
1991	6	Now	NZ$26.00
1992	6	Now	NZ$24.00
1993	7	Now	NZ$26.00
1994	7	2000	NZ$24.00
1995	6	2000	NZ$19.50
1996	7	2002	NZ$21.00
1997	6	2002	NZ$16.50

COLLARDS CHARDONNAY ROTHESAY VINEYARD ★★★★

before 1991		Prior	
1991	6	Now	NZ$44.00
1992	6	Now	NZ$41.00
1993	7	Now	NZ$44.00
1994	7	Now	NZ$41.00
1995	5	Now	NZ$27.00
1996	7	Now	NZ$35.00
1997	7	Now	NZ$32.00
1998	7	2000	NZ$30.00

COLLARDS CHARDONNAY HAWKES BAY ★★★

before 1994		Prior	
1994	6	Now	NZ$22.00
1995	6	Now	NZ$21.00
1996	6	Now	NZ$19.50
1997	7	Now	NZ$21.00
1998	7	2000	NZ$19.50

COLLARDS CHENIN BLANC ★★★★

before 1992		Prior	
1992	7	Now	NZ$21.00
1993	6	Now	NZ$17.00
1994	7	Now	NZ$18.50
1995	5	Now	NZ$12.00
1996	7	2000	NZ$16.00
1997	7	2001	NZ$14.50
1998	7	2002	NZ$13.50

COLLARDS MARLBOROUGH RIESLING ★★★

1991	6	Now	NZ$26.00
1992	7	Now	NZ$28.00
1993	6	Now	NZ$22.00
1994	7	Now	NZ$24.00

1995	Not made		
1996	7	Now	NZ$20.00
1997	7	2000	NZ$19.00
1998	7	2001	NZ$17.50

COLLARDS SAUVIGNON BLANC MARLBOROUGH

★★★★

before 1994	Prior		
1994	7	Now	NZ$23.00
1995	5	Now	NZ$15.00
1996	6	Now	NZ$16.50
1997	7	Now	NZ$18.00
1998	6	Now	NZ$14.50

COLLARDS SAUVIGNON BLANC ROTHESAY

★★★★

before 1992	Prior		
1992	7	Now	NZ$27.00
1993	7	Now	NZ$25.00
1994	6	Now	NZ$20.00
1995	5	Now	NZ$15.50
1996	6	Now	NZ$17.00
1997	7	Now	NZ$18.50
1998	7	Now	NZ$17.00

COLLARDS PINOT NOIR ★★★★

1992	6	Now	NZ$28.00
1993	6	Now	NZ$26.00
1994	7	Now	NZ$28.00
1995	Not made		
1996	6	Now	N/R
1997	6	Now	N/R
1998	6	2000	N/R

Cooks New Zealand Wine Company are owned by Corbans Wines. The "Winemaker's Reserve" was the top range. Winemaker: Kirsty Walton.

COOKS WINEMAKERS RESERVE CHARDONNAY

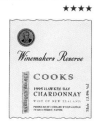

★★★★

before 1989	Prior		
1989	7	Now	NZ$37.00
1990	7	Now	NZ$34.00
1991	7	2000	NZ$32.00
1992	6	2000	NZ$25.00
1993	Not made		
1994	7	2002	NZ$25.00
1995	7	2004	NZ$23.00

No longer made.

Coolangatta Estate is an admirable resort/golfcourse /tourist operation in the Shoalhaven area of NSW. Their viticultural practices are of an exemplary standard, resulting in some impressive wines (made by Tyrrells).
Winemaker: Andrew Spinoza.

COOLANGATTA ESTATE ALEXANDER BERRY
CHARDONNAY   ★★★★

1991	6	Now	$29.00
1992	Not made		
1993	5	Now	$21.00
1994	6	Now	$23.00
1995	6	Now	$21.00
1996	6	Now	$20.00
1997	6	2000	$18.50
1998	6	2001	$17.00

Coopers Creek Vineyard is a West Auckland (New Zealand) producer whose large range includes some richly flavoured white wines of respectable quality.
Winemaker: Kim Crawford.

COOPERS CREEK CABERNET
SAUVIGNON/MERLOT   ★★★

before 1992	Prior		
1992	4	Now	NZ$16.50
1993	5	Now	NZ$19.50
1994	7	Now	NZ$25.00
1995	6	Now	N/R

COOPERS CREEK CHARDONNAY
(HAWKES BAY)   ★★★

before 1992	Prior		
1992	7	Now	NZ$36.00
1993	5	Now	NZ$24.00
1994	7	Now	NZ$31.00
1995	4	Now	NZ$16.50

COOPERS CREEK CHARDONNAY
(SWAMP RESERVE)   ★★★★

1989	6	Now	NZ$45.00
1990	5	Now	NZ$35.00
1991	4	Now	NZ$25.00
1992	7	Now	NZ$42.00
1993	Not made		
1994	7	Now	NZ$36.00
1995	5	Now	NZ$23.00

COOPERS CREEK FUME BLANC ★★★

before 1992		Prior	
1992	6	Now	NZ$21.00
1993	5	Now	NZ$16.50
1994	7	Now	NZ$21.00
1995	4	Now	NZ$11.50

COOPERS CREEK RIESLING ★★★

before 1992		Prior	
1992	5	Now	NZ$17.50
1993	5	Now	NZ$16.50
1994	7	Now	NZ$21.00
1995	4	Now	NZ$11.00

Cope-Williams is a small, cool climate Romsey (Victoria) maker, particularly well-regarded for some skilfully crafted sparkling wines. Winemaker: Michael Cope-Williams.

COPE-WILLIAMS CABERNET/MERLOT ★★★★

1988	6	Now	$36.00
1989	5	Prior	
1990	6	Now	$31.00
1991	5	Now	$24.00
1992	6	Now	$26.00
1993	6	Now	$24.00
1994	4	Now	$15.00
1995	5	Now	$17.50
1996	4	2000	N/R
1997	6	2006	N/R
1998	6	2005	N/R

COPE-WILLIAMS COAT OF ARMS CABERNET
(previously CABERNET/PINOT) ★★★

1983	6	Prior	
1984	Not made		
1985	6	Now	$25.00
1986	4	Prior	
1987	6	Now	$22.00
1988	7	Now	$23.00
1989	5	Prior	
1990	7	Now	$20.00
1991	6	Now	$16.00
1992	7	Now	$17.50

COPE-WILLIAMS CHARDONNAY ★★★

before 1988		Prior	
1988	6	Now	$38.00
1989	7	Now	$41.00
1990	6	Now	$33.00
1991	7	Now	$35.00

1992	6	Now	$28.00
1993	Not made		
1994	6	Now	$24.00
1995	7	Now	$26.00
1996	Not made		
1997	6	2000	$19.00
1998	6	2002	$18.00

COPE-WILLIAMS "ROMSEY BRUT" (METHODE CHAMPENOISE) ★★★★

before 1988		Prior	
1988	5	Now	$41.00
1989	4	Prior	
1990	7	Now	$49.00
1991	7	Now	$45.00
1992	5	Prior	
1993	6	Now	$33.00
1994	4	Now	$20.00
1995	6	Now	$28.00
1996	6	2000	$26.00
1997	7	2002	N/R
1998	7	2003	N/R

COPE-WILLIAMS PINOT NOIR ★★★

before 1988		Prior	
1988	7	Now	$49.00
1989	2	Prior	
1990	6	Now	$36.00
1991	5	Prior	
1992	7	Now	$36.00
1993	Not made		
1994	5	Now	$22.00
1995	4	Now	$16.00
1996	5	Now	$19.00
1997	7	2002	$24.00
1998	6	2002	N/R

Corbans Wines are long established New Zealand makers and marketers with a string of brands in their stable. The wines are very moderately priced for their very fine quality and reliability. Winemakers: Daniel Alcorso (Gisborne), Kirsty Walton (Hawkes Bay), Michael Kluczko (Marlborough).

CORBANS AMADEUS METHODE CHAMPENOISE ★★★★★

1987	7	Prior	
1988	Not made		
1989	6	Now	NZ$37.00
1990	7	Now	NZ$39.00
1991	7	Now	NZ$37.00
1992	7	Now	NZ$34.00
1993	6	Now	NZ$27.00
1994	No data		
1994	5	Now	NZ$19.00

CORBANS COTTAGE BLOCK CABERNET SAUVIGNON /CABERNET FRANC

★★★★

1992	5	Prior	
1993	Not made		
1994	7	2004	NZ$41.00
1995	7	2005	NZ$38.00
1996	Not made		

CORBANS COTTAGE BLOCK CHARDONNAY (GISBORNE)

★★★★★

1993	7	Now	NZ$38.00
1994	7	Now	NZ$35.00
1995	7	2000	NZ$33.00
1996	Not made		

CORBANS COTTAGE BLOCK CHARDONNAY (HAWKES BAY)

★★★★

1993	6	2000	NZ$31.00
1994	7	2002	NZ$34.00
1995	7	2002	NZ$31.00

CORBANS COTTAGE BLOCK CHARDONNAY (MARLBOROUGH)

★★★★★

1993	6	Now	NZ$41.00
1994	7	2000	NZ$44.00
1995	Not made		
1996	7	2002	NZ$38.00
1997	6	2000	NZ$30.00

CORBANS COTTAGE BLOCK MERLOT/CABERNET (MARLBOROUGH)

★★★★

1992	5	Now	NZ$37.00
1993	Not made		
1994	7	2002	NZ$45.00
1995	Not made		
1996	7	2004	NZ$38.00

CORBANS COTTAGE BLOCK NOBLE RIESLING 375ml (MARLBOROUGH)

★★★★

1991	7	2001	NZ$32.00
1992	Not made		
1993	Not made		
1994	Not made		
1995	7	2002	NZ$23.00
1996	6	2001	NZ$18.50

CORBANS COTTAGE BLOCK PINOT NOIR (MARLBOROUGH)

★★★★

1992	5	Now	NZ$34.00
1993	6	Now	NZ$38.00
1994	7	2000	NZ$42.00
1995	Not made		
1996	Not made		

CORBANS PRIVATE BIN CABERNET/MERLOT ★★★

1983	7	Now	NZ$72.00
1984	6	Prior	
1985	7	Now	NZ$62.00
1986	7	Now	NZ$56.00
1987	7	Now	NZ$52.00
1988	Not made		
1989	7	Now	NZ$45.00
1990	7	Now	NZ$42.00
1991	7	2000	NZ$39.00
1992	Not made		
1993	6	2000	NZ$28.00
1994	7	2002	NZ$31.00
1995	7	2005	NZ$28.00
1996	7	2002	NZ$26.00

CORBANS PRIVATE BIN CHARDONNAY (GISBORNE)

★★★★

1993	7	Now	NZ$36.00
1994	7	Now	NZ$33.00
1995	7	Now	NZ$31.00
1996	7	2000	NZ$28.00
1997	6	2001	NZ$22.00

CORBANS PRIVATE BIN CHARDONNAY (MARLBOROUGH)

★★★

before 1986	Prior		
1986	7	Now	NZ$54.00
1987	6	Prior	
1988	5	Prior	
1989	7	Now	NZ$43.00
1990	6	Now	NZ$34.00
1991	7	Now	NZ$37.00
1992	5	Now	NZ$24.00
1993	6	Now	NZ$27.00
1994	7	2001	NZ$29.00
1995	6	2001	NZ$23.00
1996	7	2002	NZ$25.00
1997	Not made		

CORBANS PRIVATE BIN NOBLE RIESLING 375ml

★★★

before 1989	Prior		
1989	6	Now	NZ$38.00
1990	7	Now	NZ$41.00
1991	Not made		
1992	Not made		
1993	Not made		
1994	Not made		
1995	5	Now	NZ$20.00
1996	7	2005	NZ$25.00
1997	7	2007	NZ$24.00

CORBANS PRIVATE BIN RIESLING

★★★

1986	7	Now	NZ$36.00
1987	Not made		
1988	6	Now	NZ$26.00
1989	7	Now	NZ$29.00
1990	6	Now	NZ$23.00
1991	7	2000	NZ$24.00
1992	6	2000	NZ$19.50
1993	6	2000	NZ$18.00
1994	7	2004	NZ$19.50
1995	7	2002	NZ$18.00
1996	7	2004	NZ$16.50

Coriole, in McLaren Vale, has been long known for unusually elegant reds. Of recent years the whites have improved greatly to bolster this fine maker's reputation still further. Winemaker: Stephen Hall.

CORIOLE CABERNET SAUVIGNON

★★★

before 1986	Prior		
1986	5	Now	$37.00
1987	5	Now	$35.00
1988	6	Now	$38.00
1989	6	Now	$36.00
1990	6	Now	$33.00
1991	5	Now	$25.00
1992	6	Now	$28.00
1993	6	2000	$26.00
1994	6	2001	$24.00
1995	Not made		
1996	6	2004	$21.00

CORIOLE CHARDONNAY ★★★★

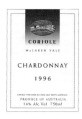

before 1989	Prior		
1989	7	Now	$45.00
1990	6	Now	$35.00
1991	5	Now	$27.00
1992	5	Now	$25.00
1993	6	Now	$28.00
1994	7	Now	$30.00

1995	6	Now	$24.00
1996	6	Now	$22.00
1997	6	2002	$20.00

CORIOLE LLOYD RESERVE SHIRAZ ★★★★★

1989	7	Now	$78.00
1990	6	Now	$62.00
1991	6	Now	$58.00
1992	7	2002	$62.00
1993	7	2003	$58.00
1994	7	2005	$54.00
1995	7	2006	$50.00
1996	7	2007	$46.00

CORIOLE REDSTONE (SHIRAZ/ CABERNET/GRENACHE) ★★★

1992	6	Now	$18.00
1993	6	Now	$17.00
1994	6	Now	$15.50
1995	6	2000	$14.50
1996	6	2002	$13.50

CORIOLE SEMILLON ★★★★

1994	6	Now	$22.00
1995	6	Now	$20.00
1996	6	2000	$18.50
1997	6	2002	$17.50

CORIOLE SHIRAZ ★★★★

before 1989		Prior	
1989	6	Now	$34.00
1990	6	Now	$31.00
1991	5	Now	$24.00
1992	7	2002	$31.00
1993	6	2001	$25.00
1994	6	2002	$23.00
1995	6	2003	$21.00
1996	6	2006	$20.00

Cowra Estate is a substantial producer taking advantage of the reputation for generous fruit earned by earlier Cowra wines from Petaluma and Rothbury. The wines are remarkably inexpensive. Winemaker: Simon Gilbert.

COWRA ESTATE CABERNET FRANC ROSE ★★★★

1995	5	Prior	
1996	5	Now	$14.50
1997	4	Now	$10.50
1998	5	Now	$12.50

COWRA ESTATE CABERNETS ★★★★

Year			Price
1988	4	Now	$15.00
1989	4	Now	$14.00
1990	Not made		
1994	5	Now	$15.00
1995	4	Now	$11.00
1996	7	Now	$18.00
1997	6	2000	$14.00

COWRA ESTATE CHARDONNAY ★★★★

Year			Price
1992	4	Now	$15.00
1993	4	Now	$14.00
1994	Not made		
1995	6	Now	$18.00
1996	5	Now	$13.50
1997	7	Now	$18.00
1998	4	2000	$9.50

Crabtree of Watervale is a Clare Valley producer previously known as Watervale Cellars. Their particularly fine wood-aged Semillon should be sought out.
Winemaker: Robert Crabtree.

CRABTREE RIESLING ★★★★

Year			Price
before 1984	Prior		
1984	7	Now	$52.00
1985	5	Now	$35.00
1986	6	Now	$39.00
1987	5	Now	$30.00
1988	7	Now	$39.00
1989	5	Now	$25.00
1990	7	Now	$33.00
1991	5	Now	$22.00
1992	5	Now	$20.00
1993	6	Now	$22.00
1994	6	2000	$21.00
1995	5	2000	$16.00
1996	6	2000	$18.00
1997	6	2002	$16.50
1998	6	2002	$15.50

CRABTREE SEMILLON ★★★★

Year			Price
1988	5	Now	$27.00
1989	7	Now	$36.00
1990	6	Now	$28.00
1991	6	Now	$26.00
1992	5	Now	$20.00
1993	5	Now	$19.00
1994	6	2000	$21.00
1995	5	2000	$16.00
1996	6	2002	$18.00
1997	6	2002	$16.50
1998	6	2002	N/R

CRABTREE SHIRAZ/CABERNET ★★★

1982	5	Prior	
1983	Not made		
1984	7	Prior	
1985	5	Prior	
1986	7	Now	$44.00
1987	6	Now	$35.00
1988	6	Now	$32.00
1989	6	Now	$30.00
1990	7	Now	$32.00
1991	5	Now	$21.00
1992	6	Now	$24.00
1993	6	2000	$22.00
1994	6	2002	$20.00
1995	6	2000	$19.00
1996	7	2002	$20.00

Craigie Knowe is a very small vineyard on the rocky soil at Cranbrook on Tasmania's east coast, and annually produce a powerful but complex Cabernet. Winemaker: John Austwick.

CRAIGIE KNOWE CABERNET SAUVIGNON ★★★★

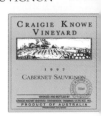

1984	5	Now	$60.00
1985	5	Now	$56.00
1986	Not made		
1987	Not made		
1988	4	Now	$36.00
1989	5	Now	$42.00
1990	5	Now	$39.00
1991	5	Now	$36.00
1992	5	Now	$33.00
1993	5	Now	$30.00
1994	6	Now	$34.00
1995	5	Now	$26.00
1996	4	Now	$19.50
1997	4	Now	$18.00

Craiglee is a re-establishment of a 19th century vineyard at Sunbury near Melbourne. Winemaker: Pat Carmody.

CRAIGLEE CHARDONNAY ★★★★

1982	5	Now	$68.00
1983	4	Now	$50.00
1984	5	Now	$58.00
1985	6	Now	$64.00
1986	6	Now	$60.00
1987	6	Now	$56.00
1988	5	Now	$43.00
1989	5	Now	$40.00
1990	5	Now	$37.00

1991	5	Now	$34.00
1992	6	2000	$38.00
1993	6	2000	$35.00
1994	6	2001	$32.00
1995	6	2001	$30.00
1996	6	2002	$28.00
1997	6	2001	$26.00

CRAIGLEE HERMITAGE ★★★★★

1979	5	Prior	
1980	5	Now	$100.00
1981	3	Now	$56.00
1982	3	Now	$50.00
1983	5	Now	$80.00
1984	6	Now	$88.00
1985	6	Now	$82.00
1986	6	Now	$76.00
1987	5	Now	$58.00
1988	6	2000	$64.00
1989	5	Now	$50.00
1990	7	2000	$64.00
1991	5	2001	$43.00
1992	5	2000	$40.00
1993	6	2000	$44.00
1994	6	2004	$41.00
1995	5	2002	$31.00
1996	6	2004	$35.00
1997	6	2007	$32.00

***Craigmoor** is an historic Mudgee winery which is now part of the Orlando Wyndham group.
Winemaker: Brett McKinnon.*

CRAIGMOOR CABERNET SAUVIGNON ★★★

before 1990		Prior	
1991	7	Now	$28.00
1992	5	Now	$19.00
1993	6	2000	$21.00
1994	6	2000	$19.50
1995	5	2002	$15.00
1996	7	2002	$19.50
1997	5	2002	$13.00
1998	5	2002	N/R

CRAIGMOOR CHARDONNAY ★★★

before 1988		Prior	
1988	7	Now	$35.00
1989	7	Now	$32.00
1990	5	Now	$21.00
1991	7	Now	$28.00
1992	6	Now	$22.00
1993	6	Now	$20.00

1994	7	Now	$22.00
1995	6	Now	$17.50
1996	6	Now	$16.00
1997	7	Now	$17.50
1998	6	2002	$14.00

CRAIGMOOR SEMILLON ★★★

1993	6	Now	$20.00
1994	5	Now	$16.00
1995	5	2000	$14.50
1996	6	2003	$16.50
1997	6	2003	$15.00
1998	5	2002	$11.50

CRAIGMOOR SHIRAZ ★★★

1988	4	Now	$20.00
1989	Not made		
1990	6	Now	$26.00
1991	6	Now	$24.00
1992	Not made		
1993	6	Now	$21.00
1994	6	Now	$19.50
1995	7	2002	$21.00
1996	6	2000	$16.50
1997	4	2001	N/R
1998	6	2003	N/R

Craneford is a Springton (Adelaide Hills) maker who produce an admirable Chardonnay. Winemaker: John Zilm.

CRANEFORD CHARDONNAY ★★★★

1986	5	Now	$29.00
1987	6	Now	$33.00
1988	6	Now	$30.00
1989	5	Now	$23.00
1990	Not made		
1991	Not made		
1992	5	Now	$18.50
1993	Not made		
1994	6	Now	$19.00
1995	4	Now	$11.50
1996	6	2000	$16.50
1997	6	2001	$15.00

CRANEFORD RIESLING ★★★★

1993	5	Now	$18.00
1994	6	Now	$20.00
1995	4	Now	$12.00
1996	6	2002	$17.00
1997	7	Now	$18.50

CRANEFORD SHIRAZ

1988	7	Now	$36.00
1989	6	Now	$29.00
1990	7	Now	$31.00
1991	6	2001	$25.00
1992	6	Now	$23.00
1993	Not made		
1994	Not made		
1995	Not made		
1996	6	2006	$17.00

★★★★

Croser is a methode champenoise wine of a quality unprecedented (for an Australian sparkling wine) when it was first released. The wine is made at Petaluma. Winemaker: Brian Croser.

CROSER

1985	4	Now	$62.00
1986	4	Now	$58.00
1987	5	Now	$66.00
1988	5	Now	$62.00
1989	Not made		
1990	7	2000	$74.00
1991	4	Now	$39.00
1992	7	2001	$64.00
1993	5	Now	$42.00
1994	6	2000	$47.00
1995	4	2000	$29.00
1996	5	2010	$33.00
1997	5	2002	$31.00

★★★★★

Cullen Wines are low key but high quality producers in an area where the fruit is so often outstanding - Margaret River. Cullen wines are powerful, individual and long-living. Winemaker: Vanya Cullen.

CULLEN CABERNET SAUVIGNON/MERLOT

1975	4	Now	$220.00
1976	5	Now	$260.00
1977	4	Now	$190.00
1978	4	Now	$175.00
1979	3	2005	$120.00
1980	5	2000	$190.00
1981	5	Now	$175.00
1982	6	Now	$195.00
1983	5	Now	$150.00
1984	6	Now	$165.00
1985	6	2000	$155.00
1986	6	2003	$140.00
1987	4	Now	$88.00
1988	6	2005	$120.00

★★★★★

1989	4	Now	$76.00
1990	6	2005	$105.00
1991	7	2010	$110.00
1992	6	2005	$90.00
1993	5	2000	$70.00
1994	6	2010	$78.00
1995	7	2020	$84.00
1996	6	2010	$66.00
1997	6	2020	$62.00

CULLEN CHARDONNAY ★★★★

1980	3	Now	$84.00
1981	5	Now	$130.00
1982	6	Now	$145.00
1983	5	Now	$110.00
1984	6	Now	$125.00
1985	5	Now	$96.00
1986	4	Now	$72.00
1987	5	Now	$82.00
1988	5	Now	$76.00
1989	3	Now	$42.00
1990	4	Now	$52.00
1991	3	Now	$36.00
1992	5	Now	$56.00
1993	5	Now	$52.00
1994	6	Now	$58.00
1995	5	2000	$45.00
1996	6	2005	$50.00
1997	6	2009	$46.00
1998	6	2010	$42.00

CULLEN PINOT NOIR ★★★★

1984	5	Now	$86.00
1985	5	Now	$80.00
1986	5	Now	$74.00
1987	4	Now	$54.00
1988	4	Now	$50.00
1989	3	Now	$35.00
1990	5	Now	$54.00
1991	4	Now	$40.00
1992	6	2000	$56.00
1993	6	2000	$52.00
1994	5	Now	$40.00
1995	6	2000	$44.00
1996	6	2001	$41.00
1997	6	2001	$38.00
1998	6	2002	$35.00

CULLEN RESERVE SAUVIGNON BLANC/SEMILLON ★★★★

1991	4	Now	$30.00
1992	5	Now	$35.00
1993	7	Now	$45.00

1994	5	Now	$30.00
1995	6	Now	$33.00
1996	6	2005	$31.00
1997	6	2000	$28.00
1998	6	2000	$26.00

Dalwhinnie Winery *is a high country Moonambel (Victoria) maker with eighteen hectares of vines. The Shiraz is magnificent, and the other wines not far behind. Winemaker: David Jones.*

DALWHINNIE CABERNET SAUVIGNON ★★★★★

1980	7	2000	$160.00
1981	5	Now	$100.00
1982	6	Now	$115.00
1983	6	Now	$105.00
1984	7	Now	$115.00
1985	5	Now	$76.00
1986	7	Now	$100.00
1987	5	Now	$66.00
1988	7	2000	$86.00
1989	5	Now	$56.00
1990	7	2000	$74.00
1991	6	2002	$58.00
1992	6	2004	$54.00
1993	7	2004	$58.00
1994	7	2006	$54.00
1995	7	2008	$50.00
1997	7	2010	$46.00

DALWHINNIE CHARDONNAY ★★★★★

1984	5	Now	$78.00
1985	6	Now	$86.00
1986	6	Now	$80.00
1987	7	Now	$86.00
1988	7	Now	$80.00
1989	4	Now	$42.00
1990	7	Now	$68.00
1991	6	Now	$54.00
1992	7	2000	$58.00
1993	6	2002	$47.00
1994	6	2002	$43.00
1995	5	2003	$33.00
1996	7	2004	$43.00
1997	6	2005	$34.00

DALWHINNIE SHIRAZ ★★★★★

1980	7	Now	$200.00
1981	5	Now	$130.00
1982	6	Now	$145.00
1983	Not made		

1984	6	Now	$125.00
1985	7	Now	$135.00
1986	6	Now	$105.00
1987	5	Now	$82.00
1988	7	2000	$105.00
1989	5	Now	$70.00
1990	7	2000	$92.00
1991	7	2004	$86.00
1992	7	2006	$78.00
1993	5	2002	$52.00
1994	7	2008	$68.00
1995	6	2008	$54.00
1996	6	2009	$50.00
1997	6	2010	$46.00

d'Arenberg are reliable, well-distributed McLaren Vale makers with a large range of respected wines.
Winemaker: Chester Osborn.

d'ARENBERG DECLARED VINTAGE FORTIFIED SHIRAZ ★★★★

1971	6	Now	$72.00
1972	Not made		
1973	7	2003	$72.00
1974	Not made		
1975	7	2006	$62.00
1976	7	2004	$56.00
1977	Not made		
1978	6	Now	$42.00
1979	Not made		
1987	7	2010	$42.00
1988	Not made		
1993	5	2010	$25.00
1994	Not made		
1995	7	2017	$31.00
1996	Not made		
1997	7	2020	$26.00

d'ARENBERG HIGH TRELLIS CABERNET SAUVIGNON ★★★★

before 1976		Prior	
1976	7	2005	$100.00
1977	6	Prior	
1978	6	2008	$74.00
1979	6	Prior	
1980	Not made		
1981	5	Prior	
1982	6	Now	$54.00
1983	5	Now	$42.00
1984	6	Prior	
1985	6	2010	$43.00
1986	6	2005	$40.00

1987	5	Now	$31.00
1988	5	2001	$28.00
1989	6	2006	$32.00
1990	6	2003	$29.00
1991	7	2010	$32.00
1992	5	2006	$21.00
1993	4	2005	$15.50
1994	5	2008	$18.00
1995	7	2012	$23.00
1996	6	2012	$18.50

d'ARENBERG IRONSTONE PRESSINGS
(GRENACHE/SHIRAZ)   ★★★★

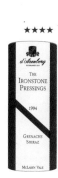

1988	5	2001	$47.00
1989	6	2002	$52.00
1990	6	2004	$48.00
1991	6	2006	$44.00
1992	6	2005	$41.00
1993	5	2005	$32.00
1994	6	2010	$35.00
1995	7	2015	$38.00
1996	6	2013	$30.00

d'ARENBERG NOBLE RIESLING (375ml)   ★★★★

1985	7	Now	$64.00
1986	Not made		
1987	6	Prior	
1988	Not made		
1989	6	Prior	
1990	Not made		
1991	6	Now	$34.00
1992	7	2002	$37.00
1993	4	Now	$19.50
1994	3	Now	$13.50
1995	5	2005	$21.00
1996	5	2007	$19.50
1997	6	2010	$21.00

d'ARENBERG OLIVE GROVE CHARDONNAY   ★★★★

before 1987	Prior		
1987	6	Now	$30.00
1988	7	Now	$32.00
1989	6	Now	$26.00
1990	6	Now	$24.00
1991	6	2000	$22.00
1992	6	2000	$20.00
1993	7	2004	$22.00
1994	7	2005	$20.00

1995	7	2005	$19.00
1996	6	2007	$15.00
1997	6	2010	$14.00

d'ARENBERG OLD VINE SHIRAZ ★★★★

1970	4	Now	$92.00
1971	6	Now	$125.00
1972	6	Prior	
1973	7	Prior	
1974	Not made		
1975	4	Prior	
1976	6	2005	$86.00
1977	Not made		
1978	5	Prior	
1979	Not made		
1980	5	Prior	
1981	Not made		
1982	5	2010	$45.00
1983	Not made		
1984	Not made		
1985	6	2005	$43.00
1986	Not made		
1987	6	Now	$37.00
1988	6	2000	$34.00
1989	6	2002	$32.00
1990	7	2005	$34.00
1991	7	2010	$32.00
1992	6	2015	$25.00
1993	4	2006	$15.50
1994	6	2008	$21.00
1995	7	2015	$23.00
1996	6	2010	$18.50

d'ARENBERG ORIGINAL SHIRAZ/GRENACHE
★★★★

1961	6	2000	$270.00
1962	Not made		
1963	7	2005	$270.00
1964	6	2002	$215.00
1965	5	Now	$165.00
1966	4	Now	$120.00
1967	7	2008	$200.00
1968	5	Now	$130.00
1969	5	Now	$120.00
1970	6	2010	$135.00
1971	6	2000	$125.00
1972	5	2001	$98.00
1973	4	Now	$72.00
1974	Not made		
1975	5	2000	$78.00

1976	7	2005	$100.00
1977	Not made		
1978	Not made		
1979	5	Now	$56.00
1980	Not made		
1981	Not made		
1982	6	2010	$54.00
1983	Not made		
1984	Not made		
1985	Not made		
1986	6	2016	$40.00
1987	7	2020	$43.00
1988	6	2015	$34.00
1989	5	2014	$26.00
1990	6	2018	$29.00
1991	7	2008	$32.00
1992	7	2020	$29.00
1993	5	2020	$19.50
1994	5	2015	$18.00
1995	7	2030	$23.00
1996	6	2025	$18.50

d'ARENBERG THE DEAD ARM SHIRAZ ★★★★★

1993	4	2000	$39.00
1994	6	2010	$54.00
1995	7	2015	$58.00
1996	6	2012	$46.00

d'ARENBERG THE CUSTODIAN GRENACHE ★★★★

1994	6	2005	$24.00
1995	7	2007	$26.00
1996	6	2006	$20.00
1997	6	2008	$19.00

d'ARENBERG THE DRY DAM RIESLING ★★★★

before 1982	Prior		
1982	6	Now	$50.00
1983	4	Prior	
1984	5	Prior	
1985	6	Now	$40.00
1986	Not made		
1987	6	2000	$35.00
1988	Not made		
1989	7	2002	$35.00
1990	6	2000	$27.00
1991	Not made		
1992	7	2005	$27.00
1993	7	2007	$25.00
1994	2	Now	$6.75

1995	6	2008	$18.50
1996	6	2010	$17.50
1997	6	2011	$16.00

d'ARENBERG THE PEPPERMINT PADDOCK
CHAMBOURCIN ★★★

1993	4	Prior	
1994	5	Now	$17.50
1995	6	Now	$19.50

*David Wynn Wines are made at the Mountadam winery
from fruit sourced from the Eden Valley.
Winemaker: Adam Wynn.*

DAVID WYNN PATRIARCH
SHIRAZ ★★★★

1990	6	Now	$56.00
1991	6	Now	$52.00
1992	7	Now	$56.00
1993	7	Now	$52.00
1994	7	Now	$49.00
1995	6	Now	$39.00
1996	7	2000	$42.00

*De Bortoli are Griffith and Yarra Valley producers whose
wide range of wines includes an astonishingly good botrytis-
affected Sauternes style.
Winemakers: Darren De Bortoli (chief), Nick Guy (Bilbul),
Stephen Webber and David Slingsby-Smith (Yarra Valley).*

DE BORTOLI "NOBLE ONE" (375 ml) ★★★★★

1982	7	Now	$74.00
1983	6	Now	$58.00
1984	5	Now	$46.00
1985	5	Now	$42.00
1986	5	Now	$39.00
1987	7	Now	$50.00
1988	6	Now	$40.00
1989	Not made		
1990	7	Now	$40.00
1991	6	Now	$32.00
1992	6	Now	$29.00
1993	7	Now	$32.00
1994	7	2000	$29.00
1995	7	2001	$27.00
1996	7	2007	$25.00

DE BORTOLI YARRA VALLEY
CABERNET SAUVIGNON ★★★★

1988	6	Now	$64.00
1989	5	Now	$49.00
1990	5	Now	$46.00

1991	6	2000	$50.00
1992	7	2002	$54.00
1993	7	2006	$50.00
1994	6	2004	$40.00
1995	7	2010	$44.00
1996	5	2004	$29.00

DE BORTOLI YARRA VALLEY CHARDONNAY

★★★★

1989	5	Now	$45.00
1990	5	Now	$42.00
1991	6	Now	$46.00
1992	6	Now	$43.00
1993	6	Now	$40.00
1994	6	2000	$37.00
1995	7	2001	$40.00
1996	7	2002	$37.00
1997	7	2004	$34.00

DE BORTOLI YARRA VALLEY PINOT NOIR   ★★★★

1994	5	Now	$36.00
1995	6	2002	$40.00
1996	7	2003	$44.00
1997	6	2005	$35.00

DE BORTOLI YARRA VALLEY
SHIRAZ ★★★★

1988	5	Now	$56.00
1989	5	Now	$52.00
1990	5	Now	$49.00
1991	Not made		
1992	6	2000	$50.00
1993	7	2002	$54.00
1994	6	2000	$43.00
1995	6	2003	$40.00
1996	5	2002	$31.00

Delamere Vineyard is a Pipers Brook (Tasmania) producer specialising in the Burgundian varieties.
Winemaker: Richard Richardson.

DELAMERE CHARDONNAY   ★★★

before 1990	Prior		
1990	7	Now	$56.00
1991	5	Now	$37.00
1992	6	Now	$41.00
1993	4	Now	$25.00
1994	5	Now	$29.00
1995	6	Now	$32.00
1996	Not made		
1997	4	Now	$18.50
1998	7	2001	$30.00

DELAMERE PINOT NOIR ★★★★

before 1988		Prior	
1988	6	Now	$50.00
1989	5	Prior	
1990	6	Now	$42.00
1991	6	Now	$39.00
1992	6	Now	$36.00
1993	5	Prior	
1994	7	Now	$36.00
1995	6	Now	$29.00
1996	6	2002	$27.00
1997	6	2001	$25.00

Delatite is a small, extremely good vineyard in Victoria's Mansfield region. Winemaker: Ros Ritchie.

DELATITE DEVIL'S RIVER
(CABERNET SAUVIGNON/MERLOT to 1986) ★★★★

1984	6	Now	$64.00
1985	5	Now	$50.00
1986	6	Now	$54.00
1987	6	Now	$50.00
1988	7	Now	$54.00
1989	4	Now	$29.00
1990	6	Now	$40.00
1991	7	Now	$44.00
1992	6	Now	$35.00
1993	5	Now	$27.00
1994	6	2000	$30.00
1995	5	2001	$23.00
1996	6	2003	$25.00
1997	6	2003	$23.00

DELATITE CHARDONNAY ★★★

1987	5	Now	$45.00
1988	5	Now	$41.00
1989	6	Now	$46.00
1990	6	Now	$43.00
1991	7	Now	$46.00
1992	6	Now	$37.00
1993	5	Now	$28.00
1994	6	2000	$31.00
1995	6	2001	$29.00
1996	6	2002	$27.00
1997	6	2000	$25.00
1998	7	2004	$27.00

DELATITE GEWURZTRAMINER

★★★★

before 1987		Prior	
1987	7	Now	$54.00
1988	6	Now	$43.00
1989	5	Now	$33.00
1990	6	Now	$37.00
1991	6	Now	$34.00
1992	6	Now	$31.00
1993	6	Now	$29.00
1994	5	2000	$22.00
1995	6	2000	$25.00
1996	7	2001	$27.00
1997	6	2002	$21.00
1998	6	2003	$20.00

DELATITE PINOT NOIR

★★★

before 1986		Prior	
1986	6	Now	$56.00
1987	5	Now	$44.00
1988	6	Now	$48.00
1989	7	Now	$52.00
1990	6	Now	$41.00
1991	Not made		
1992	7	Now	$41.00
1993	6	2000	$33.00
1994	6	2000	$30.00
1995	5	2000	$23.00
1996	6	2002	$26.00
1997	7	2003	$28.00
1998	6	2004	$22.00

DELATITE RIESLING

★★★★

1982	7	Now	$70.00
1983	6	Now	$56.00
1984	5	Now	$44.00
1985	5	Now	$40.00
1986	6	Now	$45.00
1987	7	Now	$48.00
1988	5	Now	$32.00
1989	5	Now	$29.00
1990	6	Now	$33.00
1991	7	2001	$35.00
1992	6	2002	$28.00
1993	6	2002	$26.00
1994	7	2002	$28.00
1995	5	2003	$18.50
1996	6	2006	$20.00
1997	6	2003	$19.00
1998	7	2005	$21.00

Delegat's Wine Estate is a Henderson (New Zealand) maker of some fine wines. Their "Proprietor's Reserve" range (now deleted) was dependably good. I have been asked by their management to delete all reference to both Delegat's and Oyster Bay from this book, which I feel I cannot do as they are important producers, but have withdrawn the winemaker's ratings. Winemaker: Not stated.

DELEGAT'S HAWKES BAY CHARDONNAY	★★★
DELEGAT'S HAWKES BAY CABERNET/MERLOT	★★★
DELEGAT'S HAWKES BAY SAUVIGNON BLANC	★★★
DELEGAT'S PROPRIETOR'S RESERVE CABERNET SAUVIGNON	★★★★
DELEGAT'S PROPRIETOR'S RESERVE CHARDONNAY	★★★
DELEGAT'S PROPRIETOR'S RESERVE FUME BLANC	★★★★
DELEGAT'S PROPRIETOR'S RESERVE MERLOT	★★★★
DELEGAT'S RIESLING	★★★

de Redcliffe Estates are small Auckland based makers of a limited range of graceful and rather delicate wines. Winemaker: Mark Compton.

de REDCLIFFE ESTATES
CABERNET/MERLOT　　★★★

before 1996		Prior	
1996	6	Now	NZ$20.00
1997	6	Now	NZ$18.50
1998	7	2001	NZ$20.00

de REDCLIFFE ESTATES
CHARDONNAY　　★★★★

before 1996		Prior	
1996	7	Now	NZ$19.00
1997	7	Now	NZ$17.50
1998	6	Now	N/R

de REDCLIFFE ESTATES SEMILLON/
CHARDONNAY　　★★★

before 1996		Prior	
1996	6	Now	NZ$11.50
1997	7	Now	NZ$12.50
1998	Not made		

Devil's Lair *is a substantial Margaret River vineyard owned by Southcorp and planted with the noble Bordelaise and Burgundian varieties. Winemaker: Janice McDonald.*

DEVIL'S LAIR CHARDONNAY ★★★★

before 1993		Prior	
1993	5	Now	$41.00
1994	6	Now	$45.00
1995	6	2000	$42.00
1996	6	2002	$39.00
1997	6	2004	$36.00

DEVIL'S LAIR "MARGARET RIVER" ★★★★
(CABERNET SAUVIGNON)

1990	5	Now	$52.00
1991	5	Now	$48.00
1992	5	Now	$45.00
1993	5	2000	$41.00
1994	6	2004	$46.00
1995	6	2005	$42.00
1996	5	2007	$33.00

DEVIL'S LAIR PINOT NOIR ★★★★★

1992	5	Now	$38.00
1993	6	Now	$42.00
1994	5	Now	$33.00
1995	5	Now	$30.00
1996	5	Now	$28.00
1997	6	2000	$31.00

Diamond Valley Vineyards *are high quality Yarra Valley makers who are also developing a vineyard at Phillip Island. Only the "Estate" wines are made wholly from their own fruit. Winemaker: David Lance.*

DIAMOND VALLEY VINEYARDS
BLUE LABEL CHARDONNAY ★★★

before 1994		Prior	
1994	5	Now	$20.00
1995	6	Now	$23.00
1996	7	Now	$25.00
1997	6	Now	$20.00

DIAMOND VALLEY VINEYARDS BLUE LABEL
CABERNET SAUVIGNON ★★★

1986	7	Prior	
1987	6	Now	$39.00
1988	6	Now	$36.00
1989	6	Now	$33.00

1990	5	Now	$25.00
1991	Not made		
1992	6	2000	$26.00
1993	Not made		
1994	7	2002	$26.00
1995	Not made		
1996	6	2002	$19.50

DIAMOND VALLEY VINEYARDS BLUE LABEL PINOT NOIR ★★★★

before 1990	Prior		
1990	7	Now	$36.00
1991	7	Now	$34.00
1992	6	Now	$27.00
1993	6	Now	$25.00
1994	7	Now	$27.00
1995	6	Now	$21.00
1996	7	2000	$23.00
1997	6	2001	$18.00

DIAMOND VALLEY VINEYARDS CLOSE PLANTED PINOT NOIR ★★★★★

1992	7	Now	$62.00
1993	6	2000	$50.00
1994	5	2002	$38.00
1995	7	2000	$50.00
1996	7	2003	$46.00
1997	7	2004	$43.00

DIAMOND VALLEY VINEYARDS ESTATE CABERNET ★★★★

before 1988	Prior		
1988	6	Now	$43.00
1989	6	Now	$40.00
1990	7	2000	$43.00
1991	6	Now	$34.00
1992	7	2002	$37.00
1993	Not made		
1994	6	2002	$27.00
1995	Not made		
1996	5	2004	$19.50

1989 CABERNET
CABERNET SAUVIGNON • MERLOT • CABERNET FRANC • MALBEC
ESTATE WINE

Diamond Valley Vineyards
750ml
PRODUCT OF AUSTRALIA

DIAMOND VALLEY VINEYARDS ESTATE CHARDONNAY ★★★★★

before 1991	Prior		
1991	6	Now	$43.00
1992	7	Now	$46.00
1993	6	Now	$37.00
1994	6	Now	$34.00
1995	7	2000	$37.00
1996	7	2001	$34.00
1997	7	2002	$31.00

1990 CHARDONNAY
ESTATE WINE

Diamond Valley Vineyards
750ml
PRODUCT OF AUSTRALIA

DIAMOND VALLEY VINEYARDS ESTATE
PINOT NOIR ★★★★★

before 1986	Prior		
1986	7	Now	$96.00
1987	7	Now	$88.00
1988	6	Now	$70.00
1989	5	Now	$54.00
1990	7	Now	$70.00
1991	7	Now	$64.00
1992	5	Now	$43.00
1993	7	2000	$56.00
1994	6	2001	$44.00
1995	5	2000	$34.00
1996	7	2003	$44.00

DIAMOND VALLEY VINEYARDS ★★★
WHITE DIAMOND

before 1990	Prior		
1990	Not made		
1991	Not made		
1992	6	Now	$11.50
1993	6	Now	$10.50
1994	7	Now	$11.50

eries discontinued.

*Domaine A is the label under which the elite best of Stoney
Vineyard's wines are released. The Pinot is superb.
Winemaker: Peter Althaus.*

DOMAINE A CABERNET SAUVIGNON ★★★★★

1990	6	Now	$82.00
1991	6	2001	$76.00
1992	7	2005	$82.00
1993	5	2001	$54.00
1994	7	2010	$70.00
1995	6	2005	$56.00
1996	Not made		
1997	7	2010	N/R
1998	7	2014	N/R

DOMAINE A PINOT NOIR ★★★★★★

1990	5	Prior	
1991	6	Now	$110.00
1992	7	2000	$120.00
1993	5	2000	$80.00
1994	7	2005	$100.00
1995	6	2002	$82.00
1996	Not made		
1997	7	2006	$82.00
1998	7	2010	N/R

Domaine Chandon *is the Moet et Chandon owned Yarra Valley sparkling wine vineyard. Although until 1992 the labels state "NV" for non-vintage, they bear a cuvee number which gives the year: "86.1" and "87.1" are based largely on fruit from the 1986 and 1987 vintages respectively.*
Winemakers: Dr Tony Jordan, Wayne Donaldson and Neville Rowe.

DOMAINE CHANDON GREEN POINT CHARDONNAY ★★★★

1989	5	Now	$39.00
1990	4	Now	$29.00
1991	5	Now	$33.00
1992	4	Now	$24.00
1993	5	Now	$28.00
1994	6	Now	$31.00
1995	6	Now	$29.00
1996	7	2001	$32.00

DOMAINE CHANDON nn.1 (BRUT) ★★★★★

1987	4	Now	$41.00
1988	5	Now	$48.00
1989	6	Now	$52.00
1990	7	Now	$58.00
1991	6	Now	$46.00
1992	7	Now	$49.00
1993	6	Now	$39.00
1994	7	Now	$42.00
1995	6	Now	$34.00

DOMAINE CHANDON nn.2 (BLANC DE BLANCS) ★★★★

1986	6	Now	$54.00
1987	Not made		
1988	Not made		
1989	6	Now	$43.00
1990	6	Now	$40.00
1991	7	Now	$43.00
1992	6	Now	$34.00
1993	7	Now	$37.00

DOMAINE CHANDON nn.3 (BLANC DE NOIRS) ★★★★

1988	6	Now	$42.00
1989	Not made		
1990	7	Now	$42.00
1991	6	Now	$33.00
1992	7	Now	$36.00

DOMAINE CHANDON nn.4 (ROSE) ★★★★

1990	5	Now	$42.00
1991	5	Now	$39.00
1992	6	Now	$44.00

1993	6	Now	$40.00
1994	7	Now	$44.00
1995	6	Now	$34.00

DOMAINE CHANDON nn.5
(YARRA VALLEY CUVEE)   ★★★★

before 1990		Not made	
1990	7	Now	$50.00
1991	6	Now	$40.00
1992	7	Now	$43.00
1993	6	Now	$34.00
1994	6	Now	$31.00

*Doonkuna Estate is one of the longest established of the
Canberra area producers. The quality of their wines,
particularly in recent vintages, is admirable.
Winemaker: Malcolm Burdett.*

DOONKUNA ESTATE CABERNET SAUVIGNON ★★★

1989	6	Prior	
1990	5	Now	$23.00
1991	6	Now	$26.00
1992	7	Now	$28.00
1993	5	Now	$18.50
1994	7	Now	$24.00
1995	7	2000	$22.00
1996	5	2002	$15.00

DOONKUNA ESTATE
CHARDONNAY   ★★★★

before 1993		Prior	
1993	6	Now	$23.00
1994	5	Now	$18.00
1995	6	Now	$20.00
1996	6	Now	$18.50

DOONKUNA ESTATE PINOT
NOIR   ★★★

before 1994		Prior	
1994	6	Now	$22.00
1995	7	Now	$24.00
1995	5	Now	$15.50
1996	5	Now	$14.50

DOONKUNA ESTATE
RIESLING   ★★★★

before 1992		Prior	
1993	6	Now	$14.00
1994	6	Now	$13.00
1995	6	Now	$12.00
1996	5	Now	$9.25
1997	6	Now	$10.00

DOONKUNA ESTATE SAUVIGNON BLANC ★★★★★

before 1992		Prior	
1992	6	Now	$23.00
1993	6	Now	$21.00
1994	6	Now	$20.00
1995	6	Now	$18.50
1996	6	Now	$17.00
1997	6	Now	$16.00

DOONKUNA ESTATE
SHIRAZ ★★★★

1990	5	Now	$23.00
1991	6	Now	$26.00
1992	6	Now	$24.00
1993	6	Now	$22.00
1994	7	Now	$24.00
1995	6	Now	$19.00
1996	6	2000	$18.00

Draytons are long established and much respected Pokolbin makers with a small range of reliably good wines. Winemaker: Trevor Drayton.

DRAYTONS CABERNET SAUVIGNON ★★★

1988	6	Now	$25.00
1989	Not made		
1990	Not made		
1991	7	2000	$23.00
1992	6	Now	$18.50
1993	7	2002	$20.00
1994	Not made		
1995	6	2002	$15.00

DRAYTONS CHARDONNAY ★★★

before 1986		Prior	
1986	7	Now	$37.00
1987	7	Now	$35.00
1988	4	Now	$18.50
1989	7	Now	$30.00
1990	5	Now	$19.50
1991	7	Now	$25.00
1992	7	Now	$23.00
1993	4	Now	$12.50
1994	5	Now	$14.50
1995	6	Now	$16.00

DRAYTONS CHARDONNAY/
SEMILLON ★★★

before 1987		Prior	
1987	7	Now	$30.00
1988	6	Now	$24.00
1989	6	Now	$22.00
1990	5	Now	$17.00
1991	7	Now	$22.00

1992	5	Now	$14.50
1993	6	Now	$16.00
1994	4	Now	$10.00
1995	6	Now	$14.00

DRAYTONS BIN 5555 SHIRAZ
(formerly IVANHOE HERMITAGE) ★★★

before 1988	Prior		
1988	7	Now	$33.00
1989	5	Now	$22.00
1990	5	Now	$20.00
1991	7	2000	$26.00
1992	5	Now	$17.50
1993	6	2000	$19.00
1994	4	Now	$12.00
1995	7	2005	$19.00

DRAYTON VERDELHO ★★★
before 1990	Prior		
1990	5	Now	$16.50
1991	6	Now	$18.50
1992	5	Now	$14.00
1993	7	Now	$18.50
1994	5	Now	$12.00
1995	6	Now	$13.50

DRAYTON WILLIAM SHIRAZ ★★★★
1988	7	2000	$43.00
1989	6	Now	$34.00
1990	7	2000	$37.00
1991	7	2005	$34.00
1992	Not made		
1993	6	2005	$25.00

Dromana Estate is a Mornington Peninsula producer of some of the Australia's finest wines (see also Schinus). Winemaker: Garry Crittenden.

DROMANA ESTATE CABERNET/MERLOT ★★★★★

1986	6	Now	$68.00
1987	5	Now	$52.00
1988	6	Now	$58.00
1989	5	Now	$45.00
1990	6	Now	$50.00
1991	5	Now	$39.00
1992	6	Now	$43.00
1993	6	Now	$40.00
1994	6	2001	$37.00
1995	5	2001	$28.00
1996	6	2002	$31.00

DROMANA ESTATE CHARDONNAY ★★★★★
1986	6	Now	$70.00
1987	5	Now	$54.00
1988	6	Now	$60.00

1989	6	Now	$56.00
1990	6	Now	$52.00
1991	7	2000	$56.00
1992	6	2000	$44.00
1993	6	Now	$41.00
1994	7	2002	$44.00
1995	6	2002	$35.00
1996	5	2001	$27.00
1997	5	2001	$25.00

DROMANA ESTATE PINOT NOIR ★★★★★

1986	5	Prior	
1987	5	Now	$54.00
1988	6	Now	$60.00
1989	6	Now	$56.00
1990	5	Now	$43.00
1991	7	Now	$56.00
1992	6	Now	$44.00
1993	6	Now	$41.00
1994	6	2000	$38.00
1995	6	2001	$35.00
1996	7	2001	$38.00
1997	6	2001	$30.00

Dulcinea Vineyard is a small producer at Sulky, near Ballarat in Victoria. Winemaker: Rod Stott.

DULCINEA CABERNET SAUVIGNON ★★★

1995	4	Now	$14.50
1996	6	Now	$20.00
1997	5	2000	$16.00

DULCINEA CHARDONNAY ★★★

1994	4	Now	$14.50
1995	5	Now	$16.50
1996	7	Now	$21.00
1997	6	Now	$17.00

DULCINEA PINOT NOIR ★★★

1995	4	Now	$13.50
1996	6	Now	$19.00
1997	6	Now	$18.00

Eaglehawk is the name under which moderately priced wines from the Wolf Blass empire are released. Winemaker: Wendy Stuckey.

EAGLEHAWK CHARDONNAY ★★★

before 1994		Prior	
1994	6	Now	$14.00
1995	6	Now	$13.00
1996	7	Now	$14.00
1997	6	Now	$11.00
1998	6	2000	$10.50

EAGLEHAWK RIESLING ★★★

before 1991		Prior	
1991	7	Now	$20.00
1992	6	Now	$16.00
1993	6	Now	$14.50
1994	6	Now	$13.50
1995	6	Now	$12.50
1996	7	2000	$13.50
1997	7	2002	$12.50
1998	7	2003	$11.50

EAGLEHAWK SEMILLON/ SAUVIGNON BLANC ★★

before 1996		Prior	
1996	6	Now	$12.00
1997	6	Now	$11.00
1998	7	2000	$12.00

EAGLEHAWK ESTATE SHIRAZ/ MERLOT/CABERNET ★★★

before 1991		Prior	
1991	6	Now	$19.00
1992	5	Now	$14.50
1993	6	Now	$16.00
1994	7	Now	$17.50
1995	6	Now	$13.50
1996	6	2000	$12.50
1997	6	2000	$12.00

Elderton Wines *are successful Barossa Valley makers who are enjoying the rewards of quality production and vigorous marketing. Winemaker: James Irvine.*

ELDERTON CABERNET SAUVIGNON ★★★★

1984	6	Now	$48.00
1985	Not made		
1986	6	Now	$41.00
1987	7	Now	$44.00
1988	7	Now	$41.00
1989	6	Now	$33.00
1990	6	Now	$30.00
1991	7	Now	$33.00
1992	7	Now	$30.00
1993	6	Now	$24.00
1994	6	2000	$22.00
1995	6	Now	$20.00
1996	7	2006	$22.00
1997	6	2005	$17.50

ELDERTON CABERNET/SHIRAZ/MERLOT ★★★★

1992	7	2002	$47.00
1993	Not made		
1994	7	2000	$40.00
1995	7	2001	$37.00
1996	7	2002	$35.00

ELDERTON COMMAND SHIRAZ ★★★★★

1984	5	Now	$120.00
1985	6	Now	$135.00
1986	6	Now	$125.00
1987	6	Now	$115.00
1988	6	Now	$105.00
1989	5	Now	$84.00
1990	7	Now	$105.00
1991	Not made		
1992	7	2002	$94.00
1993	6	2003	$74.00
1994	7	2005	$80.00
1995	6	2005	$64.00

ELDERTON RIESLING ★★★

before 1989	Prior		
1989	6	Now	$27.00
1990	6	Now	$25.00
1991	Not made		
1992	6	Now	$21.00
1993	6	Now	$20.00
1994	6	Now	$18.50
1995	Not made		
1996	Not made		
1997	6	2002	$14.50
1998	7	2005	$15.50

ELDERTON SHIRAZ ★★★★

1982	7	Now	$74.00
1983	5	Now	$49.00
1984	5	Now	$45.00
1985	6	Now	$50.00
1986	6	Now	$47.00
1987	6	Now	$43.00
1988	7	Now	$47.00
1989	6	Now	$37.00
1990	7	2000	$40.00
1991	7	Now	$37.00
1992	7	Now	$34.00
1993	6	2000	$27.00
1994	7	2000	$29.00
1995	6	2001	$23.00
1996	7	2005	$25.00

Elgee Park is one of the first Mornington Peninsula vineyards (established in 1972) whose graceful wines are of very good quality. Winemaker: Tod Dexter.

ELGEE PARK FAMILY RESERVE CHARDONNAY ★★★★

before 1990		Prior	
1990	7	Now	$45.00
1991	5	Now	$30.00
1992	6	Now	$33.00
1993	7	Now	$36.00
1994	6	Now	$28.00
1995	6	Now	$26.00
1996	5	Now	$20.00
1997	6	Now	$23.00

ELGEE PARK FAMILY RESERVE RIESLING ★★★

before 1989		Prior	
1989	4	Now	$15.50
1990	5	Now	$18.00
1991	4	Now	$13.50
1992	6	Now	$18.50
1993	5	Now	$14.50
1994	7	Now	$18.50
1995	6	Now	$15.00
1996	6	Now	$13.50

Elsewhere Vineyard is a Southern Tasmanian maker who produces a very highly regarded Pinot Noir. The maker is apparently reluctant to supply ratings, so these are my own. Winemaker: Andrew Hood.

ELSEWHERE VINEYARD PINOT NOIR ★★★★

1993	4	Now	$26.00
1994	5	Now	$30.00
1995	6	Now	$33.00

Eppalock Ridge (formerly Romany Rye Vineyards) are Redesdale (Bendigo district) makers with a small crush of individual wines which include an admirable Shiraz. Winemaker: Rod Hourigan.

EPPALOCK RIDGE CABERNET SAUVIGNON ★★★

1988	5	Now	$41.00
1989	Not made		
1990	5	Now	$35.00
1991	5	Now	$32.00
1992	6	2001	$36.00
1993	Not made		
1994	Not made		
1995	Not made		
1996	6	2004	$26.00
1997	5	2004	$20.00

EPPALOCK RIDGE SHIRAZ ★★★★

before 1990		Prior	
1990	5	Now	$37.00
1991	5	2000	$34.00
1992	6	Now	$38.00
1993	5	2001	$29.00
1994	5	Now	$27.00
1995	Not made		
1996	5	2004	$23.00
1997	5	2005	$22.00

Esk Valley Estate is a Hawkes Bay (New Zealand) producer under the Villa Maria aegis. Winemaker: Gordon Russell.

ESK VALLEY ESTATE MERLOT / CABERNET ★★★

1990	7	Now	NZ$29.00
1991	6	Now	NZ$23.00
1992	5	Now	NZ$18.00
1993	4	Prior	
1994	6	Now	NZ$18.50
1995	7	Now	N/R
1996	5	Now	N/R
1997	6	Now	N/R

ESK VALLEY ESTATE CHARDONNAY ★★★

before 1994		Prior	
1994	7	Now	NZ$25.00
1995	5	Now	NZ$16.50
1996	6	Now	NZ$18.50
1997	7	Now	NZ$20.00
1998	7	2000	NZ$18.50

ESK VALLEY ESTATE CHARDONNAY (RESERVE) ★★★★

before 1994		Prior	
1994	6	Now	NZ$30.00
1995	7	Now	NZ$32.00
1996	6	Now	NZ$25.00
1997	6	2000	NZ$24.00

ESK VALLEY ESTATE CHENIN BLANC ★★★

before 1994		Prior	
1994	7	Now	NZ$22.00
1995	4	Now	NZ$11.50
1996	6	Now	NZ$16.00
1997	6	2000	NZ$15.00
1998	7	2002	NZ$16.00

ESK VALLEY ESTATE MERLOT ★★★

1994	5	Now	N/R
1995	7	Now	N/R
1996	6	Now	N/R
1997	5	Now	N/R

ESK VALLEY ESTATE HAWKES BAY SAUVIGNON BLANC ★★★

before 1994	Prior		
1994	7	Now	NZ$23.00
1995	5	Prior	
1996	5	Prior	
1997	6	Now	NZ$16.00
1998	7	Now	NZ$17.50

ESK VALLEY ESTATE RESERVE MERLOT/CABERNET/MALBEC/ FRANC ★★★★

1989	6	Now	NZ$66.00
1990	6	Now	NZ$62.00
1991	7	Now	NZ$66.00
1992	6	Now	NZ$52.00
1993	Not made		
1994	6	Now	NZ$46.00
1995	7	2000	NZ$49.00
1996	7	2001	NZ$46.00
1997	6	2000	NZ$36.00

Evans and Tate are West Australian makers whose focus is now on their Redbrook vineyard at Margaret River. Winemaker: Brian Fletcher.

EVANS AND TATE MARGARET RIVER CABERNET SAUVIGNON ★★★★

1988	6	Now	$76.00
1989	5	Now	$58.00
1990	6	Now	$64.00
1991	6	Now	$60.00
1992	6	Now	$54.00
1993	7	Now	$60.00
1994	6	2001	$47.00
1995	7	2001	$50.00
1996	7	2002	$48.00
1997	7	2003	$44.00

EVANS AND TATE MARGARET RIVER CHARDONNAY ★★★★★

1987	6	Now	$68.00
1988	6	Now	$64.00
1989	7	Now	$68.00
1990	7	Now	$64.00
1991	7	Now	$58.00
1992	6	Now	$47.00

1993	7	Now	$50.00
1994	6	2000	$40.00
1995	7	Prior	
1996	6	Prior	
1997	7	2000	$37.00

EVANS AND TATE MARGARET RIVER MERLOT ★★★★

1988	6	Now	$70.00
1989	5	Now	$54.00
1990	7	Now	$70.00
1991	6	Now	$54.00
1992	7	Now	$60.00
1993	6	Now	$47.00
1994	6	2005	$44.00
1995	7	2000	$47.00
1996	7	2001	$44.00

EVANS AND TATE MARGARET RIVER SAUVIGNON BLANC (/SEMILLON) ★★★

1996	6	Now	$22.00
1997	6	Now	$20.00
1998	7	2000	$22.00

EVANS AND TATE MARGARET RIVER SEMILLON ★★★★

before 1989		Prior	
1989	7	Now	$41.00
1990	6	Now	$32.00
1991	7	Now	$35.00
1992	7	Now	$32.00
1993	7	Now	$30.00
1994	7	Now	$28.00
1995	7	Now	$25.00
1996	7	2000	$24.00
1997	7	2000	$22.00
1998	6	2000	$17.50

EVANS AND TATE MARGARET RIVER SHIRAZ ★★★★★

1985	6	Now	$94.00
1986	5	Now	$72.00
1987	7	Now	$94.00
1988	6	Now	$74.00
1989	6	Now	$68.00
1990	7	Now	$74.00
1991	6	Now	$58.00
1992	6	Now	$54.00
1993	7	Now	$58.00
1994	7	Now	$54.00
1995	7	2000	$50.00
1996	7	2001	$47.00
1997	6	2002	$37.00

EVANS AND TATE TWO VINEYARDS CHARDONNAY ★★★

1990	6	Now	$37.00
1991	5	Now	$29.00
1992	6	Now	$32.00
1993	6	Now	$29.00
1994	6	Now	$27.00
1995	6	Now	$25.00
1996	5	Now	$19.50
1997	6	Now	$22.00
1998	7	2000	$23.00

Eyton on Yarra is a new and well-funded Yarra Valley winery and restaurant enterprise of considerable promise. Winemaker: Matt Aldridge.

EYTON ON YARRA CABERNET/MERLOT ★★★★

1995	4	2004	$25.00
1996	3	2005	$17.50
1997	5	2006	$27.00

EYTON ON YARRA CHARDONNAY ★★★★

1993	5	Prior	
1994	6	Now	$35.00
1995	4	Now	$22.00
1996	4	Now	$20.00
1997	6	Now	$28.00
1998	5	2001	$22.00

EYTON ON YARRA PINOT/ CHARDONNAY BRUT ★★★★

1993	6	Now	$39.00
1994	5	Now	$30.00
1995	5	2000	$28.00

EYTON ON YARRA PINOT NOIR ★★★★★

1995	4	2001	$25.00
1996	3	2000	$17.50
1997	5	2004	$27.00

Fergussons are Yarra Valley makers whose estate grown wines are densely flavoured and emphatic. Winemaker: Chris Keyes.

FERGUSSONS CABERNET SAUVIGNON ★★★★

before 1982		Prior	
1982	7	Now	$100.00
1983	7	Now	$94.00
1984	3	Now	$37.00
1985	Not made		
1986	7	Now	$74.00
1987	6	Now	$60.00
1988	Destroyed by fire		

1989	Destroyed by fire		
1990	7	Now	$54.00
1991	6	Now	$44.00
1992	7	2010	$47.00
1993	6	2010	$37.00
1994	6	2010	$35.00
1995	6	2010	$32.00
1996	6	2010	$30.00
1997	6	2020	$27.00
1998	6	2020	N/R

FERGUSSONS CHARDONNAY ★★★★

before 1992	Prior		
1992	6	Now	$44.00
1993	5	Now	$34.00
1994	6	Now	$37.00
1995	6	Now	$35.00
1996	6	2005	$32.00
1997	7	2005	$35.00
1998	7	2001	$32.00

FERGUSSONS SHIRAZ ★★★

before 1982	Prior		
1982	6	Now	$88.00
1983	7	Now	$94.00
1984	4	Prior	
1985	Not made		
1986	7	Now	$74.00
1987	5	Now	$49.00
1988	Destroyed by fire		
1989	Destroyed by fire		
1990	Not made		
1991	6	Now	$44.00
1992	6	2005	$40.00
1993	6	Now	$37.00
1994	7	2005	$40.00
1995	5	2005	$27.00
1996	7	2005	$35.00
1997	7	2005	$32.00
1998	7	2020	N/R

Fermoy Estate is a Margaret River maker whose exceedingly elegant Cabernet Sauvignon is complemented by a graceful Pinot and a most intriguing Merlot. Winemaker: Michael Kelly.

FERMOY ESTATE
CABERNET SAUVIGNON ★★★★★

1988	6	Now	$47.00
1989	6	Now	$44.00
1990	5	Now	$34.00
1991	6	2000	$38.00
1992	7	2000	$41.00
1993	6	2001	$32.00
1994	6	2001	$30.00
1995	6	2002	$28.00

FERMOY ESTATE MERLOT ★★★★

1991	6	Now	$36.00
1992	7	2000	$39.00
1993	Not made		
1994	6	2001	$28.00
1995	5	Now	$22.00
1996	5	2002	$20.00

FERMOY ESTATE PINOT NOIR ★★★★

1990	5	Now	$30.00
1991	6	Now	$33.00
1992	5	Now	$25.00
1993	6	Now	$28.00
1994	7	Now	$31.00
1995	6	Now	$24.00
1996	Not made		
1997	Not made		

Fox Creek Wines is a recently established McLaren maker with high quality aspirations.
Winemakers: Sarah and Sparky Marquis.

FOX CREEK RESERVE CABERNET ★★★★

1995	6	2000	$33.00
1996	7	2002	$35.00
1997	6	2003	$28.00

FOX CREEK RESERVE SHIRAZ ★★★★

1994	6	2001	$50.00
1995	5	2001	$38.00
1996	7	2005	$50.00
1997	6	2005	$40.00

FOX CREEK VERDELHO ★★★

1995	4	Prior	
1996	5	Now	$16.00
1997	7	Now	$21.00
1998	7	Now	$19.00

Fox River is the second label of Mount Barker's respected maker Goundrey Wines. Winemaker: Keith Brown.

FOX RIVER CLASSIC RED ★★

1995	6	Now	$14.50
1996	5	Now	$11.00
1997	6	2001	$12.50

FOX RIVER CLASSIC WHITE ★★

1996	6	Now	$12.50
1997	7	Now	$13.50
1998	7	Now	$12.50

Frankland Estate in Western Australia's Frankland River region is a grower turned winemaker whose product is well worth seeking out. Winemakers: Judi Cullam and Barrie Smith.

FRANKLAND ESTATE CABERNET SAUVIGNON

★★★★

1991	5	Now	$27.00
1992	5	Now	$25.00
1993	6	Now	$28.00
1994	6	Now	$25.00
1995	6	Now	$24.00
1996	6	2001	$22.00

FRANKLAND ESTATE CHARDONNAY

★★★★

1992	5	Now	$27.00
1993	5	Now	$25.00
1994	6	Now	$28.00
1995	6	Now	$25.00
1996	5	Now	$20.00
1997	7	2000	$25.00

FRANKLAND ESTATE ISOLATION RIDGE RIESLING

★★★★★

1991	7	Now	$41.00
1992	5	Now	$27.00
1993	6	2002	$30.00
1994	6	2003	$28.00
1995	5	Now	$22.00
1996	6	2004	$24.00
1997	6	2008	$22.00
1998	7	2010	$24.00

FRANKLAND ESTATE ISOLATION RIDGE SHIRAZ

★★★★

1991	5	Prior	
1992	5	Now	$20.00
1993	6	2000	$23.00
1994	6	2002	$21.00
1995	6	2002	$19.50
1996	7	2006	$21.00

FRANKLAND ESTATE OLMO'S REWARD (CAB.FRANC/MERLOT/MALBEC/CAB.SAUVIGNON) ★★★★

1992	6	Now	$36.00
1993	6	2001	$33.00
1994	7	2004	$36.00
1995	7	2005	$33.00

Fraser Vineyard is a small Hunter Valley maker with a growing range of stylish, well-made wines. Winemaker: Peter Fraser.

FRASER VINEYARD CHARDONNAY ★★★

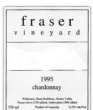

before 1991	Prior		
1991	6	Now	$24.00
1992	5	Prior	
1993	6	Now	$20.00
1994	6	Now	$19.00
1995	6	Now	$17.50
1996	6	Now	$16.00

FRASER VINEYARD SHIRAZ ★★★

before 1992	Prior		
1992	5	Now	$21.00
1993	5	Now	$19.50
1994	5	Now	$18.00
1995	6	Now	$20.00
1996	6	2000	$18.50

Galah Wine, in spite of the name, is neither a joke nor made from or by Galahs. In essence this operation is an underpriced mail-order negociant label controlled and administered by Stephen George of Ashton Hills fame (q.v.). Wines can be purchased only by writing to Box 231 Ashton 5137. Winemaker/Wine Selector: Stephen George.

GALAH WINE CLARE VALLEY SHIRAZ ★★★★

1986	6	Now	$38.00
1987	6	Now	$35.00
1988	7	Now	$38.00
1989	7	Now	$35.00
1990	7	Now	$33.00
1991	5	Now	$21.00
1992	7	Now	$28.00
1993	6	Now	$22.00
1994	7	Now	$24.00
1995	6	Now	$19.00
1996	6	2000	$17.50
1997	6	2002	$16.50

GALAH CLARE VALLEY CABERNET/MALBEC

★★★★

1986	7	Now	$44.00
1987	6	Now	$35.00
1988	6	Now	$32.00
1989	7	Now	$35.00
1990	Not made		
1991	5	Now	$21.00
1992	7	Now	$28.00

1993	6	Now	$22.00
1994	7	Now	$24.00
1995	Not made		
1996	7	2001	$20.00
1997	6	2004	$16.00

Garden Gully Vineyards *in Victoria's Great Western district is a syndicate-owned operation producing very agreeable wines, sometimes from sourced grapes, but the following wines are usually estate grown.*
Winemakers: Brian Fletcher and Warren Randall.

GARDEN GULLY SHIRAZ ★★★

before 1991	Prior		
1991	6	Now	$30.00
1992	Not made		
1993	5	Now	$22.00
1994	6	2000	$24.00
1995	7	2005	$26.00
1996	7	2002	$24.00
1997	6	2004	$19.00

GARDEN GULLY SPARKLING BURGUNDY ★★★★

1991	6	Now	$42.00
1992	5	Now	$33.00
1993	5	Now	$30.00
1994	7	2004	$39.00
1995	Not made		
1996	6	2004	$29.00
1997	7	2008	$31.00

GARDEN GULLY RIESLING ★★★

1992	6	Now	$19.50
1993	Not made		
1994	6	Now	$17.00
1995	Not made		
1996	Not made		
1997	5	2002	$11.00
1998	7	2004	$14.50

Garrett, Andrew *- see Andrew Garrett.*

Geoff Weaver *(formerly Stafford Ridge) is the label under which wines are released from the Lenswood (high Adelaide Hills) vineyard of the gifted winemaker.*
Winemaker: Geoff Weaver.

GEOFF WEAVER CHARDONNAY ★★★★★

before 1991	Prior		
1991	6	2000	$62.00
1992	4	2000	$38.00
1993	6	Now	$54.00
1994	5	Now	$41.00

1995	6	2001	$46.00
1996	6	2002	$42.00
1997	5	2002	$33.00

GEOFF WEAVER RIESLING

★★★★

before 1992	Prior		
1992	4	Now	$26.00
1993	4	Prior	
1994	4	2000	$22.00
1995	5	2002	$25.00
1996	6	2002	$28.00
1997	6	2003	$26.00
1998	5	2004	$20.00

GEOFF WEAVER SAUVIGNON BLANC

★★★★

1989	6	Now	$47.00
1990	6	Prior	
1991	5	Prior	
1992	4	Prior	
1993	4	Prior	
1994	5	Prior	
1995	5	Now	$24.00
1996	5	Now	$22.00
1997	6	Now	$25.00
1998	5	2000	$19.50

Glazebrook is a Hawkes Bay (New Zealand) small, high quality maker with a range of austere but stylish wines. Winemaker: Alwyn Corban.

GLAZEBROOK (formerly ALWYN) CHARDONNAY

★★★★

before 1991	Prior		
1991	7	Now	NZ$37.00
1992	7	Now	NZ$35.00
1993	6	Now	NZ$27.00
1994	7	Now	NZ$30.00
1995	7	Now	NZ$27.00

GLAZEBROOK RESERVE (CABERNET/MERLOT)

★★★★

before 1989	Prior		
1989	7	Now	NZ$46.00
1990	6	Now	NZ$37.00
1991	7	Now	NZ$39.00
1992·	6	Now	NZ$31.00
1993	6	Now	NZ$29.00
1994	6	2000	NZ$27.00
1995	7	2000	NZ$29.00

GLAZEBROOK STABLES CHARDONNAY ★★★

before 1991	Prior		
1991	7	Now	NZ$23.00
1992	6	Now	NZ$18.50
1993	6	Now	NZ$17.00
1994	7	Now	NZ$18.50
1995	5	Now	N/R
1996	7	Now	N/R

GLAZEBROOK STABLES SAUVIGNON BLANC ★★★

before 1994	Prior		
1994	6	Now	NZ$20.00
1995	5	Now	NZ$16.00
1996	6	Now	NZ$18.00

GLAZEBROOK STABLES RED CABERNET/MERLOT)
★★★

before 1990	Prior		
1990	6	Now	NZ$24.00
1991	5	Now	NZ$18.50
1992	5	Now	NZ$17.00
1993	5	Now	NZ$15.50
1994	5	Now	N/R
1995	6	Now	N/R

Glenara Wines *are Adelaide Hills makers whose vineyard is 400 metres above sea level. The wines are stylish and elegant. Winemaker: Trevor Jones.*

GLENARA CABERNET ROSE ★★★

before 1996 .	Prior		
1996	7	Now	$15.00
1997	7	Now	$14.00

GLENARA RIESLING ★★★★

1989	7	Now	$28.00
1990	7	Now	$26.00
1991	6	Now	$20.00
1992	7	Now	$22.00
1993	7	Now	$20.00
1994	7	Now	$19.00
1995	7	2000	$17.50
1996	7	2001	$16.00
1997	7	2002	$15.00

Gnangara - *see Evans and Tate.*

Goldwater Estate *on New Zealand's Waiheke Island are justly renowned for their graceful, intense and complex Cabernet blend - one of the country's most sought-after wines. Winemaker: Kim Goldwater.*

GOLDWATER ESTATE CABERNET
SAUVIGNON/MERLOT/CABERNET FRANC ★★★★★

1983	6	Now NZ$130.00
1984	5	Prior
1985	6	Prior
1986	Not made	
1987	7	Now NZ$110.00

1988	5	Now	NZ$74.00
1989	6	Prior	
1990	7	2000	NZ$88.00
1991	7	2002	NZ$82.00
1992	6	Now	NZ$64.00
1993	7	2005	NZ$70.00
1994	7	2010	NZ$64.00
1995	6	2005	NZ$52.00
1996	6	2006	NZ$48.00

Goona Warra Vineyard is a re-establishment of a then elaborate 19th century vineyard at Sunbury in Victoria's Macedon region. Winemaker: John Barnier.

GOONA WARRA
CABERNET FRANC ★★★★
before 1993		Prior	
1993	6	Now	$29.00
1994	5	2000	$22.00
1995	6	2001	$25.00
1996	5	2000	$19.50
1997	6	2003	N/R

GOONA WARRA
CHARDONNAY ★★★★
before 1993		Prior	
1993	5	Now	$26.00
1994	4	Now	$19.50
1995	5	2000	$22.00
1996	6	2002	$25.00
1997	6	2003	$23.00
1998	7	2004	$25.00

GOONA WARRA PINOT NOIR
★★★★
before 1995		Prior	
1995	6	2000	$29.00
1996	5	2001	$22.00
1997	6	2002	$25.00
1998	7	2003	N/R

GOONA WARRA SEMILLON
★★★★
before 1996		Prior	
1996	6	2003	$21.00
1997	6	2004	$20.00
1998	6	2005	N/R

Goundrey Wines were the pioneers of the Mount Barker area on the South Coast of Western Australia. Their 100 hectares of prime vineyards give them a formidable basis for an increasing impact on the quality market. Winemaker: Keith Brown.

GOUNDREY CHENIN BLANC ★★★
1994	5	Prior	
1995	Not made		
1996	Not made		
1997	5	Now	$17.00
1998	6	Now	$19.00

GOUNDREY RESERVE CABERNET SAUVIGNON

★★★★

before 1985		Prior	
1985	7	Now	$86.00
1986	5	Now	$58.00
1987	5	Now	$52.00
1988	5	Now	$49.00
1989	6	Now	$54.00
1990	4	Now	$34.00
1991	5	Now	$39.00
1992	6	2001	$43.00
1993	5	2000	$33.00
1994	6	2002	$37.00
1995	6	2003	$34.00
1996	7	2003	$37.00

GOUNDREY RESERVE CHARDONNAY

★★★★

before 1994		Prior	
1994	6	Now	$32.00
1995	7	Now	$35.00
1996	5	Now	$23.00
1997	6	Now	$26.00

GOUNDREY RESERVE RIESLING

★★★★

before 1990		Prior	
1990	5	Now	$29.00
1991	6	Now	$33.00
1992	6	Now	$30.00
1993	5	Now	$23.00
1994	6	Now	$26.00
1995	6	Now	$24.00
1996	5	Now	$18.50
1997	7	Now	$24.00

GOUNDREY RESERVE SAUVIGNON BLANC

★★★

before 1994		Prior	
1994	6	Now	$25.00
1995	6	Now	$23.00
1996	5	Now	$18.00
1997	7	Now	$23.00

GOUNDREY RESERVE SHIRAZ

★★★★

1988	5	Now	$39.00
1989	4	Prior	
1990	Not made		
1991	5	Now	$31.00
1992	7	Now	$40.00
1993	6	Now	$32.00
1994	6	2000	$29.00
1995	7	2005	$32.00
1996	7	2010	$29.00

GOUNDREY UNWOODED CHARDONNAY ★★★

1996	3	Now	$11.50
1997	5	Now	$18.00
1998	7	Now	$23.00

Grand Cru - see Karl Seppelt Estate.

Granite Hills in Victoria's Baynton area are cool climate makers of intensely flavoured wines.
Winemaker: Llew Knight.

GRANITE HILLS CABERNET SAUVIGNON ★★★★

before 1982		Prior	
1982	5	Now	$74.00
1983	4	Prior	
1984	4	Prior	
1985	4	Prior	
1986	5	Now	$54.00
1987	4	Now	$40.00
1988	4	Now	$37.00
1989	4	Now	$34.00
1990	Not made		
1991	5	2000	$37.00
1992	5	2000	$34.00
1993	Not made		
1994	4	2002	$23.00
1995	6	2005	$32.00
1996	6	2006	$30.00
1997	6	2010	$28.00

GRANITE HILLS CHARDONNAY ★★★★

1986	5	Now	$47.00
1987	4	Prior	
1988	4	Now	$32.00
1989	4	Now	$30.00
1990	5	Now	$34.00
1991	4	Now	$25.00
1992	4	Now	$23.00
1993	5	2000	$27.00
1994	5	2000	$25.00
1995	6	2002	$28.00
1996	7	2006	$30.00
1997	6	2006	$24.00

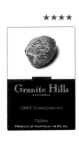

GRANITE HILLS RIESLING ★★★★

1986	7	Now	$49.00
1987	4	Now	$26.00
1988	6	Now	$36.00
1989	4	Now	$22.00
1990	7	2000	$36.00
1991	5	Now	$24.00
1992	5	Now	$22.00
1993	6	2002	$24.00

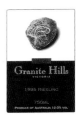

1994	5	2000	$19.00
1995	6	2004	$21.00
1996	6	2006	$19.50
1997	6	2008	$18.00

GRANITE HILLS SHIRAZ ★★★★

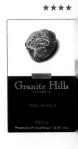

before 1986	Prior		
1986	6	Now	$64.00
1987	4	Now	$39.00
1988	7	2000	$64.00
1989	4	Now	$33.00
1990	Not made		
1991	5	2000	$36.00
1992	5	2002	$33.00
1993	Not made		
1994	Not made		
1995	6	2007	$32.00
1996	5	2008	$24.00
1997	7	2010	$32.00

Grant Burge is a family owned and operated Barossa Valley based producer whose substantial range of wines includes a very fine Shiraz - "Meshach".
Winemaker: Grant Burge.

GRANT BURGE CAMERON VALE CABERNET SAUVIGNON ★★★

1988	6	Now	$39.00
1989	5	Now	$30.00
1990	6	Now	$33.00
1991	7	Now	$36.00
1992	6	Now	$28.00
1993	7	2000	$31.00
1994	6	2000	$24.00
1995	6	2001	$22.00
1996	6	2002	$21.00
1997	6	2002	$19.50

GRANT BURGE CHARDONNAY ★★★★

1988	7	Now	$42.00
1989	6	Now	$33.00
1990	6	Now	$31.00
1991	5	Now	$24.00
1992	6	Now	$26.00
1993	7	Now	$29.00
1994	6	Now	$23.00
1995	5	Now	$17.50
1996	6	Now	$19.50
1997	6	2000	$18.00
1998	6	2002	$17.00

GRANT BURGE EDEN VALLEY RIESLING ★★★

1988	7	Now	$35.00
1989	6	Now	$27.00
1990	7	Now	$30.00
1991	6	Now	$23.00
1992	5	Now	$18.50
1993	5	Now	$17.00
1994	5	Now	$15.50
1995	5	Now	$14.50
1996	6	2000	$16.00
1997	7	2002	$17.50
1998	7	2005	$16.00

GRANT BURGE MERLOT ★★★★

1988	6	Now	$35.00
1989	6	Now	$33.00
1990	7	Now	$35.00
1991	7	Now	$33.00
1992	6	Now	$26.00
1993	5	Now	$20.00
1994	6	Now	$22.00
1995	6	Now	$20.00
1996	6	2000	$19.00
1997	5	2001	$15.00

GRANT BURGE MESHACH SHIRAZ ★★★★★

1988	6	Now	$130.00
1989	Not made		
1990	7	2004	$130.00
1991	7	2005	$120.00
1992	6	2005	$96.00
1993	6	2006	$88.00
1994	6	2006	$82.00
1995	7	2008	$88.00

GRANT BURGE SAUVIGNON BLANC ★★★

before 1990	Prior		
1990	5	Now	$26.00
1991	5	Now	$24.00
1992	5	Now	$22.00
1993	6	Now	$24.00
1994	5	Now	$19.00
1995	5	Now	$17.50
1996	5	Now	$16.00
1997	6	Now	$18.00
1998	6	2000	$16.50

GRANT BURGE SEMILLON ★★★

1988	5	Now	$29.00
1989	5	Now	$27.00
1990	5	Now	$25.00
1991	5	Now	$23.00
1992	5	Now	$21.00
1993	6	Now	$24.00
1994	5	Now	$18.50
1995	5	Now	$17.00
1996	6	Now	$19.00
1997	6	2000	$17.50
1998	7	2002	$19.00

GRANT BURGE SHIRAZ ★★★★

1988	6	Now	$38.00
1989	6	Now	$35.00
1990	7	Now	$38.00
1991	7	Now	$35.00
1992	6	Now	$28.00
1993	6	2000	$26.00
1994	5	2001	$20.00
1995	7	2004	$26.00
1996	7	2005	$24.00

Grosset Wines is a Clare Valley maker whose wines are of remarkable finesse and elegance. Winemaker: Jeffrey Grosset.

GROSSET GAIA (BORDEAUX BLEND) ★★★★

1989	5	Now	$47.00
1990	6	2000	$52.00
1991	6	Now	$49.00
1992	7	2003	$52.00
1993	6	2001	$42.00
1994	7	2005	$45.00
1995	7	2007	$42.00
1996	6	2005	$33.00

GROSSET PICCADILLY (CHARDONNAY) ★★★★

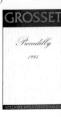

before 1989		Prior	
1989	5	Now	$52.00
1990	6	Now	$58.00
1991	6	Now	$54.00
1992	6	Now	$50.00
1993	6	2000	$46.00
1994	6	2002	$43.00
1995	6	2002	$40.00
1996	7	2004	$43.00
1997	7	2004	$40.00

GROSSET POLISH HILL RIESLING ★★★★★

1981	4	Now	$54.00
1982	6	Now	$76.00
1983	4	Now	$47.00
1984	5	Now	$54.00
1985	5	Now	$50.00
1986	6	Now	$56.00
1987	6	Now	$52.00
1988	5	Now	$40.00
1989	4	Now	$30.00
1990	6	2002	$41.00
1991	5	Now	$32.00
1992	6	2002	$35.00
1993	6	2003	$33.00
1994	7	2005	$35.00
1995	7	2005	$33.00
1996	7	2007	$30.00
1997	7	2005	$28.00

GROSSET SEMILLON SAUVIGNON BLANC ★★★

before 1993		Prior	
1993	7	Now	$35.00
1994	6	Now	$28.00
1995	6	2000	$26.00
1996	6	Now	$24.00
1997	7	2000	$26.00

GROSSET WATERVALE RIESLING ★★★★

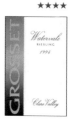

before 1986		Prior	
1986	6	Now	$45.00
1987	6	Now	$42.00
1988	5	Now	$32.00
1989	5	Now	$30.00
1990	6	Now	$33.00
1991	6	Now	$30.00
1992	6	Now	$28.00
1993	7	2000	$30.00
1994	7	2002	$28.00
1995	7	2003	$26.00
1996	6	2004	$21.00
1997	7	2005	$22.00

Grove Mill is a Marlborough (New Zealand) producer whose early mainstay was a beguiling Riesling. The development of the Landsdowne Chardonnay shows an intention to aspire to extreme quality. Winemaker: David Pearce.

GROVE MILL LANDSDOWNE CHARDONNAY ★★★★★

before 1994		Prior	
1994	6	Now	NZ$34.00
1995	Not made		
1996	6	Now	N/R
1997	Not made		

115

GROVE MILL MARLBOROUGH CHARDONNAY

★★★★

before 1996		Prior	
1996	6	Now	NZ$26.00
1997	6	Now	NZ$24.00
1998	6	2000	NZ$23.00

GROVE MILL MARLBOROUGH GEWURZTRAMINER ★★★

before 1996		Prior	
1996	5	Now	NZ$23.00
1997	5	Now	NZ$22.00
1998	Not made		

GROVE MILL PINOT GRIS ★★

before 1996		Prior	
1996	5	Now	NZ$21.00
1997	6	Now	NZ$24.00
1998	Not made		

GROVE MILL MARLBOROUGH RIESLING ★★★★

before 1994		Prior	
1994	7	Now	NZ$27.00
1995	4	Prior	
1996	6	Now	NZ$20.00
1997	6	Now	NZ$18.50
1998	6	2001	NZ$17.50

GROVE MILL MARLBOROUGH SAUVIGNON BLANC ★★★★

before 1995		Prior	
1995	5	Now	NZ$19.50
1996	6	Now	NZ$21.00
1997	6	Now	NZ$20.00
1998	6	Now	NZ$18.50

Hamilton - see Richard Hamilton.

Hanging Rock Winery is the Macedon area vineyard and winery of the redoubtable John Ellis. The wines are made both from his own fruit and from selected cool-climate fruit. Winemaker: John Ellis.

HANGING ROCK HEATHCOTE SHIRAZ ★★★★

1987	7	Now	$68.00
1988	5	Now	$45.00
1989	4	Now	$33.00
1990	6	Now	$46.00
1991	7	2000	$50.00
1992	7	2002	$46.00
1993	Not made		
1997	7	2007	$39.00

HANGING ROCK JIM JIM ESTATE-GROWN SAUVIGNON BLANC ★★★★

1987	4	Now	$37.00
1988	6	Now	$50.00
1989	4	Prior	
1990	6	Now	$44.00
1991	Not made		
1992	6	Now	$37.00
1993	7	Now	$40.00
1994	6	Now	$32.00
1995	6	Now	$29.00
1996	6	Now	$27.00
1997	5	Now	$21.00

HANGING ROCK VICTORIA CHARDONNAY ★★★

1987	4	Now	$25.00
1988	5	Now	$29.00
1989	5	Prior	
1990	6	Now	$30.00
1991	6	Now	$28.00
1992	6	Now	$26.00
1993	6	Now	$24.00
1994	5	Now	$18.50
1995	5	Now	$17.00
1996	5	Now	$16.00
1997	6	Now	$17.50

Hardy's (now BRL Hardy) is one of the vinous corporate giants with vineyards in McLaren Vale, Barossa Valley, Keppoch and the Riverland.
Winemakers: Stephen Pannell and Tom Newton.

HARDY EILEEN HARDY CHARDONNAY ★★★★

1986	7	Now	$76.00
1987	6	Now	$60.00
1988	6	Now	$56.00
1989	7	Now	$60.00
1990	7	Now	$56.00
1991	6	Now	$45.00
1992	7	Now	$49.00
1993	5	Now	$32.00
1994	7	Now	$42.00
1995	6	2000	$33.00
1996	7	2001	$36.00
1997	7	2002	$33.00

HARDY EILEEN HARDY SHIRAZ ★★★★★

1970	7	Now	$410.00
1971	6	Now	$320.00
1972	4	Prior	

1973	6	Now	$280.00
1974	4	Prior	
1975	6	Now	$240.00
1976	6	Now	$220.00
1977	4	Prior	
1978	Not made		
1979	7	Now	$205.00
1980	6	Now	$160.00
1981	7	Now	$175.00
1982	6	Now	$140.00
1983	Not made		
1984	4	Now	$80.00
1985	5	Now	$92.00
1986	6	Now	$100.00
1987	7	Now	$110.00
1988	7	Now	$100.00
1989	6	Now	$82.00
1990	7	2000	$88.00
1991	7	2005	$82.00
1992	6	2005	$64.00
1993	7	2007	$70.00
1994	6	2006	$56.00
1995	7	2008	$60.00

HARDY SIR JAMES VINTAGE ★★★★

1992	3	Now	$19.00
1994	4	Now	$23.00
1995	5	Now	$27.00

HARDY VINTAGE PORT ★★★★

1965	6	Now	$125.00
1966	6	Now	$115.00
1967	5	Now	$90.00
1968	6	Now	$100.00
1969	7	Now	$105.00
1970	6	Now	$86.00
1971	7	Now	$92.00
1972	6	Now	$74.00
1973	5	Now	$56.00
1974	4	Now	$42.00
1975	7	2000	$68.00
1976	7	Now	$62.00
1977	5	Now	$42.00
1978	6	2000	$46.00
1979	5	Now	$36.00
1980	5	Now	$33.00
1981	7	2005	$43.00
1982	5	2000	$28.00
1983	5	2005	$26.00
1984	Not made		

1985	Not made		
1986	Not made		
1987	6	2010	$23.00
1988	6	2010	$21.00
1989	No data		
1993	6	2013	$18.50

Hawkesbridge Estate, in New Zealand's Marlborough region produces a remarkably fine Chardonnay, well worth seeking out. Winemakers: Mike and Judy Veal.

HAWKESBRIDGE CHARDONNAY ★★★★★

1995	5	Now	NZ$18.50
1996	7	Now	NZ$24.00
1997	7	Now	NZ$22.00
1998	7	Now	NZ$21.00

HAWKESBRIDGE
SAUVIGNON BLANC ★★★

1994	7	Now	NZ$28.00
1995	4	Now	NZ$15.00
1996	6	Now	NZ$21.00
1997	6	Now	NZ$19.50
1998	6	Now	NZ$18.00

Heemskerk is a well-planned cool climate vineyard and winery in the Pipers Brook area near Launceston. It is now owned by Pipers Brook Vineyards. Winemaker: Dr Andrew Pirie.

HEEMSKERK CABERNETS ★★★★

1976	7	Now	$105.00
1977	4	Now	$56.00
1978	5	Now	$64.00
1979	4	Now	$48.00
1980	4	Now	$44.00
1981	4	Now	$41.00
1982	5	Now	$47.00
1983	5	Now	$44.00
1984	5	Now	$41.00
1985	6	Now	$45.00
1986	6	Now	$42.00
1987	4	Now	$26.00
1988	5	Now	$30.00
1989	3	Now	$16.50
1990	6	Now	$31.00
1991	5	Now	$23.00
1992	6	Now	$26.00
1993	7	Now	$28.00
1994	No data		
1995	6	2002	$21.00

HEEMSKERK CHARDONNAY ★★★★

before 1984		Prior	
1984	6	Now	$76.00
1985	5	Now	$58.00
1986	6	Now	$66.00
1987	6	Now	$60.00
1988	6	Now	$56.00
1989	6	Now	$52.00
1990	6	Now	$48.00
1991	6	Now	$45.00
1992	6	Now	$41.00
1993	6	Now	$38.00
1994	No data		
1995	6	Now	$33.00
1996	5	Now	$25.00

HEEMSKERK PINOT NOIR ★★★★

1984	4	Now	$54.00
1985	Not made		
1986	Not made		
1987	5	Now	$54.00
1988	5	Now	$50.00
1989	5	Now	$46.00
1990	6	Now	$50.00
1991	6	Now	$47.00
1992	Not made		
1993	Not made		
1994	5	Now	$31.00
1995	5	Now	$29.00
1996	7	2001	$38.00

HEEMSKERK RIESLING ★★★★

1984	5	Now	$58.00
1985	4	Now	$44.00
1986	4	Now	$40.00
1987	4	Now	$37.00
1988	4	Now	$34.00
1989	Not made		
1990	5	Now	$37.00
1991	5	Now	$34.00
1992	6	Now	$38.00
1993	6	Now	$35.00
1994	Not made		
1995	4	Now	$20.00
1996	5	Now	$23.00
1997	4	Now	$17.00
1998	5	2000	$20.00

Heggies *is a very good vineyard at 550 metres up in the Eden Valley, owned by S. Smith and Sons who also own the labels Yalumba and Pewsey Vale. Winemaker: Simon Adams.*

HEGGIES VINEYARD BOTRYTIS RIESLING (375ml)

★★★★

before 1992	Prior		
1992	6	Now	$23.00
1993	Not made		
1994	6	Now	$19.50
1995	5	Now	$15.00
1996	7	Now	$19.50
1997	7	Now	$18.00
1998	6	Now	$14.50

HEGGIES VINEYARD CHARDONNAY

★★★★

before 1992	Prior		
1992	7	Now	$36.00
1993	6	Now	$29.00
1994	6	Now	$26.00
1995	5	Now	$20.00
1996	6	Now	$23.00
1997	7	2000	$24.00

HEGGIES VINEYARD MERLOT

★★★★

1990	6	Now	$33.00
1991	5	Now	$25.00
1992	6	Now	$28.00
1993	7	2000	$30.00
1994	6	2002	$24.00
1995	5	2001	$18.50

HEGGIES VINEYARD RIESLING

★★★★

before 1992	Prior		
1992	6	Now	$24.00
1993	5	Now	$19.00
1994	6	Now	$21.00
1995	6	Now	$19.50
1996	6	Now	$18.00
1997	5	Now	$14.00
1998	6	2000	$15.50

HEGGIES VINEYARD VIOGNIER

★★★★

before 1993	Prior		
1993	7	Now	$30.00
1994	6	Now	$23.00
1995	5	Now	$18.00
1996	6	Now	$20.00
1997	7	Now	$22.00
1998	6	Now	$17.50

Helm Wines are well-established Murrumbateman (A.C.T.) producers whose wines have helped create considerable interest in the region. Winemaker: Ken Helm.

HELM CABERNET SAUVIGNON (/MERLOT from 1989) ★★★★

before 1983		Prior	
1983	7	Now	$58.00
1984	6	Now	$47.00
1985	5	Now	$36.00
1986	7	Now	$47.00
1987	6	Now	$37.00
1988	7	Now	$40.00
1989	7	Now	$37.00
1990	7	2000	$34.00
1991	7	2000	$32.00
1992	6	2000	$25.00
1993	6	2000	$23.00
1994	6	2000	$21.00
1995	7	2002	$23.00
1996	6	2001	$18.50
1997	7	2001	$20.00

HELM CHARDONNAY (NON-OAKED) ★★★

1990	7	Now	$31.00
1991	6	Now	$25.00
1992	7	Now	$27.00
1993	7	Now	$25.00
1994	6	Now	$19.50
1995	7	Now	$21.00
1996	6	Now	$17.00
1997	6	Now	$15.50
1998	7	Now	$17.00

HELM (CABERNET BLEND) ★★★★

1994	7	Now	$25.00
1995	Not made		
1996	7	2000	$21.00
1997	7	2000	$20.00

HELM RIESLING ★★★

1988	7	Now	$34.00
1989	5	Prior	
1990	7	Now	$29.00
1991	6	Now	$23.00
1992	7	Now	$25.00
1993	7	Now	$23.00
1994	6	Now	$18.00
1995	7	2002	$19.50
1996	7	2002	$18.00
1997	7	2000	$17.00
1998	7	2000	$15.50

***Henschke,** a family-owned winery established for five generations in the Keyneton and Eden Valley area of the Barossa ranges, produce some of Australia's finest wines. Winemaker: Stephen Henschke.*

HENSCHKE CABERNET SAUVIGNON CYRIL HENSCHKE

★★★★★

before 1988		Prior	
1988	5	Now	$115.00
1989	7	Now	$150.00
1990	6	Now	$120.00
1991	6	Now	$110.00
1992	4	Now	$68.00
1993	7	2003	$110.00
1994	7	2004	$100.00
1995	5	2005	$68.00

HENSCHKE HILL OF GRACE

✴✴✴✴✴✴

1958	4	Prior	
1959	7	Now	$2980.00
1960	5	Prior	
1961	3	Prior	
1962	6	Now	$2020.00
1963	2	Prior	
1964	5	Now	$1440.00
1965	6	Prior	
1966	6	Now	$1480.00
1967	7	Now	$1600.00
1968	4	Prior	
1969	1	Prior	
1970	3	Prior	
1971	4	Prior	
1972	7	2000	$1080.00
1973	6	Now	$860.00
1974	Not made		
1975	3	Prior	
1976	4	Prior	
1977	5	Prior	
1978	7	Now	$680.00
1979	5	Now	$450.00
1980	5	Prior	
1981	4	Prior	
1982	6	2007	$430.00
1983	4	Now	$260.00
1984	7	2009	$430.00
1985	5	2010	$280.00
1986	7	2011	$370.00
1987	6	2012	$290.00
1988	7	2013	$320.00
1989	5	2009	$210.00
1990	7	2010	$270.00

1991	6	2011	$215.00
1992	6	2012	$200.00
1993	5	2008	$150.00
1994	7	2009	$200.00

HENSCHKE EDEN VALLEY
"JULIUS" RIESLING ★★★★

before 1994		Prior	
1994	5	Now	$26.00
1995	6	2000	$29.00
1996	5	2001	$22.00
1997	6	2002	$25.00
1998	5	2003	$19.00

HENSCHKE LENSWOOD ABBOTT'S PRAYER ★★★★★

1989	5	Now	$72.00
1990	6	2000	$80.00
1991	6	2000	$74.00
1992	4	2000	$46.00
1993	7	2001	$74.00
1994	6	2002	$60.00
1995	6	2003	$54.00

HENSCHKE LOUIS EDEN VALLEY SEMILLON ★★★★

before 1989		Prior	
1989	6	Now	$56.00
1990	5	2000	$43.00
1991	4	Prior	
1992	6	2000	$44.00
1993	5	2001	$34.00
1994	4	2001	$25.00
1995	6	2002	$35.00
1996	6	2004	$33.00
1997	5	2003	$25.00
1998	6	2006	$28.00

HENSCHKE MOUNT EDELSTONE ★★★★★

before 1978		Prior	
1978	6	Now	$250.00
1979	3	Prior	
1980	5	Now	$180.00
1981	4	Now	$130.00
1982	7	2007	$215.00
1983	5	2000	$140.00
1984	6	2009	$160.00
1985	4	2000	$98.00
1986	7	2006	$160.00
1987	5	2012	$100.00
1988	7	2008	$135.00
1989	5	2004	$90.00

1990	7	2010	$115.00
1991	5	2006	$76.00
1992	6	2006	$86.00
1993	5	2008	$66.00
1994	7	2009	$86.00
1995	4	2005	$45.00
1996	6	2006	$62.00

Hickinbotham *of Dromana is a 10 hectare vineyard and winery in the Mornington Peninsula, using its own and local contract grown grapes.*
Winemaker: Andrew Hickinbotham.

HICKINBOTHAM CHARDONNAY ★★★

1992	7	Now	$35.00
1993	7	2000	$33.00
1994	6	Now	$26.00
1995	5	2005	$20.00
1996	6	2002	$22.00
1997	7	2005	$24.00

HICKINBOTHAM MERLOT ★★★★

1991	6	Now	$30.00
1992	7	Now	$33.00
1993	7	2010	$30.00
1994	6	2000	$24.00
1995	6	2005	$22.00

HICKINBOTHAM PINOT NOIR ★★★★

1991	6	Now	$32.00
1992	6	Prior	
1993	7	Now	$32.00
1994	6	2000	$25.00
1995	Not made		
1996	7	Now	$25.00
1997	7	2001	$23.00

Hidden Valley *is the second label of St Peters Winery and Distillery, the premium label being Wilton Estate (q.v.)*
Winemaker: Adrian Sheridan.

HIDDEN VALLEY CLASSIC DRY WHITE ★★

1991	6	Now	$10.50
1992	6	Now	$9.75
1993	6	Now	$9.00
1994	5	Now	$6.75
1995	6	Now	$7.75

HIDDEN VALLEY SHIRAZ/ CABERNET/MERLOT ★★

1991	7	Now	$15.00
1992	6	Now	$12.00
1993	6	Now	$11.00
1994	6	Now	$10.00
1995	6	Now	$9.50

Hill-Smith Estate is a high Barossa ranges vineyard owned and operated by the Hill Smith family.
Winemaker: Hugh Reimers.

HILL-SMITH ESTATE CHARDONNAY ★★★★

before 1994		Prior	
1994	6	Now	$23.00
1995	7	Now	$24.00
1996	6	Now	$19.50
1997	5	Now	$15.00
1998	6	2000	$17.00

HILL-SMITH ESTATE SAUVIGNON BLANC ★★★

before 1996		Prior	
1996	5	Now	$14.00
1997	5	Now	$13.00
1998	7	Now	$17.00

Hillstowe Wines are Adelaide Hills based makers with exemplary vineyards in McLaren Vale and the high Adelaide Hills. Winemaker: Chris Laurie.

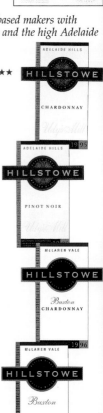

HILLSTOWE ADELAIDE HILLS UDY'S MILL CHARDONNAY ★★★★

1992	6	Now	$36.00
1993	6	Now	$33.00
1994	5	Now	$26.00
1995	6	Now	$29.00
1996	6	Now	$26.00

HILLSTOWE ADELAIDE HILLS UDY'S MILL PINOT NOIR ★★★★

1991	6	2001	$40.00
1992	4	2000	$25.00
1993	6	2003	$34.00
1994	5	2004	$27.00
1995	5	2004	$25.00

HILLSTOWE MCLAREN VALE BUXTON CHARDONNAY ★★★

1991	6	Now	$24.00
1992	5	Now	$19.00
1993	6	Now	$21.00
1994	5	Now	$19.50
1995	5	Now	$15.00
1996	6	Now	$16.50

HILLSTOWE MCLAREN VALE BUXTON MERLOT/CABERNET ★★★

1991	5	2001	$23.00
1992	5	2002	$21.00
1993	6	2005	$24.00
1994	6	2005	$22.00
1995	Not made		
1996	6	2006	$19.00

HILLSTOWE MCLAREN VALE
BUXTON SAUVIGNON BLANC

			★★★
1992	6	Now	$23.00
1993	Not made		
1994	6	Now	$20.00
1995	6	Now	$18.50
1996	6	Now	$17.00
1997	6	Now	$16.00

HJT Vineyards are Glenrowan (North-East Victoria) makers established by the late Harry Tinson of Baileys Bundarra fame. Winemaker: Wendy Tinson.

HJT CHARDONNAY

			★★★
1989	6	Now	$28.00
1990	6	2000	$26.00
1991	6	2003	$24.00
1992	6	2000	$22.00
1993	5	Now	$17.50
1994	5	2003	$16.00
1995	6	2003	$18.00
1996	6	2004	$16.50

Hollick Wines are Coonawarra small makers whose large range of wines includes one of the best Cabernets that this premium area has seen.
Winemakers: Ian Hollick and Matt Pellew.

HOLLICK BOTRYTIS RIESLING (375ml)

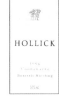

			★★★★
1985	6	Now	$50.00
1986	Not made		
1987	Not made		
1988	Not made		
1989	6	Now	$37.00
1990	7	2000	$40.00
1991	Not made		
1992	6	2002	$29.00
1993	Not made		
1994	6	2004	$25.00
1995	Not made		
1996	7	2006	$25.00
1997	6	2007	$20.00
1998	Not made		

HOLLICK "COONAWARRA"
(CABERNET/MERLOT/CAB. FRANC)   ★★★★

before 1986	Prior		
1986	5	Now	$41.00
1987	5	Prior	

1988	7	Now	$49.00
1989	6	Now	$39.00
1990	7	2000	$42.00
1991	7	2001	$39.00
1992	6	2002	$31.00
1993	6	2003	$28.00
1994	7	2004	$31.00
1995	5	2003	$20.00
1996	6	2004	$23.00
1997	6	2005	$21.00

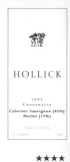

HOLLICK CHARDONNAY (RESERVE) ★★★★

1984	4	Now	$40.00
1985	4	Prior	
1986	6	Prior	
1987	5	Prior	
1988	5	Prior	
1989	6	Prior	
1990	7	Now	$44.00
1991	7	Now	$41.00
1992	6	Now	$32.00
1993	6	Now	$30.00
1994	6	Now	$28.00
1995	6	Now	$26.00
1996	5	Now	$20.00
1997	6	2002	$22.00

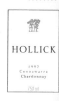

HOLLICK PINOT NOIR ★★★★

before 1990		Prior	
1990	6	Now	$29.00
1991	Not made		
1992	6	Now	$24.00
1993	6	Now	$23.00
1994	Not made		
1995	6	Now	$19.50
1996	6	2000	$18.00
1997	6	2001	$17.00

HOLLICK RIESLING ★★★★

before 1991		Prior	
1991	6	Now	$25.00
1992	7	Now	$27.00
1993	Not made		
1994	5	Now	$17.00
1995	6	2000	$18.50
1996	Not made		
1997	6	2001	$16.00
1998	6	2002	$15.00

HOLLICK RAVENSWOOD (CABERNET SAUVIGNON) ★★★★★

1988	6	2003	$84.00
1989	6	2004	$78.00
1990	7	2005	$84.00
1991	7	2006	$78.00
1992	7	2007	$72.00
1993	7	2009	$66.00
1994	7	2009	$62.00
1995	Not made		
1996	7	2011	$52.00
1997	Not made		
1998	7	2013	N/R

HOLLICK SHIRAZ/ CABERNET/MALBEC ★★★

1991	6	Prior	
1992	6	Now	$24.00
1993	6	Now	$22.00
1994	7	Now	$24.00
1995	6	Now	$19.00
1996	6	Now	$17.50
1997	6	2001	$16.50

HOLLICK WILGHA SHIRAZ ★★★

1988	6	Now	$62.00
1989	5	Now	$48.00
1990	6	Now	$54.00
1991	6	Now	$50.00
1992	6	Now	$46.00
1993	6	2000	$42.00
1994	6	2002	$39.00
1995	Not made		
1996	7	2006	$39.00
1997	6	2007	$31.00

Houghtons are the largest producers in Western Australia with vineyards in the Swan Valley, Moondah Brook (q.v.), Frankland River, Mount Barker and Pemberton. The wines have earned a consistent reputation for reliability over the years. Winemaker: Paul Lapsley.

HOUGHTON GOLD RESERVE CHARDONNAY ★★★

before 1988	Prior		
1988	5	Now	$23.00
1989	6	Now	$26.00
1990	5	Now	$20.00
1991	5	Now	$18.50
1992	7	2000	$24.00
1993	5	Now	$16.00
1994	6	Now	$18.00
1995	7	2000	$19.00

No longer made.

HOUGHTON GOLD RESERVE VERDELHO ★★★

before 1991		Prior	
1991	6	2000	$20.00
1992	Not made		
1993	7	2005	$20.00
1994	7	2000	$18.50
1995	6	2005	$14.50

No longer made.

HOUGHTON WHITE BURGUNDY
★★

before 1991		Prior	
1991	7	2000	$21.00
1992	4	Now	$11.00
1993	6	2000	$15.00
1994	5	Now	$11.50
1995	5	2000	$11.00
1996	5	Now	$10.00
1997	5	Now	$9.25

Howard Park *is a tiny Denmark (Western Australia) producer. The wines are meticulously made, and incidentally bear most beautiful and unusual labels.*
Winemaker: Michael Kerrigan.

HOWARD PARK CABERNET
SAUVIGNON/MERLOT ★★★★★

1986	7	Now	$140.00
1987	6	Now	$110.00
1988	6	Now	$100.00
1989	6	Now	$94.00
1990	7	2000	$100.00
1991	7	Now	$94.00
1992	7	2002	$88.00
1993	6	2000	$70.00
1994	7	2004	$74.00
1995	6	2002	$60.00
1996	6	2004	$54.00

HOWARD PARK CHARDONNAY ★★★★

1993	5	Now	$39.00
1994	7	Prior	
1995	6	Prior	
1996	6	2000	$37.00
1997	6	2000	$35.00

HOWARD PARK RIESLING ★★★★

1986	7	Now	$54.00
1987	6	Now	$44.00
1988	6	Now	$41.00
1989	6	Now	$38.00
1990	7	Now	$41.00
1991	6	Now	$32.00
1992	7	Now	$35.00
1993	6	Now	$27.00

1994	6	2000	$25.00
1995	6	2000	$23.00
1996	6	2000	$22.00
1997	7	2000	$23.00
1998	6	2002	$19.00

The Hugo Winery is yet another McLaren Flat maker to stun the winelover with a quality most would have thought unachievable for the area until a few years ago.
Winemaker: John Hugo.

HUGO CABERNET SAUVIGNON ★★★★

1988	7	Now	$42.00
1989	6	Now	$33.00
1990	7	Now	$36.00
1991	6	Now	$29.00
1992	7	2000	$31.00
1993	6	2000	$24.00
1994	7	2002	$26.00
1995	6	2002	$21.00
1996	7	2004	$23.00
1997	6	2004	$18.00
1998	7	2006	N/R

HUGO CHARDONNAY ★★★★

before 1987	Prior		
1987	7	Now	$50.00
1988	6	Now	$40.00
1989	6	Now	$37.00
1990	6	Now	$35.00
1991	6	Now	$32.00
1992	7	Now	$35.00
1993	6	Now	$27.00
1994	7	2001	$30.00
1995	6	2002	$23.00
1996	6	2002	$22.00
1997	7	Now	$23.00
1998	6	2000	$18.50

HUGO RIESLING ★★★

before 1989	Prior		
1989	7	Now	$25.00
1990	5	Now	$16.50
1991	6	Now	$18.50
1992	Not made		
1993	6	Now	$15.50
1994	Not made		
1995	7	Now	$15.50
1996	6	2001	$12.50

HUGO SHIRAZ ★★★★

before 1986	Prior		
1986	7	Now	$50.00
1987	6	Now	$40.00
1988	6	Now	$37.00

1989	6	Now	$34.00
1990	7	Now	$37.00
1991	6	Now	$29.00
1992	7	Now	$32.00
1993	6	Now	$25.00
1994	6	2002	$23.00
1995	6	2002	$21.00
1996	7	2004	$23.00
1997	6	2004	$18.50
1998	7	2006	N/R

Hungerford Hill, part of Southcorp Wines, are middle sized Hunter Valley based producers of a range of table wines from the NSW fruit. Winemaker: Ian Walsh.

HUNGERFORD HILL YOUNG/
COWRA CABERNET SAUVIGNON
★★★

1994	5	Now	$18.50
1995	6	2000	$20.00
1996	6	2001	$19.00
1997	7	2002	$21.00
1998	6	2003	N/R

HUNGERFORD HILL COWRA
CHARDONNAY ★★★

before 1996	Prior		
1996	5	Now	$16.00
1997	6	Now	$18.00
1998	5	Now	$14.00

HUNGERFORD HILL SEMILLON ★★★

1995	5	Now	$17.50
1996	6	Now	$19.50
1997	Not made		
1998	5	Now	$14.00

HUNGERFORD HILL TUMBARUMBA
SAUVIGNON BLANC ★★★

before 1995	Prior		
1995	6	Now	$22.00
1996	5	Now	$17.00
1997	6	Now	$19.00
1998	6	Now	$18.00

Huntaway Reserve is the label under which the New Zealand giant Corbans release varietals chosen from the three Corbans winemaking regions of Gisborne, Hawkes Bay and Marlborough. The wines are unvaryingly very good. Winemaker: Michael Kluczko.

HUNTAWAY RESERVE
CHARDONNAY (GISBORNE) ★★★★

1994	No data		
1995	7	Now	NZ$25.00
1996	7	Now	NZ$23.00
1997	5	2000	NZ$15.50

132

HUNTAWAY RESERVE
MERLOT & CABERNET BLENDS ★★★★★

1994	7	Now	NZ$27.00
1995	7	Now	NZ$25.00
1996	7	2000	NZ$23.00
1997	5	2001	NZ$15.00

HUNTAWAY RESERVE
PINOT GRIS ★★★★

1996	5	Prior	
1997	5	Now	NZ$18.00
1998	6	Now	NZ$20.00

Hunter's Wines are small makers in New Zealand's
Marlborough area, a vignoble at the forefront of the recent
quality revolution. Winemaker: Gary Duke.

HUNTER'S CHARDONNAY ★★★★

before 1993		Prior	
1993	4	Now	NZ$23.00
1994	6	Now	NZ$32.00
1995	5	Now	NZ$24.00
1996	6	2000	NZ$27.00
1997	6	2002	NZ$25.00

HUNTER'S SAUVIGNON
BLANC ★★★★

before 1996		Prior	
1996	6	Now	NZ$20.00
1997	6	Now	NZ$19.00
1998	5	Now	N/R

HUNTER'S SAUVIGNON BLANC
(OAK AGED) ★★★★

before 1994		Prior	
1994	6	Now	NZ$29.00
1995	Not made		
1996	6	Now	NZ$25.00
1997	5	Now	NZ$19.50
1998	6	Now	NZ$21.00

Huntington Estate is one of the more impressive of the
Mudgee producers, well established and distinctively styled.
Winemaker: Susie Roberts.

HUNTINGTON ESTATE CABERNET
SAUVIGNON/MERLOT ★★★★

before 1984		Prior	
1984	7	Now	$45.00
1985	6	Now	$36.00
1986	7	Now	$39.00
1987	5	Now	$25.00
1988	6	Now	$28.00
1989	6	Now	$26.00
1990	7	Now	$28.00

133

1991	7	Now	$26.00
1992	6	Now	$21.00
1993	6	Now	$19.50
1994	6	Now	$18.00
1995	6	2001	$16.50
1996	Not made		
1997	6	2003	$14.00
1998	Not made		

HUNTINGTON ESTATE
CABERNET SAUVIGNON ★★★★

before 1981	Prior		
1981	7	Now	$54.00
1982	6	Now	$42.00
1983	6	Now	$39.00
1984	7	Now	$42.00
1985	6	Now	$34.00
1986	7	Now	$36.00
1987	5	Now	$24.00
1988	6	Now	$27.00
1989	6	Now	$25.00
1990	7	Now	$27.00
1991	6	Now	$21.00
1992	6	Now	$19.50
1993	6	Now	$18.00
1994	6	Now	$17.00
1995	6	2001	$15.50
1996	5	2000	$12.00
1997	7	2003	N/R
1998	6	2004	N/R

HUNTINGTON ESTATE SHIRAZ ★★★

before 1981	Prior		
1981	7	Now	$50.00
1982	6	Now	$40.00
1983	6	Now	$37.00
1984	7	Now	$40.00
1985	6	Now	$31.00
1986	7	Now	$34.00
1987	5	Now	$22.00
1988	6	Now	$25.00
1989	7	Now	$27.00
1990	6	Now	$21.00
1991	6	Now	$20.00
1992	6	Now	$18.50
1993	7	2000	$20.00
1994	6	Now	$15.50
1995	6	2001	$14.50
1996	3	Now	N/R
1997	7	2003	N/R
1998	6	2004	N/R

Idyll Vineyard *was the first planted in the re-establishment of the Geelong vignoble. The wines are supple and attractive. Winemaker: Daryl Sefton.*

BONE IDYLL (SHIRAZ) ★★★

before 1990		Prior	
1990	5	Now	$24.00
1991	5	Now	$23.00
1992	6	Now	$25.00
1993	5	Now	$19.50
1994	5	Now	$18.00
1995	6	Now	$20.00
1996	5	Now	$15.50
1997	7	Now	$20.00
1998	6	Now	$16.00

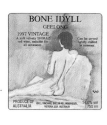

IDYLL BLUSH (ROSE) ★★★★

before 1992		Prior	
1992	5	Now	$18.50
1993	5	Now	$17.00
1994	5	Now	$16.00
1995	6	Now	$17.50
1996	6	Now	$16.50
1997	Not made		
1998	6	Now	$14.00

IDYLL CABERNET SAUVIGNON
(CABERNET SAUVIGNON/SHIRAZ until 1987) ★★★★

before 1980		Prior	
1980	6	Now	$70.00
1981	7	Now	$76.00
1982	6	Now	$60.00
1983	5	Now	$47.00
1984	4	Now	$35.00
1985	5	Now	$40.00
1986	6	Now	$45.00
1987	5	Now	$34.00
1988	5	Now	$32.00
1989	5	Now	$29.00
1990	6	Now	$33.00
1991	6	Now	$30.00
1992	6	2000	$28.00
1993	5	2000	$21.00
1994	6	2000	$24.00
1995	6	2003	$22.00
1996	6	2003	$20.00
1997	7	2005	$22.00

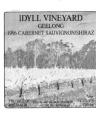

IDYLL CHARDONNAY ★★★

1989	5	Prior	
1990	6	Now	$30.00
1991	5	Now	$23.00
1992	5	Now	$22.00

1993	6	Now	$24.00
1994	5	Now	$18.50
1995	6	Now	$20.00
1996	5	Now	$16.00
1997	5	Now	$15.00
1998	6	Now	$16.50

IDYLL GEWURZTRAMINER ★★★★

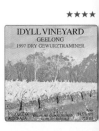

before 1990		Prior	
1990	5	Now	$24.00
1991	6	Now	$27.00
1992	5	Now	$21.00
1993	6	Now	$23.00
1994	5	Now	$18.00
1995	6	Now	$20.00
1996	6	Now	$18.50
1997	6	Now	$17.00
1998	6	Now	$15.50

IDYLL SHIRAZ ★★★★

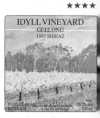

1990	7	Now	$37.00
1991	5	Now	$24.00
1992	5	Now	$22.00
1993	5	Now	$21.00
1994	6	2000	$23.00
1995	6	2003	$21.00
1996	6	2003	$20.00
1997	7	2005	$21.00

Ingoldby Wines are McLaren Flat makers whose flagship wine is a fine Cabernet Sauvignon. The operation is now owned by Mildara Blass. Winemaker: Phillip Reschke.

INGOLDBY CABERNET SAUVIGNON ★★★★

before 1985		Prior	
1985	7	Now	$37.00
1986	6	Now	$29.00
1987	7	Now	$32.00
1988	6	Now	$25.00
1989	7	Now	$27.00
1990	7	Now	$25.00
1991	7	2002	$23.00
1992	6	2002	$18.50
1993	7	2005	$20.00
1994	7	2005	$18.50
1995	6	2002	$14.50
1996	6	2004	$13.50
1997	6	2004	$12.50

INGOLDBY CHARDONNAY ★★★★

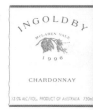

before 1993		Prior	
1993	6	Now	$18.00
1994	5	Now	$13.50
1995	7	Now	$18.00
1996	7	Now	$16.50
1997	6	2000	$13.00
1998	7	2001	$14.00

INGOLDBY SHIRAZ ★★★★

1988	6	Now	$26.00
1989	7	Now	$28.00
1990	7	Now	$26.00
1991	5	2005	$17.50
1992	6	2005	$19.50
1993	7	2005	$21.00
1994	7	2002	$19.50
1995	6	2001	$15.50
1996	6	2002	$14.00
1997	6	2003	$13.00

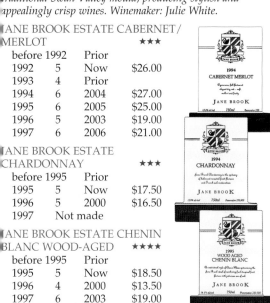

Ironbark Ridge in Queensland's Ipswich region is a small maker producing just one remarkably sophisticated wine - a complex and elegant Chardonnay. Winemaker: Adam Chapman.

IRONBARK RIDGE CHARDONNAY ★★★★

before 1994		Prior	
1994	6	Now	$22.00
1995	6	Now	$20.00
1996	6	Now	$19.00

Jane Brook Estate is a Swan Valley producer not in the traditional Swan Valley mould, producing stylish and appealingly crisp wines. Winemaker: Julie White.

JANE BROOK ESTATE CABERNET / MERLOT ★★★

before 1992		Prior	
1992	5	Now	$26.00
1993	4	Prior	
1994	6	2004	$27.00
1995	6	2005	$25.00
1996	5	2003	$19.00
1997	6	2006	$21.00

JANE BROOK ESTATE CHARDONNAY ★★★

before 1995		Prior	
1995	5	Now	$17.50
1996	5	2000	$16.50
1997	Not made		

JANE BROOK ESTATE CHENIN BLANC WOOD-AGED ★★★★

before 1995		Prior	
1995	5	Now	$18.50
1996	4	2000	$13.50
1997	6	2003	$19.00
1998	7	2005	$21.00

JANE BROOK ESTATE METHODE CHAMPENOISE CHARDONNAY ★★★

1992	4	Prior	
1993	Not made		
1994	6	Prior	
1995	5	2001	$19.00

JANE BROOK ESTATE METHODE CHAMPENOISE SHIRAZ ★★★

1992	5	2000	$36.00
1993	Not made		
1994	Not made		
1995	Not made		
1996	5	2002	$26.00
1996	6	2006	$29.00

JANE BROOK ESTATE SAUVIGNON BLANC ★★★

before 1997		Prior	
1997	6	2001	$17.50
1998	6	2004	$16.50

JANE BROOK ESTATE SHIRAZ ★★★★

before 1995		Prior	
1995	7	2005	$25.00
1996	6	2003	$19.50
1997	5	2002	$15.00

Jansz is the Methode Champenoise wine created by Heemskerk in association with their then partners Louis Roederer of Reims. It is 50/50 Pinot Noir and Chardonnay, the vintage being identifiable by the cuvee number (cuvee 89 is 1989, etc), with the addition of 15% of oak-aged older material. Winemaker: Steve Goodwin.

JANSZ METHODE CHAMPENOISE ★★★★

1989	5	Now	$31.00
1990	6	Now	$35.00
1991	6	Now	$32.00
1992	6	Now	$30.00
1993	7	Now	$32.00

Jasper Hill is a cool climate producer in Victoria's Heathcote area. The wines are both convincing and impressive. Winemaker: Ron Laughton.

JASPER HILL EMILY'S PADDOCK SHIRAZ/CABERNET FRANC ★★★★

1982	5	Now	$155.00
1983	4	Now	$110.00
1984	5	Now	$130.00
1985	6	Now	$145.00
1986	7	Now	$160.00

1987	6	Now	$125.00
1988	6	Now	$115.00
1989	5	Now	$90.00
1990	7	2002	$115.00
1991	7	2003	$105.00
1992	7	2003	$100.00
1993	7	2003	$92.00
1994	7	2005	$86.00
1995	7	2007	$80.00
1996	7	2006	$74.00

ASPER HILL GEORGIA'S PADDOCK SHIRAZ ★★★★

1982	6	Now	$125.00
1983	5	Now	$98.00
1984	5	Now	$90.00
1985	6	Now	$100.00
1986	7	Now	$105.00
1987	Not made		
1988	6	Now	$80.00
1989	5	Now	$62.00
1990	7	2000	$80.00
1991	7	2000	$74.00
1992	7	2000	$68.00
1993	7	2002	$62.00
1994	7	2003	$58.00
1995	7	2005	$54.00
1996	7	2006	$50.00

ASPER HILL RIESLING ★★★

1984	6	Now	$44.00
1985	6	Now	$41.00
1986	5	Now	$32.00
1987	Not made		
1988	Not made		
1989	6	Now	$30.00
1990	7	Now	$32.00
1991	7	Now	$30.00
1992	7	Now	$28.00
1993	7	Now	$26.00
1994	7	2000	$24.00
1995	Not made		
1996	7	2001	$20.00
1997	7	2002	$19.00

im Barry Wines are Clare Valley makers with a sizeable *range of reliable wines including one of the world's best *hiraz. Winemaker: Mark Barry.*

IM BARRY ARMAGH SHIRAZ ✸✸✸✸✸

1985	5	2002	$215.00
1986	Not made		
1987	6	2007	$220.00

139

1988	6	2005	$205.00
1989	7	2010	$220.00
1990	7	2010	$205.00
1991	6	2003	$160.00
1992	7	2005	$175.00
1993	7	2015	$160.00
1994	6	2006	$130.00
1995	7	2007	$140.00
1996	7	2010	$130.00

JIM BARRY CABERNET/MERLOT ★★★

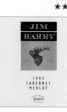

before 1989		Prior	
1989	6	Now	$19.50
1990	6	Now	$18.00
1991	6	Now	$16.50
1992	6	Now	$15.50
1993	6	Now	$14.50
1994	7	Now	$15.50
1995	6	Now	$12.00
1996	7	Now	$13.00

Not made after 1996

JIM BARRY CABERNET SAUVIGNON ★★★

before 1985		Prior	
1985	5	Now	$33.00
1986	6	Now	$36.00
1987	6	Now	$34.00
1988	5	Now	$26.00
1989	7	Now	$34.00
1990	6	Now	$27.00
1991	Not made		
1992	7	2000	$27.00
1993	6	2002	$21.00
1994	7	2005	$23.00
1995	6	2006	$18.00
1996	6	2007	$17.00
1997	6	2008	$15.50

JIM BARRY CHARDONNAY ★★★

before 1990		Prior	
1990	6	Now	$21.00
1991	6	Now	$19.50
1992	6	Now	$18.00
1993	7	Now	$19.50
1994	No data		
1995	6	Now	$14.00
1996	6	Now	$13.00
1997	7	2000	$14.00

JIM BARRY McCRAE WOOD SHIRAZ

★★★★

1992	6	2000	$37.00
1993	7	2002	$40.00
1994	6	2005	$31.00
1995	7	2005	$34.00
1996	7	2005	$31.00

JIM BARRY WATERVALE RIESLING ★★★

1980	6	Now	$52.00
1981	4	Now	$32.00
1982	5	Now	$37.00
1983	5	Now	$34.00
1984	5	Now	$31.00
1985	5	Now	$29.00
1986	6	Now	$32.00
1987	5	Now	$25.00
1988	5	Now	$23.00
1989	7	2000	$30.00
1990	4	Now	$16.00
1991	4	Now	$14.50
1992	7	2000	$24.00
1993	6	Now	$19.00
1994	6	2000	$17.50
1995	6	2000	$16.00
1996	6	2000	$15.00
1997	6	2000	$14.00
1998	7	Now	$15.00

Jud's Hill is one of the Clare Valley's respected makers.
Winemaker: Brian Barry.

JUD'S HILL CABERNET SAUVIGNON ★★★★

before 1992	Prior		
1992	7	2000	$24.00
1993	7	2000	$22.00
1994	7	2002	$20.00
1995	7	2000	$19.00
1996	7	2002	$18.00

JUD'S HILL MERLOT ★★★★★

1992	7	Now	$47.00
1993	Not made		
1994	7	2000	$40.00
1995	Not made		
1996	7	2002	$35.00

JUD'S HILL RIESLING ★★★

before 1994	Prior		
1994	7	2000	$20.00
1995	7	Prior	
1996	7	2000	$17.00
1997	7	2001	$16.00
1998	7	2002	$15.00

***Kangaroo Island Wines** is an operation owned by Gumeracha Cellars, who also own the Chain of Ponds label. The grapes are grown on Kangaroo Island's only producing vineyard - the Florance vineyard. Winemaker: Caj Amadio.*

KANGAROO ISLAND
CABERNET/MERLOT ★★★★

Year			
1991	5	Prior	
1992	5	Now	$22.00
1993	6	Now	$24.00
1994	7	2000	$26.00
1995	6	2000	$21.00
1996	6	2002	$19.50

***The Karina Vineyard** is a beautifully tended small vineyard in the Dromana area of the Mornington Peninsula. Winemaker: Graeme Pinney.*

KARINA VINEYARD CABERNET/MERLOT ★★★★

before 1991		Prior	
1991	7	Now	$32.00
1992	6	Now	$26.00
1993	6	Now	$24.00
1994	7	Now	$26.00
1995	6	2000	$20.00
1996	6	2000	$19.00
1997	7	2002	$20.00

KARINA VINEYARD
CHARDONNAY ★★★★★

1993	7	Now	$27.00
1994	6	Now	$22.00
1995	7	Now	$23.00
1996	5	Now	$15.50
1997	7	2002	$20.00
1998	7	2003	N/R

KARINA VINEYARD RIESLING
★★★★

before 1994		Prior	
1994	7	Now	$27.00
1995	7	Now	$25.00
1996	6	Now	$20.00
1997	7	Now	$21.00
1998	6	2000	$17.00

KARINA VINEYARD
SAUVIGNON BLANC ★★★★

before 1994		Prior	
1994	6	Now	$24.00
1995	7	Now	$26.00
1996	7	Now	$24.00
1997	6	Now	$19.00
1998	6	2000	$17.50

Karl Seppelt Estate (formerly Grand Cru) is a small Springton (Eden Valley) producer whose wines are worthy of considerable respect. Winemaker: Karl Seppelt.

KARL SEPPELT ESTATE CABERNET SAUVIGNON ★★★★

before 1991	Prior		
1991	No data		
1992	No data		
1993	6	2000	$21.00
1994	7	2005	$22.00
1996	7	2007	$21.00

KARL SEPPELT ESTATE CHARDONNAY ★★★

before 1994	Prior		
1994	6	Now	$17.50
1995	7	2000	$19.00
1996	7	2001	$17.50

KARL SEPPELT ESTATE CHARDONNAY BRUT ★★★★

1990	6	Now	$20.00
1991	7	Now	$22.00
1992	7	2000	$21.00

KARL SEPPELT ESTATE SHIRAZ ★★★

1986	5	Prior	
1987	Not made		
1988	5	Now	$22.00
1989	5	Now	$21.00
1990	Not made		
1996	7	2005	$25.00

KARL SEPPELT ESTATE SPARKLING SHIRAZ ★★★★

before 1992	Prior		
1992	6	Now	$29.00
1993	Not made		
1994	6	2001	$25.00

Karriview, in Western Australia's Denmark region, pioneered the area's production of Pinot Noir and Chardonnay with their 1989 vintage. Their quality is such that others will surely follow. Winemaker: John Wade.

KARRIVIEW CHARDONNAY ★★★★

before 1993	Prior		
1993	6	Now	$50.00
1994	5	Prior	
1995	7	2000	$50.00
1996	6	2001	$40.00
1997	7	2003	$43.00

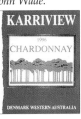

KARRIVIEW PINOT NOIR

★★★★

before 1994		Prior	
1994	7	Now	$39.00
1995	5	2000	$26.00
1996	6	2003	$29.00

Katnook are Coonawarra makers of wines of extremely impressive quality. Winemaker: Wayne Stehbens.

KATNOOK CABERNET SAUVIGNON

★★★★★

1980	6	Now	$140.00
1981	5	Now	$110.00
1982	5	Now	$100.00
1983	4	Now	$76.00
1984	5	Now	$88.00
1985	5	Now	$82.00
1986	6	Now	$90.00
1987	5	Now	$70.00
1988	5	Now	$64.00
1989	Not made		
1990	6	Now	$66.00
1991	6	Now	$62.00
1992	6	Now	$56.00
1993	5	Now	$44.00
1994	6	2001	$49.00
1995	5	2001	$38.00
1996	6	2003	$42.00

KATNOOK CHARDONNAY

★★★★

1980	5	Now	$105.00
1981	4	Now	$80.00
1982	5	Now	$92.00
1983	4	Now	$68.00
1984	5	Now	$80.00
1985	5	Now	$74.00
1986	6	Now	$82.00
1987	5	Now	$62.00
1988	5	Now	$58.00
1989	6	Now	$64.00
1990	7	Now	$70.00
1991	5	Now	$47.00
1992	6	Now	$52.00
1993	5	Now	$40.00
1994	7	Now	$52.00
1995	7	Now	$48.00
1996	6	Now	$38.00

KATNOOK ESTATE CHARDONNAY BRUT

★★★★

1984	5	Now	$56.00
1985	5	Now	$52.00
1986	5	Now	$49.00

1987	5	Now	$45.00
1988	Not made		
1989	Not made		
1990	6	Now	$43.00
1991	Not made		
1992	Not made		
1993	6	Now	$34.00
1994	5	Now	$26.00

KATNOOK MERLOT ★★★★

1987	4	Now	$49.00
1988	5	Now	$56.00
1989	Not made		
1990	5	Now	$48.00
1991	Not made		
1992	6	Now	$50.00
1993	5	Now	$38.00
1994	6	Now	$42.00
1995	5	2000	$33.00
1996	7	2003	$42.00

KATNOOK RIESLING ★★★

1980	6	Now	$56.00
1981	5	Now	$43.00
1982	5	Now	$40.00
1983	Not made		
1984	5	Now	$34.00
1985	5	Now	$32.00
1986	6	Now	$35.00
1987	5	Now	$27.00
1988	6	Now	$30.00
1989	6	Now	$28.00
1990	Not made		
1994	6	Now	$24.00
1995	5	Now	$18.50
1996	6	Now	$20.00
1997	7	2000	$22.00

KATNOOK SAUVIGNON BLANC ★★★

before 1991	Prior		
1991	6	Now	$38.00
1992	6	Now	$35.00
1993	5	Now	$27.00
1994	6	Now	$30.00
1995	7	Now	$33.00
1996	7	Now	$30.00
1997	6	Now	$24.00

***Kays** are long established and respected McLaren Vale producers with a large range of traditionally styled wines. Winemaker: Colin Kay.*

KAYS AMERY BLOCK 6 SHIRAZ ★★★★

before 1986		Prior	
1986	7	Now	$74.00
1987	5	Prior	
1988	5	Prior	
1989	6	Now	$50.00
1990	7	Now	$54.00
1991	7	2000	$50.00
1992	7	2002	$47.00
1993	6	2000	$37.00
1994	7	2001	$40.00
1995	7	2002	$37.00
1996	7	2004	$34.00
1997	7	2005	$32.00

KAYS AMERY CABERNET SAUVIGNON ★★★

before 1992		Prior	
1992	7	2000	$36.00
1993	5	Now	$24.00
1994	7	2004	$31.00
1995	5	2001	$20.00
1996	7	2004	$26.00
1997	6	2005	$21.00

KAYS AMERY GRENACHE ★★★

1994	5	Now	$18.50
1995	7	Now	$24.00
1996	6	Now	$19.00
1997	6	Now	$18.00

KAYS AMERY SHIRAZ ★★★★

1992	6	Now	$31.00
1993	5	Now	$24.00
1994	6	2000	$26.00
1995	7	2002	$29.00
1996	7	2004	$26.00
1997	6	2003	$21.00

***Kellybrook Winery** is a Yarra Valley producer whose peerless cider-making mastery unfairly limits the respect accorded the very fine wines. The sparkling wine is particularly recommendable. Winemaker: Darren Kelly.*

KELLYBROOK CABERNET SAUVIGNON (/MERLOT) ★★★★

before 1987		Prior	
1987	4	Now	$31.00
1988	6	Now	$43.00
1989	Not made		

1990	Not made		
1991	5	2001	$28.00
1992	6	2001	$32.00
1993	6	2002	$29.00
1994	6	2002	$27.00
1995	Not made		
1996	6	2003	$23.00
1997	7	2007	$25.00

KELLYBROOK CHARDONNAY ★★★

before 1992	Prior		
1992	4	Now	$21.00
1993	5	Now	$24.00
1994	6	Now	$27.00
1995	6	Now	$25.00
1996	6	Now	$23.00
1997	6	2000	$21.00
1998	5	2001	$16.50

KELLYBROOK PINOT NOIR ★★★

1991	5	Now	$29.00
1992	6	Now	$32.00
1993	5	Now	$25.00
1994	5	Now	$23.00
1995	5	Now	$21.00
1996	5	2000	$19.50
1997	5	2001	$18.00

KELLYBROOK PINOT NOIR/CHARDONNAY
METHODE CHAMPENOISE ★★★★★

1988	5	Now	$34.00
1989	5	Now	$32.00
1990	6	Now	$35.00
1991	6	Now	$33.00
1992	6	Now	$30.00
1993	6	Now	$28.00
1994	6	Now	$26.00

KELLYBROOK SHIRAZ ★★★★

1984	6	Prior	
1985	Not made		
1986	Not made		
1987	Not made		
1988	6	Now	$43.00
1989	Not made		
1990	Not made		
1991	5	Now	$28.00
1992	Not made		
1993	5	Now	$24.00
1994	7	2000	$32.00

147

1995	4	Now	$17.00
1996	6	2003	$23.00
1997	7	2004	$25.00

Killerby Vineyards, *formerly Leschenault, is a Capel (Western Australia) area producer whose change of name was accompanied by a marked quality improvement.*
Winemaker: Paul Boulden.

KILLERBY CABERNET SAUVIGNON ★★★★

before 1988		Prior	
1988	Not made		
1989	6	Now	$46.00
1990	Not made		
1991	5	Prior	
1992	6	Prior	
1993	6	Now	$34.00
1994	5	2001	$26.00
1995	5	2000	$24.00
1996	5	2000	$22.00
1997	6	2002	$25.00

KILLERBY CHARDONNAY ★★★★★

before 1989		Prior	
1989	5	Now	$62.00
1990	4	Prior	
1991	5	Now	$52.00
1992	5	Now	$49.00
1993	4	Now	$36.00
1994	6	2000	$50.00
1995	5	2000	$39.00
1996	6	2001	$43.00
1997	7	2002	$47.00
1998	6	2003	$37.00

KILLERBY SEMILLON ★★★★

before 1989		Prior	
1989	6	Now	$47.00
1990	4	Prior	
1991	5	2000	$34.00
1992	5	Now	$31.00
1993	4	Now	$23.00
1994	6	Now	$32.00
1995	5	Now	$25.00
1996	6	2000	$27.00
1997	4	2002	$17.00
1998	5	2000	$19.50

KILLERBY SHIRAZ ★★★★

1989	3	Prior	
1990	Not made		
1991	5	Now	$37.00
1992	4	Now	$27.00
1993	5	Now	$32.00

1994	6	Now	$35.00
1995	6	2000	$33.00
1996	5	2000	$25.00
1997	5	2002	$23.00

Kings Creek Vineyard *in the Mornington Peninsula is a very small producer of three charming wines. Winemaker: Brian Cole.*

KINGS CREEK CABERNET SAUVIGNON ★★★★

1985	4	Now	$38.00
1986	Not made		
1987	6	Now	$49.00
1988	Not made		
1989	6	Now	$42.00
1990	5	Now	$32.00
1991	Not made		
1992	5	Now	$28.00
1993	6	2001	$31.00
1994	6	2001	$28.00
1995	5	2001	$22.00
1996	5	201	$20.00

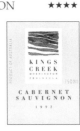

KINGS CREEK CHARDONNAY ★★★★

1985	4	Now	$40.00
1986	5	Now	$46.00
1987	7	Now	$60.00
1988	Not made		
1989	7	Now	$50.00
1990	5	Now	$34.00
1991	7	Now	$44.00
1992	6	Now	$35.00
1993	7	Now	$38.00
1994	7	2000	$35.00
1995	7	Now	$32.00
1996	7	Now	$30.00
1997	6	Now	$24.00

KINGS CREEK PINOT NOIR ★★★

1985	4	Now	$43.00
1986	Not made		
1987	6	Now	$54.00
1988	Not made		
1989	6	Now	$47.00
1990	5	Now	$36.00
1991	6	Now	$40.00
1992	7	Now	$44.00
1993	5	Now	$29.00
1994	6	Now	$32.00
1995	7	Now	$35.00
1996	7	Now	$32.00
1997	5	Now	$21.00

***Knappstein Lenswood Vineyards** is the name under which Tim Knappstein is producing high quality wines from his Lenswood (Adelaide Hills) plantings. Winemaker: Tim Knappstein.*

KNAPPSTEIN LENSWOOD CHARDONNAY ★★★★★

1991	7	Now	$50.00
1992	5	Now	$34.00
1993	5	Now	$31.00
1994	5	Now	$29.00
1995	7	2000	$37.00
1996	7	2001	$35.00

KNAPPSTEIN LENSWOOD PINOT NOIR ★★★★

1991	4	Now	$38.00
1992	4	Now	$35.00
1993	6	Now	$49.00
1994	6	2000	$45.00
1995	5	2000	$35.00
1996	7	2002	$45.00

KNAPPSTEIN LENSWOOD SAUVIGNON BLANC
★★★

1993	7	Now	$37.00
1994	5	Now	$24.00
1995	5	Now	$23.00
1996	6	Now	$25.00
1997	6	Now	$23.00

***Knappstein Wines** (formerly Tim Knappstein Wines) is a good quality producer in the Clare Valley. In 1995 a new 120 acre vineyard, Yertabulti, was developed. Winemaker: Andrew Hardy.*

KNAPPSTEIN CABERNET/MERLOT ★★★

1985	5	Now	$39.00
1986	6	Now	$44.00
1987	4	Prior	
1988	6	Now	$38.00
1989	5	Prior	
1990	6	Prior	
1991	7	2000	$35.00
1992	6	2000	$27.00
1993	6	Now	$25.00
1994	7	2000	$27.00
1995	6	Now	$22.00
1996	6	2000	$20.00

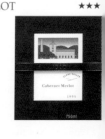

KNAPPSTEIN CABERNET SAUVIGNON ★★★★

before 1985		Prior	
1985	5	Now	$44.00
1986	7	Now	$58.00
1987	4	Now	$30.00
1988	6	Now	$42.00
1989	6	Now	$39.00

1990	7	Now	$42.00
1991	Not made		
1992	Not made		
1993	6	2003	$29.00
1994	7	2005	$31.00
1995	6	2006	$25.00

KNAPPSTEIN CHARDONNAY

before 1994		Prior	★★★★
1994	6	Now	$20.00
1995	7	Now	$22.00
1996	5	2000	$15.00

KNAPPSTEIN GEWURZTRAMINER

before 1994		Prior	★★★
1994	7	Now	$16.50
1995	7	Prior	
1996	5	Prior	
1997	6	Now	$11.50

KNAPPSTEIN RIESLING   ★★★

before 1985		Prior	
1985	7	2000	$36.00
1986	6	2000	$29.00
1987	6	2000	$27.00
1988	6	2000	$25.00
1989	6	Now	$23.00
1990	7	Now	$25.00
1991	5	2000	$16.50
1992	6	2000	$18.00
1993	6	2000	$17.00
1994	6	2000	$15.50
1995	7	2001	$17.00
1996	6	2001	$13.50
1997	7	2003	$14.50

KNAPPSTEIN SHIRAZ   ★★★★

1994	6	2000	$31.00
1995	6	2002	$29.00
1996	6	2003	$27.00

Knight's Granite Hills - see Granite Hills.

Krondorf is a Barossa winery processing grapes from far afield as well as from the original Tanunda area vineyard. It is owned by Mildara Blass. Winemaker: Nick Walker.

KRONDORF BAROSSA RIESLING
★★★

before 1991		Prior	
1991	6	Now	$17.00
1992	7	Now	$18.50
1993	6	Now	$14.50
1994	5	Now	$11.50
1995	7	2000	$14.50

1996	7	2000	$13.50
1997	7	2002	$12.50
1998	7	2001	$11.50

KRONDORF CHARDONNAY ★★★

before 1991		Prior	
1991	6	Now	$16.00
1992	5	Now	$12.50
1993	6	Now	$13.50
1994	7	Now	$15.00
1995	7	Now	$13.50
1996	7	Now	$12.50
1997	7	2001	$11.50

KRONDORF FAMILY RESERVE CHARDONNAY

★★★★

1985	7	Now	$45.00
1986	7	Now	$41.00
1987	5	Prior	
1988	5	Now	$25.00
1989	6	Now	$28.00
1990	7	Now	$30.00
1991	6	Now	$24.00
1992	6	Now	$22.00
1993	6	Now	$20.00
1994	7	Now	$22.00
1995	6	Now	$17.50
1996	7	2001	$19.00
1997	6	2001	$15.00

KRONDORF FAMILY RESERVE
SHOW CABERNET ★★★★

1991	5	Now	$20.00
1992	6	Now	$23.00
1993	5	2000	$17.50
1994	7	2002	$23.00
1995	6	2004	$18.00
1996	7	2004	$19.50

KRONDORF SEMILLON ★★★

before 1991		Prior	
1991	6	Now	$18.00
1992	5	Now	$14.00
1993	6	Now	$15.50
1994	5	Now	$12.00
1995	6	Now	$13.50

1996	7	2000	$14.50
1997	7	2000	$13.50
1998	7	2001	$12.50

KRONDORF SHIRAZ ★★★
1993	5	Now	$16.00
1994	5	2000	$15.00
1995	4	2000	$11.00
1996	6	2001	$15.50
1997	5	2000	$12.00

Kumeu River is a respected New Zealand producer at Kumeu (west of Auckland), owned and operated by the Brajkovich family. The wines are sensitively crafted and individual. Winemaker: Michael Brajkovich MW.

KUMEU RIVER CHARDONNAY ★★★★★
before 1991		Prior	
1991	7	Now	NZ$58.00
1992	5	Prior	
1993	7	Now	NZ$50.00
1994	7	Now	NZ$47.00
1995	6	Prior	
1996	7	Now	NZ$40.00
1997	7	2000	NZ$37.00
1998	7	2001	NZ$34.00

KUMEU RIVER CHARDONNAY (MATE'S VINEYARD) ★★★★★
1993	6	Now	NZ$50.00
1994	7	Now	NZ$54.00
1995	6	Now	NZ$43.00
1996	7	2000	NZ$46.00
1997	7	2001	NZ$43.00
1998	7	2002	NZ$39.00

KUMEU RIVER MERLOT/CABERNET ★★★★
before 1987		Prior	
1987	7	Now	NZ$76.00
1988	Not made		
1989	5	Prior	
1990	7	Now	NZ$60.00
1991	7	Now	NZ$56.00
1992	5	Prior	
1993	6	Now	NZ$41.00
1994	7	Now	NZ$44.00
1995	6	Now	NZ$35.00
1996	7	2002	NZ$38.00
1997	Not made		
1998	7	2006	NZ$32.00

KUMEU RIVER SAUVIGNON/ SEMILLON
★★★★

before 1996		Prior	
1996	7	Now	NZ$29.00
1997	6	Now	NZ$23.00
1998	7	2000	NZ$25.00

Lake George Winery was the seminal Canberra district winemaking venture, and has remained small and markedly individual. Winemaker: Dr Edgar Riek.

LAKE GEORGE CHARDONNAY
★★★

before 1995		Prior	
1995	5	Now	$32.00
1996	5	2000	$30.00

LAKE GEORGE MERLOT ★★★

1991	4	Now	$35.00
1992	3	Prior	
1994	3	Prior	
1994	4	2000	$27.00
1995	5	2000	$32.00
1996	6	2002	$36.00

LAKE GEORGE PINOT NOIR ★★★

before 1991		Prior	
1991	3	Now	$32.00
1992	3	Prior	
1993	3	Now	$27.00
1994	4	Now	$34.00
1995	5	2000	$40.00
1996	5	2000	$37.00

Lakes Folly is a superb small vineyard at Pokolbin. The wines are among the most sought-after in Australia. Winemaker: Stephen Lake.

LAKES FOLLY CABERNET SAUVIGNON ★★★★★

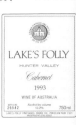

before 1972		Prior	
1972	7	Now	$440.00
1973	5	Prior	
1974	3	Prior	
1975	6	Prior	
1976	5	Prior	
1977	5	Prior	
1978	6	Prior	
1979	4	Prior	
1980	5	Now	$170.00
1981	6	Now	$185.00
1982	4	Prior	
1983	5	Prior	
1984	3	Prior	
1985	6	Now	$135.00
1986	5	Prior	
1987	6	Now	$115.00
1988	5	Now	$92.00

1989	7	2004	$115.00
1990	5	Now	$78.00
1991	6	2003	$86.00
1992	5	2000	$66.00
1993	7	2008	$86.00
1994	7	2009	$80.00
1995	5	2002	$52.00
1996	7	2012	$68.00
1997	6	2009	$54.00

LAKES FOLLY CHARDONNAY ★★★★★

before 1981		Prior	
1981	7	Now	$200.00
1982	6	Prior	
1983	7	Prior	
1984	3	Prior	
1985	5	Prior	
1986	7	Now	$135.00
1987	5	Prior	
1988	5	Prior	
1989	6	Now	$94.00
1990	5	Prior	
1991	6	Now	$80.00
1992	6	Now	$74.00
1993	6	Prior	
1994	7	2002	$74.00
1995	6	2000	$58.00
1996	7	2006	$64.00
1997	6	2004	$50.00
1998	5	2003	N/R

Lark Hill is a Canberra district maker of the area's best wines, a fact not probably unconnected with the vineyard's altitude - over 800 metres. Winemaker: Sue Carpenter.

LARK HILL CABERNET/MERLOT ★★★★

1991	6	Now	$34.00
1992	5	Now	$26.00
1993	7	2000	$34.00
1994	6	2001	$27.00
1995	7	2003	$29.00
1996	6	2003	$23.00

LARK HILL CHARDONNAY ★★★★

before 1991		Prior	
1991	6	Now	$37.00
1992	5	Now	$28.00
1993	7	2000	$37.00
1994	5	Now	$24.00
1995	6	Now	$27.00
1996	7	2000	$29.00
1997	7	2001	$27.00

LARK HILL METHODE CHAMPENOISE ★★★★

1993	6	Now	$31.00
1994	6	Now	$29.00
1995	6	2000	$27.00

LARK HILL PINOT NOIR ★★★★★

1994	5	Now	$26.00
1995	5	Now	$24.00
1996	6	2000	$27.00
1997	7	2001	$29.00

LARK HILL RIESLING ★★★★

before 1993		Prior	
1993	6	Now	$22.00
1994	7	Now	$23.00
1995	5	Prior	
1996	6	Now	$17.00
1997	7	2000	$18.50
1998	5	2000	$12.50

Leasingham is a 100 year old Clare Valley producer now owned and operated by BRL Hardy. Winemaker: Richard Rowe.

LEASINGHAM BIN 7 RIESLING ★★★

1994	4	Now	$11.50
1995	4	Now	$10.50
1996	6	Now	$14.50
1997	7	2002	$16.00

LEASINGHAM BIN 37 CHARDONNAY ★★★

1992	4	Now	$15.50
1993	4	Now	$14.50
1994	4	Now	$13.00
1995	4	Now	$12.00
1996	5	Now	$14.00
1997	6	2000	$16.00

LEASINGHAM BIN 56 CABERNET SAUVIGNON/MALBEC ★★★

before 1980		Prior	
1980	7	Now	$74.00
1981	7	Now	$68.00
1982	5	Now	$46.00
1983	7	Now	$58.00
1984	7	Now	$54.00
1985	5	Now	$36.00
1986	5	Now	$33.00
1987	5	Now	$31.00
1988	6	Now	$34.00
1989	7	2000	$37.00
1990	7	2005	$34.00
1991	6	2000	$27.00
1992	6	2000	$25.00

1993	5	2000	$19.50
1994	7	2000	$25.00
1995	6	2000	$20.00
1996	5	2000	$15.50

LEASINGHAM BIN 61 SHIRAZ ★★★

1988	5	Now	$29.00
1989	4	Now	$22.00
1990	7	Now	$35.00
1991	7	Now	$33.00
1992	7	2000	$30.00
1993	5	2000	$20.00
1994	7	2005	$26.00
1995	6	2004	$20.00
1996	5	2004	$16.00

LEASINGHAM CLASSIC CLARE
CABERNET SAUVIGNON ★★★★

1991	6	Now	$42.00
1992	7	Now	$45.00
1993	6	2000	$36.00
1994	7	2005	$38.00
1995	6	2004	$30.00

LEASINGHAM CLASSIC CLARE SHIRAZ ★★★★

1991	7	2001	$46.00
1992	6	2000	$36.00
1993	5	2000	$28.00
1994	7	2010	$36.00
1995	6	2007	$29.00

Leconfield, a 25 hectare Coonawarra vineyard owned and operated by the Hamilton Wine Group, specialises in premium Cabernets. Winemaker: Ralph Fowler.

LECONFIELD CABERNET SAUVIGNON ★★★★

before 1982	Prior		
1982	6	Now	$96.00
1983	Not made		
1984	4	Prior	
1985	Not made		
1986	4	Prior	
1987	Not made		
1988	5	Now	$50.00
1989	4	Now	$37.00
1990	6	2000	$52.00
1991	7	2003	$56.00
1992	5	2002	$37.00
1993	6	2004	$41.00
1994	7	2005	$44.00
1995	5	2001	$29.00
1996	6	2006	$32.00
1997	7	2008	$35.00
1998	5	2009	N/R

LECONFIELD CHARDONNAY ★★★

before 1991		Prior	
1991	6	Now	$32.00
1992	5	Now	$25.00
1993	6	Now	$27.00
1994	6	2000	$25.00
1995	4	Now	$15.50
1996	6	2001	$22.00
1997	5	2002	$17.00
1998	4	2003	N/R

LECONFIELD MERLOT ★★★★

1991	7	2000	$38.00
1992	6	2001	$30.00
1993	6	2002	$28.00
1994	7	2003	$30.00
1995	6	2004	$24.00
1996	6	2005	$22.00

LECONFIELD RIESLING ★★★★

1990	5	Now	$29.00
1991	5	Now	$27.00
1992	6	Now	$30.00
1993	5	Now	$23.00
1994	7	Now	$30.00
1995	5	Now	$20.00
1996	7	Now	$25.00
1997	6	2001	$20.00
1998	5	2000	$15.50

LECONFIELD SHIRAZ ★★★★

before 1990		Prior	
1990	6	Now	$44.00
1991	5	Now	$34.00
1992	5	2000	$31.00
1993	6	2001	$35.00
1994	5	Now	$27.00
1995	7	2005	$35.00
1996	6	2006	$28.00
1997	7	2007	$30.00
1998	5	2003	N/R

Leeuwin Estate is Australia's largest extreme quality producer, the grapes being grown on their 90 hectare Margaret River vineyard. Their habit of affixing an Art Series label to the best vintages (at very substantial prices) makes the lesser labelled wines remarkably good buying. Winemaker: Bob Cartwright.

LEEUWIN ESTATE CABERNET SAUVIGNON ★★★★

before 1981		Prior	
1981	5	Now	$140.00
1982	7	Now	$185.00
1983	5	Prior	
1984	5	Prior	
1985	6	Now	$125.00
1986	6	Prior	

1987	7	Now	$125.00
1988	6	Now	$100.00
1989	7	Now	$110.00
1990	5	Now	$72.00
1991	6	Now	$80.00
1992	6	2000	$74.00
1993	5	Now	$56.00
1994	5	2000	$52.00
1995	6	2002	$58.00
1996	5	2001	$45.00
1997	6	2003	N/R

LEEUWIN ESTATE CHARDONNAY ✹✹✹✹✹

1980	6	Now	$270.00
1981	6	Now	$250.00
1982	7	Now	$270.00
1983	6	Now	$215.00
1984	6	Now	$200.00
1985	7	Now	$215.00
1986	6	Now	$170.00
1987	7	Now	$185.00
1988	6	Now	$145.00
1989	6	Now	$135.00
1990	5	Now	$100.00
1991	6	Now	$115.00
1992	6	Now	$105.00
1993	6	Now	$100.00
1994	6	Now	$92.00
1995	6	Now	$86.00
1996	5	2001	$66.00
1997	5	2001	$60.00

LEEUWIN ESTATE PINOT NOIR ★★★★★

before 1990		Prior	
1990	5	Now	$58.00
1991	6	Now	$64.00
1992	5	Now	$50.00
1993	4	Now	$37.00
1994	5	Now	$43.00
1995	6	Now	$47.00
1996	6	Now	$44.00
1997	5	2000	$34.00

LEEUWIN ESTATE RIESLING

★★★★

before 1990		Prior	
1990	6	Now	$41.00
1991	6	Now	$38.00
1992	5	Now	$29.00
1993	5	Now	$27.00
1994	5	Now	$25.00
1995	6	Now	$28.00
1996	6	Now	$26.00
1997	5	Now	$20.00
1998	6	Now	$22.00

LEEUWIN ESTATE SAUVIGNON BLANC ★★★

before 1994		Prior	
1994	5	Now	$35.00
1995	6	Now	$39.00
1996	6	Now	$36.00
1997	5	Now	$27.00
1998	6	Now	$31.00

Lehmann - see Peter Lehmann.

Lenton Brae is a Margaret River vineyard and winery (designed and built by the architect/owner). Wine quality has been a little patchy, but the better vintages show much promise. Winemaker: Edward Tomlinson.

LENTON BRAE CABERNET SAUVIGNON ★★★★

1988	5	Now	$58.00
1989	4	Now	$43.00
1990	5	Now	$50.00
1991	6	2000	$56.00
1992	4	Now	$34.00
1993	3	Now	$24.00
1994	5	2002	$37.00
1995	6	2004	$41.00
1996	7	2007	$44.00
1997	6	2005	$35.00

LENTON BRAE CABERNET/MERLOT ★★★

1991	4	Prior	
1992	Not made		
1993	4	Now	$22.00
1994	5	Now	$26.00
1995	5	Now	$24.00
1996	6	Now	$26.00
1997	5	2001	$20.00

LENTON BRAE CHARDONNAY ★★★

before 1994		Prior	
1994	4	Now	$28.00
1995	4	2000	$26.00
1996	6	2000	$36.00
1997	7	2003	$39.00
1998	6	2003	$31.00

LENTON BRAE SAUVIGNON BLANC ★★★

before 1995		Prior	
1995	6	Now	$25.00
1996	5	Now	$19.50
1997	5	Now	$18.50
1998	5	Now	$17.00

LENTON BRAE SEMILLON/ SAUVIGNON BLANC ★★★

before 1992		Prior	
1992	5	Now	$24.00
1993	6	Prior	
1994	4	Prior	
1995	7	2000	$26.00
1996	6	Now	$21.00
1997	5	Now	$16.00
1998	6	2000	$18.00

Leo Buring is a Barossa Valley based maker in the Southcorp Wines aegis. They are particularly renowned for their uniquely beautiful premium Rhine Rieslings - wines which possess remarkable longevity. Winemaker: Geoff Henriks.

LEO BURING LEONAY EDEN VALLEY RIESLING ★★★★★

before 1972		Prior	
1972	7	Now	$170.00
1973	7	Prior	
1974	Not made		
1975	6	Now	$115.00
1976	6	Prior	
1977	5	Prior	
1978	5	Prior	
1979	7	Now	$100.00
1980	6	Now	$80.00
1981	4	Now	$49.00
1982	5	Now	$56.00
1983	Not made		
1984	6	Now	$58.00
1985	Not made		
1986	5	Now	$42.00
1987	5	Now	$39.00
1988	7	Now	$50.00
1989	5	Now	$33.00
1990	7	2000	$43.00
1991	7	2003	$40.00
1992	5	2004	$26.00
1993	Not made		
1994	6	2005	$27.00
1995	6	2005	$25.00
1996	Not made		
1997	7	2008	N/R

LEO BURING RESERVE BIN BAROSSA/COONAWARRA CABERNET SAUVIGNON ★★★

1984	7	Now	$60.00
1985	5	Now	$40.00
1986	6	Now	$44.00
1987	4	Now	$27.00
1988	7	Now	$44.00

161

1989	4	Now	$23.00
1990	6	Now	$32.00
1991	7	2000	$35.00
1992	5	Now	$23.00
1993	6	2000	$26.00
1994	6	2002	$24.00
1995	5	2002	$18.50
1996	6	2004	$20.00
1997	7	2006	N/R

Leydens Vale *is the label under which Blue Pyrenees Estate (qv) release a range of reasonably priced varietals from grapes grown virtually anywhere in the better areas of Australia.*
Winemaker: Kim Hart.

LEYDENS VALE PINOT NOIR

★★★

1993	4	Now	$18.00
1994	5	Now	$20.00
1995	5	Now	$19.00
1996	6	2000	$21.00

LEYDENS VALE SHIRAZ ★★★

1993	4	Now	$20.00
1994	5	Now	$23.00
1995	4	Now	$17.00
1996	5	2000	$20.00

Lillydale Vineyards *is a respected Yarra Valley operation now owned by McWilliams.*
Winemakers: Jim Brayne and Max McWilliam.

LILLYDALE VINEYARDS
CABERNET/MERLOT

★★★★

before 1993		Prior	
1993	5	Now	$21.00
1994	6	2002	$24.00
1995	5	2001	$18.50
1996	6	2002	$20.00
1997	7	2004	$22.00
1998	6	2004	N/R

LILLYDALE VINEYARDS
CHARDONNAY ★★★★

before 1993		Prior	
1993	5	Now	$20.00
1994	5	Now	$19.00
1995	5	Now	$17.50
1996	6	2000	$19.50
1997	6	2001	$18.00
1998	6	2002	$16.50

LILLYDALE VINEYARDS PINOT NOIR ★★★★

before 1997		Prior	
1997	6	Now	$20.00
1998	5	2001	N/R

LILLYDALE VINEYARDS SAUVIGNON BLANC ★★★

before 1998		Prior	
1998	6	Now	$15.50

Lindemans, part of Southcorp Wines, is a very large maker with holdings in the Hunter Valley, Coonawarra, Clare, Padthaway and North West Victoria. In spite of their necessarily substantial production of high volume lines, they consistently make small quantities of very fine wines. Winemakers: Patrick Auld (Hunter Valley), Greg Clayfield (Coonawarra and Padthaway), Phillip John (Overall).

LINDEMANS HUNTER RIVER SHIRAZ ★★★★

1975	5	Now	$62.00
1976	Not made		
1977	5	Now	$54.00
1978	5	Now	$50.00
1979	6	Now	$54.00
1980	7	Now	$60.00
1981	Not made		
1982	5	Now	$36.00
1983	7	Now	$47.00
1984	Not made		
1985	4	Now	$23.00
1986	7	Now	$37.00
1987	7	Now	$35.00
1988	5	Now	$23.00
1989	5	Now	$21.00
1990	6	2002	$23.00
1991	7	2005	$25.00
1992	Not made		
1993	Not made		
1994	6	2005	$17.50
1995	6	2007	$16.00
1996	5	2009	$12.50
1997	6	2010	N/R
1998	6	2012	N/R

LINDEMANS HUNTER RIVER CHABLIS
(UNOAKED CHARDONNAY from 1994) ★★★★

1975	6	Now	$74.00
1976	4	Now	$45.00
1977	5	Now	$52.00
1978	6	Now	$58.00
1979	7	Now	$62.00
1980	5	Now	$42.00

1981	5	Now	$39.00
1982	4	Now	$28.00
1983	5	Now	$33.00
1984	5	Now	$31.00
1985	3	Now	$17.00
1986	6	Now	$31.00
1987	7	Now	$34.00
1988	4	Now	$18.00
1989	4	Now	$16.50
1990	5	Now	$19.50
1991	7	Now	$25.00
1992	6	Now	$20.00
1993	5	2000	$15.50
1994	5	2001	$14.00
1995	7	2004	$18.50
1996	5	2005	$12.00
1997	Not made		
1998	Not made		

LINDEMANS HUNTER RIVER CHARDONNAY

★★★★

1981	5	Now	$40.00
1982	4	Now	$30.00
1983	5	Now	$34.00
1984	4	Now	$25.00
1985	4	Now	$23.00
1986	5	Now	$27.00
1987	5	Now	$25.00
1988	7	Now	$33.00
1989	6	Now	$26.00
1990	5	Now	$20.00
1991	7	Now	$26.00
1992	7	Now	$24.00
1993	6	Now	$19.00
1994	5	2000	$14.50
1995	7	2004	$19.00
1996	5	2005	$12.50
1997	Not made		
1998	6	2005	N/R

LINDEMANS HUNTER RIVER
RESERVE PORPHYRY

★★★★

1975	6	Now	$50.00
1976	Not made		
1977	5	Now	$35.00
1978	6	Now	$39.00
1979	Not made		
1980	Not made		
1981	Not made		
1982	4	Now	$19.00
1983	6	Now	$27.00
1984	Not made		
1985	Not made		
1986	Not made		

1987	6	Now	$19.50
1988	5	Now	$15.00
1989	5	Now	$14.00
1990	6	Now	$15.50
1991	Not made		
1992	Not made		
1993	6	Now	$12.50
1994	6	Now	$11.50
1995	6	2004	$10.50
1996	Not made		
1997	Not made		
1998	Not made		

LINDEMANS HUNTER RIVER SEMILLON ★★★★

1975	5	Now	$100.00
1976	4	Now	$76.00
1977	5	Now	$88.00
1978	5	Now	$82.00
1979	7	Now	$105.00
1980	6	Now	$84.00
1981	4	Now	$52.00
1982	4	Now	$48.00
1983	5	Now	$54.00
1984	4	Now	$41.00
1985	5	Now	$47.00
1986	6	Now	$52.00
1987	7	Now	$56.00
1988	5	Now	$38.00
1989	5	Now	$35.00
1990	5	Now	$32.00
1991	7	Now	$42.00
1992	6	Now	$33.00
1993	5	2000	$25.00
1994	5	2002	$23.00
1995	7	2004	$31.00
1996	5	2005	$20.00
1997	Not made		
1998	7	2008	$24.00

LINDEMANS LIMESTONE HIRAZ/CABERNET ★★★★★

1976	7	Now	$130.00
1977	5	Now	$88.00
1978	6	Now	$98.00
1979	6	Now	$90.00
1980	7	Now	$98.00
1981	5	Now	$64.00
1982	7	Now	$84.00
1983	Not made		
1984	5	Now	$50.00
1985	6	Now	$56.00
1986	7	Now	$62.00

1987	6	Now	$49.00
1988	6	Now	$45.00
1989	5	Now	$35.00
1990	7	2000	$45.00
1991	7	2004	$42.00
1992	6	2005	$33.00
1993	7	2006	$36.00
1994	6	2007	$28.00
1995	Not made		
1996	5	2006	N/R
1997	5	2008	N/R
1998	6	2010	N/R

LINDEMANS PADTHAWAY CHARDONNAY ★★★

1980	4	Now	$38.00
1981	Not made		
1982	4	Now	$33.00
1983	6	Now	$45.00
1984	5	Now	$35.00
1985	6	Now	$39.00
1986	6	Now	$36.00
1987	7	Now	$39.00
1988	7	Now	$36.00
1989	6	Now	$28.00
1990	7	Now	$31.00
1991	7	Now	$28.00
1992	5	2000	$19.00
1993	6	2002	$21.00
1994	7	2003	$23.00
1995	6	2005	$18.00
1996	6	2005	$16.50
1997	7	2006	$18.00
1998	6	2007	$14.50

LINDEMANS PADTHAWAY PINOT NOIR ★★

before 1987	Prior		
1987	5	Now	$29.00
1988	5	Now	$27.00
1989	5	Now	$25.00
1990	6	Now	$28.00
1991	6	Now	$25.00
1992	5	Now	$20.00
1993	5	Now	$18.50
1994	6	2000	$20.00
1995	6	2000	$19.00
1996	5	2002	$14.50
1997	6	2003	$16.00
1998	6	2004	N/R

LINDEMANS PADTHAWAY SAUVIGNON BLANC ★★

1989	6	Now	$32.00
1990	Not made		
1991	6	Now	$28.00

1992	5	Now	$21.00
1993	5	Now	$20.00
1994	6	Now	$22.00
1995	7	Now	$24.00
1996	5	Now	$15.50
1997	6	2000	$17.50
1998	5	2000	$13.50

LINDEMANS PYRUS COONAWARRA RED BLEND

★★★★★

1985	7	Now	$78.00
1986	6	Now	$62.00
1987	6	Now	$58.00
1988	6	Now	$52.00
1989	Not made		
1990	6	2000	$46.00
1991	7	2003	$49.00
1992	5	2003	$32.00
1993	6	2004	$36.00
1994	6	2005	$33.00
1995	6	2007	$31.00
1996	6	2008	$29.00
1997	6	2009	N/R

LINDEMANS ST GEORGE CABERNET SAUVIGNON

★★★★★

1976	6	Now	$140.00
1977	5	Now	$110.00
1978	6	Now	$120.00
1979	5	Now	$96.00
1980	7	Now	$120.00
1981	5	Now	$82.00
1982	6	Now	$90.00
1983	Not made		
1984	5	Now	$64.00
1985	7	Now	$84.00
1986	6	Now	$66.00
1987	5	Now	$52.00
1988	6	Now	$56.00
1989	5	Now	$44.00
1990	7	2000	$56.00
1991	7	2004	$52.00
1992	5	2005	$35.00
1993	6	2006	$39.00
1994	6	2007	$36.00
1995	5	2006	$28.00
1996	5	2000	$26.00
1997	6	2005	N/R

Long Gully Estate is a Healesville (Yarra Valley) producer some of whose releases to date have been impressive. Winemaker: Peter Florance.

LONG GULLY CABERNET SAUVIGNON   ★★★★

1984	6	Now	$50.00
1985	6	Now	$46.00
1986	6	Now	$43.00
1987	6	Prior	
1988	7	2003	$43.00
1989	4	Prior	
1990	5	Now	$26.00
1991	6	2000	$29.00
1992	7	2002	$31.00
1993	7	2003	$29.00
1994	6	2002	$23.00
1995	6	2004	$21.00
1996	6	2005	$20.00

LONG GULLY CHARDONNAY   ★★★★

1984	6	Now	$50.00
1985	6	Now	$47.00
1986	6	Now	$44.00
1987	6	Now	$40.00
1988	7	Now	$44.00
1989	7	Now	$40.00
1990	5	Prior	
1991	6	Prior	
1992	7	Now	$32.00
1993	6	Now	$25.00
1994	7	Now	$27.00
1995	7	2000	$25.00
1996	6	2001	$20.00
1997	7	2001	$22.00

LONG GULLY PINOT NOIR   ★★★

1986	6	Now	$45.00
1987	5	Prior	
1988	6	Now	$38.00
1989	7	Now	$42.00
1990	5	Now	$27.00
1991	6	Now	$30.00
1992	7	Now	$33.00
1993	6	2000	$26.00
1994	6	2001	$24.00
1995	6	2002	$22.00
1996	7	2003	$24.00
1997	7	2005	$22.00

LONG GULLY RIESLING   ★★★★

1986	5	Now	$29.00
1987	6	Now	$33.00
1988	7	Now	$35.00
1989	4	Prior	

1990	5	Prior	
1991	5	Prior	
1992	6	Now	$22.00
1993	7	Now	$24.00
1994	6	Now	$19.00
1995	6	Now	$17.50
1996	6	Now	$16.50
1997	7	2000	$18.00

LONG GULLY SAUVIGNON BLANC ★★★

before 1991		Prior	
1991	6	Now	$27.00
1992	7	Now	$30.00
1993	6	Prior	
1994	6	Now	$22.00
1995	6	Now	$20.00
1996	7	Now	$22.00

LONG GULLY SHIRAZ ★★★

1989	5	Prior	
1990	7	Now	$34.00
1991	7	Now	$31.00
1992	6	Now	$25.00
1993	7	Now	$27.00
1994	6	Now	$21.00
1995	7	Now	$23.00
1996	7	2000	$21.00

Longleat are long established Goulburn Valley growers with close ties to Chateau Tahbilk. Winemaker: Mark Schulz.

LONGLEAT CABERNET SAUVIGNON ★★★

1985	5	Now	$35.00
1986	7	Now	$46.00
1987	5	Now	$30.00
1988	6	Now	$34.00
1989	5	Now	$26.00
1990	7	2000	$34.00
1991	7	2000	$31.00
1992	7	2000	$29.00
1993	No data		
1994	No data		
1995	5	2002	$16.50

LONGLEAT SHIRAZ ★★★

1985	6	Now	$39.00
1986	6	Now	$36.00
1987	7	Now	$39.00
1988	6	Now	$31.00
1989	5	Now	$24.00
1990	7	Now	$31.00
1991	7	Now	$28.00

1992	Not made		
1993	6	2000	$21.00
1994	5	2000	$16.00

Longridge *of Hawkes Bay (NZ) is a modestly priced label in the Corbans wine empire. The Chardonnay is remarkable value. Winemaker: Kirsty Walton.*

LONGRIDGE CABERNET SAUVIGNON/ MERLOT ★★★

before 1989	Prior		
1989	6	Now	NZ$28.00
1990	6	Now	NZ$25.00
1991	7	Now	NZ$28.00
1992	6	Now	NZ$22.00
1993	6	Now	NZ$20.00
1994	7	2000	NZ$22.00
1995	7	2002	NZ$20.00
1996	7	2002	NZ$19.00
1997	5	2000	NZ$12.50

LONGRIDGE CHARDONNAY ★★★★

before 1990	Prior		
1990	6	Now	NZ$27.00
1991	7	Now	NZ$29.00
1992	6	Now	NZ$23.00
1993	5	Now	NZ$18.00
1994	7	2000	NZ$23.00
1995	6	2001	NZ$18.50
1996	7	2002	NZ$20.00
1997	4	Now	NZ$10.50
1998	7	2001	NZ$17.00

LONGRIDGE SAUVIGNON BLANC ★★★

before 1991	Prior		
1991	7	Now	NZ$24.00
1992	6	Now	NZ$19.50
1993	5	Now	NZ$15.00
1994	7	Now	NZ$19.50
1995	7	Now	NZ$18.00
1996	7	Now	NZ$16.50
1997	4	Now	NZ$8.75
1198	7	2000	NZ$14.50

LONGRIDGE GEWURZTRAMINER
★★★

before 1995	Prior		
1995	7	2002	NZ$18.50
1996	7	2004	NZ$17.00
1997	7	2001	NZ$16.00
1998	7	2002	NZ$15.00

McAlister Vineyards is a Longford (Gippsland) maker producing just the one wine, a Bordeaux styled red from four of the five noble Bordeaux varieties (no Malbec). Winemaker: Peter Edwards.

The McALISTER ★★★★★

before 1980		Prior	
1980	5	Now	$130.00
1981	Not made		
1982	2	Prior	
1983	Not made		
1984	6	Now	$115.00
1985	5	Prior	
1986	6	Now	$100.00
1987	7	2000	$110.00
1988	6	2000	$86.00
1989	5	Now	$66.00
1990	7	2005	$86.00
1991	7	2005	$80.00
1992	6	2000	$64.00
1993	7	2005	$68.00
1994	7	2005	$64.00
1995	7	2010	$58.00
1996	5	2005	$39.00
1997	6	2010	$43.00

McWilliams Mount Pleasant - see Mount Pleasant.

McWilliams is a large company with vineyards in the Hunter Valley, Yarra Valley, Coonawarra, Young and the Murrumbidgee Irrigation Area. Winemaker: Jim Brayne.

McWILLIAMS HANWOOD CABERNET SAUVIGNON ★★

before 1992		Prior	
1992	6	Now	$15.00
1993	5	Now	$11.50
1994	5	Now	$10.50
1995	5	Now	$10.00
1996	6	Now	$11.00
1997	6	Now	$10.00
1998	6	Now	$9.50

McWILLIAMS HANWOOD CHARDONNAY ★★

before 1994		Prior	
1994	5	Now	$10.50
1995	5	Now	$10.00
1996	6	Now	$11.00
1997	6	Now	$10.00
1998	6	Now	$9.50

171

Main Ridge Estate was the first of the Mornington Peninsula (Victoria) makers to achieve commercial production. Since then the wines have achieved a beauty and reliability to establish an enviable reputation for this maker. Winemaker: Nat White.

MAIN RIDGE ESTATE CABERNET/MERLOT ★★★★

before 1988		Prior	
1988	5	Now	$22.00
1989	4	Now	$30.00
1990	6	2000	$42.00
1991	6	2001	$39.00
1992	5	2000	$30.00
1993	7	2005	$39.00
1994	7	2006	$36.00
1995	6	2003	$28.00

MAIN RIDGE ESTATE CHARDONNAY ★★★★★

before 1988		Prior	
1988	6	Now	$74.00
1989	5	Now	$58.00
1990	6	2000	$64.00
1991	6	2001	$58.00
1992	6	2002	$54.00
1993	6	2003	$50.00
1994	7	2004	$54.00
1995	6	2005	$44.00
1996	7	2004	$47.00
1997	7	2007	$44.00

MAIN RIDGE ESTATE HALF ACRE PINOT NOIR
★★★★★

before 1988		Prior	
1988	6	Now	$76.00
1989	4	Prior	
1990	5	Now	$54.00
1991	6	Now	$60.00
1992	6	2000	$56.00
1993	6	2001	$52.00
1994	7	2004	$56.00
1995	6	2005	$45.00
1996	7	2006	$49.00
1997	7	2007	$45.00

Malcolm Creek Vineyard is a small maker at Kersbrook in the Adelaide Hills, established as a "hobby" for winemaking identity Reg Tolley. Winemaker: Reg Tolley.

MALCOLM CREEK CABERNET
SAUVIGNON ★★★

before 1993		Prior	
1993	6	2003	$17.50
1994	6	2004	$16.00

172

1995	6	2005	$15.00
1996	7	2006	N/R
1997	7	2007	N/R
1998	6	2008	N/R

MALCOLM CREEK CHARDONNAY ★★★

before 1994		Prior	
1994	7	Now	$19.50
1995	6	Now	$15.50
1996	6	Now	$14.50
1997	7	2000	N/R
1998	7	2001	N/R

Marienberg Wines *was established decades ago by Ursula Pridham. The operation's purchase by Hill International Wines has breathed new life into the name.*
Winemaker: Grant Burge.

MARIENBERG CABERNET SAUVIGNON ★★★

before 1992		Prior	
1992	7	Now	$29.00
1993	6	Now	$23.00
1994	5	Now	$17.50
1995	6	2000	$19.50
1996	7	2002	$21.00
1997	6	2002	$16.50

MARIENBERG CHARDONNAY ★★★

1994	6	Now	$21.00
1995	6	Now	$20.00
1996	6	Now	$18.50
1997	5	Now	$14.00

MARIENBERG CLASSIC CABERNET/MOURVEDRE/GRENACHE ★★★

1995	5	Now	$11.00
1996	6	Now	$12.50
1997	6	2000	$11.50

MARIENBERG CLASSIC RIESLING ★★★

before 1995		Prior	
1995	6	Now	$12.50
1996	6	Now	$11.50
1997	6	Now	$10.50

MARIENBERG LAVINIA DRY WHITE ★★

1992	5	Prior	
1993	6	Now	$12.50
1994	6	Now	$11.50
1995	6	Now	$10.50

MARIENBERG SEMILLON/CHARDONNAY ★★★

before 1995	Prior	
1995	6	Now	$19.00
1996	6	Now	$17.50
1997	6	Now	$16.50

MARIENBERG SHIRAZ

★★★

before 1994	Prior	
1994	6	Now	$19.50
1995	6	Now	$18.00
1996	7	2000	$19.50
1997	6	2002	$15.50

Marsh Estate is an unirrigated Pokolbin vineyard originally established by Quentin Taperell, but acquired by Peter Marsh in 1978. Winemaker: Peter Marsh.

MARSH ESTATE CABERNET SAUVIGNON ★★★

before 1990	Prior	
1990	6	Now	$29.00
1991	7	Now	$31.00
1992	6	Now	$25.00
1993	6	Now	$23.00
1994	7	2000	$25.00
1995	6	2000	$20.00
1996	6	2000	$18.50
1997	6	2001	$17.00

MARSH ESTATE CHARDONNAY ★★★

before 1991	Prior	
1991	7	Now	$31.00
1992	6	Now	$25.00
1993	6	Now	$23.00
1994	7	2000	$25.00
1995	6	Now	$20.00
1996	6	2000	$18.50
1997	6	2001	$17.00

MARSH ESTATE SHIRAZ VAT R ★★★

1981	6	Now	$62.00
1982	5	Now	$48.00
1983	5	Now	$44.00
1984	5	Now	$41.00
1985	6	Now	$45.00
1986	6	Now	$42.00
1987	6	Now	$39.00
1988	6	Now	$36.00
1989	6	Now	$33.00
1990	6	Now	$31.00
1991	7	Now	$33.00
1992	6	Now	$26.00
1993	6	Now	$24.00
1994	7	2000	$26.00
1995	6	2000	$21.00

| 1996 | 6 | 2000 | $19.50 |
| 1997 | 6 | 2001 | $18.00 |

*The Martinborough Vineyard is a very good small maker of some of New Zealand's most graceful wines.
Winemaker: Larry McKenna.*

The MARTINBOROUGH VINEYARD CHARDONNAY

before 1989		Prior		★★★★
1989	7	Now	NZ$64.00	
1990	5	Now	NZ$42.00	
1991	6	Now	NZ$47.00	
1992	5	Prior		
1993	5	Prior		
1994	6	Now	NZ$37.00	
1995	5	Now	NZ$28.00	
1996	6	2001	NZ$32.00	
1997	6	2003	NZ$29.00	

The MARTINBOROUGH VINEYARD PINOT NOIR

1986	6	Now	NZ$88.00	★★★★
1987	5	Prior		
1988	7	Prior		
1989	7	Now	NZ$82.00	
1990	5	Prior		
1991	6	Now	NZ$60.00	
1992	4	Now	NZ$37.00	
1993	4	Now	NZ$34.00	
1994	5	Now	NZ$40.00	
1995	5	Now	NZ$37.00	
1996	6	2001	NZ$41.00	
1997	6	2005	NZ$38.00	

The MARTINBOROUGH VINEYARD RIESLING

1987	6	Now	NZ$40.00	★★★★
1988	7	Now	NZ$44.00	
1989	6	Now	NZ$34.00	
1990	5	Prior		
1991	6	Now	NZ$29.00	
1992	6	Now	NZ$27.00	
1993	5	Now	NZ$21.00	
1994	6	Now	NZ$23.00	
1995	3	Prior		
1996	7	2000	NZ$23.00	
1997	6	2002	NZ$18.50	
1998	7	2002	NZ$20.00	

*Massoni is a 1.5 hectare vineyard at Red Hill in the Mornington Peninsula, and is now owned by Ian Home, who created the renowned Yellowglen sparkling wines.
Winemaker: Ian Home.*

MASSONI RED HILL CHARDONNAY

				★★★★
before 1994		Prior		
1994	7	Now	$45.00	
1995	5	Now	$29.00	

| 1996 | 6 | Now | $33.00 |
| 1997 | 7 | 2002 | $35.00 |

MASSONI RED HILL PINOT NOIR
★★★★

before 1994		Prior	
1994	7	2000	$47.00
1995	6	2000	$37.00
1996	6	2001	$34.00
1997	7	2002	$37.00

Matawhero is an individualistic but sometimes extremely fine New Zealand vineyard and winery in the Gisborne region. There has been no input from the winemaker in recent years, but the wines are too important to exclude. Winemaker: Denis Irwin.

MATAWHERO CHARDONNAY
★★★★

before 1989		Prior	
1989	6	Now	NZ$32.00
1990	6	Now	NZ$30.00
1991	6	Now	NZ$27.00
1992	Not made		
1993	7	Now	NZ$28.00

MATAWHERO GEWURZTRAMINER
★★★★

before 1990		Prior	
1990	5	Now	NZ$24.00
1991	4	Now	NZ$18.00
1992	7	Now	NZ$29.00
1993	6	Now	NZ$23.00
1994	7	Now	NZ$25.00
1995	7	Now	N/R

MATAWHERO SAUVIGNON BLANC
★★★★

before 1991		Prior	
1991	6	Now	NZ$30.00
1992	No data		
1993	7	Now	NZ$30.00
1994	6	Now	NZ$23.00
1995	7	Now	NZ$25.00

Matua Valley Wines is a reliable Kumeu (New Zealand) maker with vineyards at Waimauku and Hawkes Bay. Their range is formidable. Winemaker: Ross Spence.

MATUA VALLEY CABERNET SAUVIGNON
★★★★

1985	7	Now	NZ$66.00
1986	7	Now	NZ$60.00
1987	5	Now	NZ$40.00
1988	Not made		
1989	6	Now	NZ$42.00
1990	5	Now	NZ$32.00
1991	7	Now	NZ$42.00
1992	5	Now	NZ$27.00
1993	7	2000	NZ$36.00

1994	No data		
1995	No data		
1996	6	2002	NZ$24.00

MATUA VALLEY JUDD ESTATE CHARDONNAY

★★★★

before 1989	Prior		
1989	6	Now	NZ$36.00
1990	7	Now	NZ$39.00
1991	6	Now	NZ$31.00
1992	7	Now	NZ$34.00
1993	5	Now	NZ$22.00
1994	7	Now	NZ$29.00
1995	No data		
1996	5	2000	NZ$17.50

MATUA VALLEY MERLOT

★★★★

1987	7	Now	NZ$54.00
1988	5	Now	NZ$37.00
1989	7	Now	NZ$47.00
1990	5	Now	NZ$31.00
1991	7	Now	NZ$41.00
1992	6	Now	NZ$32.00
1993	7	Now	NZ$35.00
1994	No data		
1995	No data		
1996	6	2002	NZ$24.00

MATUA VALLEY RESERVE
SAUVIGNON BLANC

★★★

before 1991	Prior		
1991	7	Now	NZ$26.00
1992	7	Now	NZ$24.00
1993	7	Now	NZ$22.00
1994	7	Now	NZ$21.00
1995	No data		
1996	5	2002	NZ$12.50

Maxwell Wines and Mead is a McLaren Vale producer of just that. Their wines are elegant, convincing and underpriced. Winemaker: Mark Maxwell.

MAXWELL CABERNET SAUVIGNON

★★★

before 1990	Prior		
1990	6	Now	$29.00
1991	6	Now	$27.00
1992	5	Now	$20.00
1993	5	2000	$19.00
1994	6	2002	$21.00
1995	6	2001	$19.50
1996	7	Now	$21.00

MAXWELL CABERNET/MERLOT ★★★

1988	6	Now	$29.00
1989	Not made		
1990	5	Now	$20.00

1991	4	Now	$15.00
1992	6	Now	$21.00
1993	5	Now	$16.00
1994	7	Now	$21.00
1995	6	Now	$16.50
1996	7	Now	$18.00
1997	6	Now	$14.50

MAXWELL CHARDONNAY ★★★

before 1994		Prior	
1994	6	Now	$18.50
1995	7	Now	$20.00
1996	5	Now	$13.00
1997	7	Now	$17.00

MAXWELL SHIRAZ ★★★★

before 1991		Prior	
1991	6	Now	$37.00
1992	5	Now	$28.00
1993	5	Now	$26.00
1994	7	2002	$34.00
1995	6	Now	$27.00
1996	6	2000	$25.00
1997	6	2000	$23.00

MAXWELL UNWOODED SEMILLON ★★★

1991	5	Now	$18.00
1992	6	Now	$20.00
1993	5	Now	$15.50
1994	6	Now	$17.00
1995	7	Now	$18.50
1996	6	Now	$14.50
1997	6	Now	$13.50
1998	6	Now	$12.50

Meadowbank Wines are well established growers in the Bushy Park region in southern Tasmania.
Winemaker: Greg O'Keefe.

MEADOWBANK CHARDONNAY ★★★★

1990	4	Now	$27.00
1991	4	Now	$25.00
1992	6	Prior	
1993	5	Now	$27.00
1994	5	Now	$25.00
1995	6	2004	$27.00
1996	3	2001	$12.50
1997	5	2000	$19.50
1998	6	2005	$22.00

MEADOWBANK PINOT NOIR ★★★★

1990	4	Now	$23.00
1991	4	Now	$21.00
1992	6	2000	$30.00

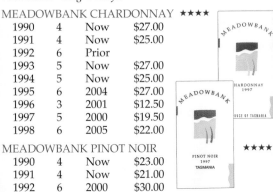

1993	7	2005	$32.00
1994	6	2000	$26.00
1995	6	2000	$24.00
1996	3	Now	$11.00
1997	5	2000	$17.00
1998	6	2001	N/R

MEADOWBANK RIESLING ★★★★

1980	5	Now	$62.00
1981	5	Now	$58.00
1982	4	Prior	
1983	6	Now	$60.00
1984	Not made		
1985	Not made		
1986	6	2000	$47.00
1987	4	Prior	
1988	6	2000	$40.00
1989	6	2000	$37.00
1990	4	Prior	
1991	5	Now	$27.00
1992	6	2000	$30.00
1993	6	2000	$27.00
1994	4	Prior	
1995	4	Now	$15.50
1996	5	Now	$18.00
1997	6	2004	$20.00

Meerea Park in the Hunter Valley's Singleton area is a small producer of admirable barrel-fermented Chardonnay. Winemaker: Rhys Eather.

MEEREA PARK CHARDONNAY ★★★★

1991	5	Prior	
1992	6	Now	$33.00
1993	5	Now	$25.00
1994	6	Now	$28.00
1995	5	Now	$21.00
1996	6	2001	$24.00
1997	6	2002	$22.00

Merricks Estate is a Mornington Peninsula maker with a small range of fine wines. Winemaker: Alex White

MERRICKS ESTATE CABERNET SAUVIGNON ★★★★

1984	5	Now	$33.00
1985	Not made		
1986	6	Now	$34.00
1987	4	Now	$21.00
1988	6	Now	$29.00
1989	6	Now	$27.00
1990	7	2000	$29.00
1991	6	2000	$23.00
1992	6	2000	$22.00
1993	7	2005	$23.00

MERRICKS ESTATE CHARDONNAY ★★★★

1986	5	Now	$49.00
1987	5	Now	$46.00
1988	5	Now	$42.00
1989	6	Now	$47.00
1990	6	Now	$44.00
1991	6	Now	$40.00
1992	7	Now	$44.00
1993	7	Now	$40.00
1994	7	Now	$37.00
1995	5	Now	$24.00
1996	6	Now	$27.00
1997	5	Now	$21.00

MERRICKS ESTATE SHIRAZ ★★★

1984	5	Now	$47.00
1985	5	Now	$43.00
1986	Not made		
1987	Not made		
1988	7	Now	$48.00
1989	6	Now	$38.00
1990	7	Now	$41.00
1991	6	Now	$33.00
1992	6	Now	$30.00
1993	7	2000	$33.00
1994	Not made		
1995	4	2000	$16.00

Metala is a long respected label now in the hands of Mildara Blass. Winemaker: Nigel Dolan.

METALA CABERNET SAUVIGNON / SHIRAZ ★★★★

before 1986	Prior		
1986	7	Now	$40.00
1987	6	Now	$31.00
1988	7	Now	$34.00
1989	6	Now	$27.00
1990	6	Now	$25.00
1991	6	Now	$23.00
1992	7	2000	$25.00
1993	7	2000	$23.00
1994	6	2001	$18.50
1995	6	2002	$17.00
1996	7	2004	$18.50
1997	7	2005	$17.00

METALA ORIGINAL PLANTINGS SHIRAZ ★★★★

1994	6	2006	$28.00
1995	6	2008	$26.00
1996	7	2010	$28.00

Milburn Park is the label reserved for the premium output of Irymple maker Alambie wines. Winemaker: Bob Shields.

Mildara is a large and long-established producer whose wines have for decades been at the upper end of the quality spectrum. Winemaker: Gavin Hogg.

MILDARA ALEXANDERS ★★★★

1985	6	2000	$50.00
1986	7	2004	$54.00
1987	5	Now	$36.00
1988	7	2006	$47.00
1989	Not made		
1990	6	2005	$34.00
1991	5	2000	$26.00
1992	7	2006	$34.00
1993	6	2005	$27.00

Series discontinued.

MILDARA COONAWARRA CABERNET SAUVIGNON ★★★★

before 1979	Prior		
1979	7	Now	$84.00
1980	6	Prior	
1981	7	Now	$72.00
1982	6	Prior	
1983	Not made		
1984	5	Prior	
1985	6	Now	$45.00
1986	6	Now	$42.00
1987	5	Now	$32.00
1988	7	Now	$42.00
1989	5	Now	$28.00
1990	7	2000	$36.00
1991	7	2001	$33.00
1992	7	2004	$31.00
1993	5	2001	$20.00
1994	6	2004	$22.00
1995	5	2002	$17.50
1996	7	2006	$22.00

MILDARA JAMIESONS RUN CHARDONNAY ★★★

before 1992	Prior		
1992	7	Now	$27.00
1993	6	Now	$22.00
1994	6	Now	$20.00
1995	5	Now	$15.50
1996	6	Now	$17.00
1997	6	Now	$16.00
1998	6	2000	$15.00

MILDARA JAMIESONS RUN COONAWARRA (DRY RED) ★★★

1985	6	Prior	
1986	6	Now	$36.00
1987	5	Prior	

1988	7	Now	$36.00
1989	5	Now	$24.00
1990	7	Now	$31.00
1991	7	Now	$28.00
1992	6	Now	$22.00
1993	7	2002	$24.00
1993	6	2001	$19.50
1994	6	2004	$18.00
1995	5	2002	$14.00
1996	7	2005	$18.00

MILDARA ROBERTSON'S WELL COONAWARRA CABERNET ★★★★

1992	7	2000	$27.00
1993	6	2000	$21.00
1994	7	2000	$23.00
1995	6	2002	$18.50
1996	7	2004	$20.00

The Millton Vineyard is a Poverty Bay (New Zealand) producer of small amounts of very fine wines. Winemaker: James Millton.

The MILLTON VINEYARD CHARDONNAY (BARREL FERMENTED) ★★★★

1986	6	Now	NZ$56.00
1987	6	Now	NZ$52.00
1988	6	Now	NZ$49.00
1989	6	Now	NZ$45.00
1990	6	Now	NZ$42.00
1991	5	Now	NZ$32.00
1992	7	Now	NZ$42.00
1993	5	Now	NZ$27.00
1994	6	2000	NZ$31.00
1995	5	Now	NZ$23.00
1996	6	Now	NZ$26.00
1997	6	2000	NZ$24.00

The MILLTON VINEYARD CHENIN BLANC (BARREL FERMENTED) ★★★★

1986	6	Now	NZ$49.00
1987	5	Now	NZ$38.00
1988	5	Now	NZ$35.00
1989	6	Now	NZ$39.00
1990	4	Now	NZ$24.00
1991	6	Now	NZ$33.00
1992	6	Now	NZ$31.00
1993	6	Now	NZ$28.00
1994	7	Now	NZ$31.00
1995	Not made		
1996	5	2000	NZ$19.00
1997	6	2000	NZ$21.00

The MILLTON VINEYARD RIESLING ★★★

1987	7	Now	NZ$33.00
1988	7	Now	NZ$30.00
1989	6	Now	NZ$24.00
1990	5	Now	NZ$18.50
1991	6	Now	NZ$20.00
1992	6	Now	NZ$19.00
1993	5	Now	NZ$15.00
1994	7	Now	N/R
1995	Not made		
1996	5	Now	N/R
1997	6	Now	N/R

Miramar is a Mudgee winery producing sensitively made wines with good balance and fruit. Winemaker: Ian MacRae.

MIRAMAR CABERNET SAUVIGNON ★★★

before 1984	Prior		
1984	7	Now	$52.00
1985	6	Now	$41.00
1986	7	Now	$45.00
1987	5	Now	$29.00
1988	5	Now	$27.00
1989	Not made		
1990	5	Now	$23.00
1991	6	Now	$26.00
1992	Not made		
1993	Not made		
1994	6	Now	$20.00
1995	7	2005	$22.00
1996	6	2005	$18.00

MIRAMAR CHARDONNAY ★★★

before 1990	Prior		
1990	5	Now	$21.00
1991	6	Now	$24.00
1992	6	Now	$22.00
1993	7	Now	$24.00
1994	6	Now	$19.00
1995	5	Now	$14.50
1996	6	Now	$16.00

MIRAMAR FUME BLANC ★★★

before 1993	Prior		
1993	6	Now	$18.50
1994	6	Now	$17.00
1995	6	Now	$16.00
1996	6	Now	$15.00

MIRAMAR ROSE ★★

before 1994	Prior		
1994	6	Now	$11.50
1995	6	Now	$10.50
1996	6	Now	$10.00

MIRAMAR SEMILLON ★★

before 1990		Prior	
1990	6	Now	$19.50
1991	5	Now	$15.00
1992	6	Now	$16.50
1993	6	Now	$15.00
1994	6	Now	$14.00
1995	6	Now	$13.00
1996	6	Now	$12.00

MIRAMAR SHIRAZ ★★★

before 1980		Prior	
1980	7	Now	$64.00
1981	5	Prior	
1982	5	Prior	
1983	6	Now	$44.00
1984	6	Now	$40.00
1985	5	Now	$31.00
1986	Not made		
1987	Not made		
1988	6	Now	$29.00
1989	6	Now	$27.00
1990	6	Now	$25.00
1991	6	Now	$23.00
1992	Not made		
1993	6	Now	$20.00
1994	7	2000	$22.00
1995	6	2000	$17.00
1996	6	2000	$16.00

Mitchell Cellars is a small Clare Valley maker with two high quality vineyards in the area. Winemaker: Andrew Mitchell.

MITCHELL CELLARS
CABERNET SAUVIGNON ★★★★

1976	6	Now	$92.00
1977	6	Now	$84.00
1978	Not made		
1979	4	Now	$48.00
1980	7	Now	$78.00
1981	6	Now	$62.00
1982	7	Now	$66.00
1983	5	Now	$44.00
1984	7	Now	$58.00
1985	6	Now	$46.00
1986	7	Now	$49.00
1987	6	Now	$39.00
1988	6	Now	$36.00
1989	Not made		
1990	7	2000	$36.00
1991	6	2000	$29.00

184

1992	5	2000	$22.00
1993	6	2002	$24.00
1994	7	2003	$26.00
1995	5	2003	$17.50
1996	6	2004	$19.50

MITCHELL CELLARS PEPPERTREE VINEYARD SHIRAZ ★★★★

1984	6	Now	$49.00
1985	5	Now	$38.00
1986	6	Now	$42.00
1987	7	Now	$46.00
1988	5	Now	$30.00
1989	5	Now	$28.00
1990	7	Now	$36.00
1991	6	Now	$29.00
1992	7	Now	$31.00
1993	7	2000	$29.00
1994	6	2001	$23.00
1994	5	2001	$17.50
1996	7	2003	$23.00

MITCHELL CELLARS WATERVALE RIESLING ★★★★

1979	4	Now	$38.00
1980	6	Now	$52.00
1981	4	Now	$32.00
1982	7	Now	$52.00
1983	5	Now	$35.00
1984	7	Now	$45.00
1985	6	Now	$36.00
1986	6	Now	$33.00
1987	6	Now	$31.00
1988	5	Now	$23.00
1989	6	Now	$26.00
1990	6	Now	$24.00
1991	6	Now	$22.00
1992	6	Now	$21.00
1993	7	Now	$22.00
1994	7	Now	$21.00
1995	5	Now	$13.50
1996	6	2001	$15.50
1997	6	2002	$14.00

MITCHELL CELLARS SEMILLON ★★★

before 1990		Prior	
1990	6	Now	$23.00
1991	6	Now	$21.00
1992	6	Now	$20.00
1993	7	Now	$21.00
1994	7	Now	$20.00
1995	5	Now	$13.00
1996	6	Now	$14.50
1997	6	2000	$13.50

***Mitchelton** in Victoria's Goulburn Valley is a highly respected medium-sized producer of some of the State's better wines. Winemaker: Don Lewis.*

MITCHELTON BLACKWOOD PARK RIESLING ★★★★

before 1981		Prior	
1981	7	Now	$54.00
1982	6	Now	$43.00
1983	6	Prior	
1984	6	Now	$37.00
1985	6	Now	$34.00
1986	6	Now	$32.00
1987	5	Now	$24.00
1988	6	Now	$27.00
1989	6	Now	$25.00
1990	6	Now	$23.00
1991	7	2000	$25.00
1992	7	2005	$23.00
1993	5	Now	$15.50
1994	6	2002	$17.00
1995	7	2005	$18.50
1996	6	2006	$14.50
1997	6	2006	$13.50

MITCHELTON CABERNET SAUVIGNON ★★★★

before 1985		Prior	
1985	7	Now	$62.00
1986	7	Now	$58.00
1987	7	Now	$52.00
1988	6	Now	$42.00
1989	6	Now	$39.00
1990	7	2002	$42.00
1991	7	2003	$39.00
1992	6	2005	$31.00
1993	7	2005	$33.00
1994	6	2008	$26.00
1995	6	2010	$24.00
1996	6	2010	$23.00

MITCHELTON CHARDONNAY ★★★★

1983	5	Prior	
1984	5	Now	$49.00
1985	5	Now	$46.00
1986	6	Now	$50.00
1987	6	Now	$47.00
1988	6	Now	$44.00
1989	7	Now	$47.00
1990	7	Now	$44.00
1991	7	Now	$40.00
1992	7	2005	$37.00
1993	6	2000	$29.00
1994	7	2000	$32.00

1995	7	2005	$29.00
1996	6	2005	$23.00
1997	7	2005	$25.00

MITCHELTON MARSANNE ★★★★

1979	5	Now	$60.00
1980	6	Now	$66.00
1981	5	Now	$52.00
1982	6	Now	$56.00
1983	5	Now	$44.00
1984	6	Now	$49.00
1985	5	Now	$38.00
1986	7	Now	$49.00
1987	6	Now	$39.00
1988	7	Now	$42.00
1989	6	Now	$33.00
1990	7	2000	$36.00
1991	6	2000	$28.00
1992	6	2005	$26.00
1993	6	2008	$24.00
1994	7	2010	$26.00

MITCHELTON PRINT LABEL ★★★★★

1980	6	Now	$135.00
1981	6	Now	$125.00
1982	6	Now	$115.00
1983	Not made		
1984	5	Now	$82.00
1985	6	Now	$92.00
1986	Not made		
1987	6	2000	$78.00
1988	Not made		
1989	Not made		
1990	7	2005	$74.00
1991	6	2005	$58.00
1992	7	2008	$62.00
1993	6	2010	$50.00
1994	7	2010	$54.00
1995	7	2010	$50.00

MITCHELTON SEMILLON (CLASSIC RELEASE) ★★★★

1980	5	Prior	
1981	7	Now	$66.00
1982	6	Now	$52.00
1983	6	Now	$49.00
1984	7	Now	$52.00
1985	6	Now	$42.00
1986	7	Now	$45.00
1987	Not made		
1988	6	Now	$33.00

187

1989	Not made		
1990	Not made		
1991	7	Now	$30.00

Montana Wines are New Zealand's biggest producers, with vineyards at Marlborough and Gisborne. No information has been received from the winemaker for some years, so I have removed the old ratings. Winemaker: Jeff Clarke.

MONTANA MARLBOROUGH
CABERNET SAUVIGNON ★★★

MONTANA MARLBOROUGH CHARDONNAY ★★★

MONTANA MARLBOROUGH
SAUVIGNON BLANC ★★★

Montrose Wines in Mudgee have been acquired by the Orlando Wyndham group, sharing a common winemaker with Craigmoor. Winemaker: Brett McKinnon.

MONTROSE BLACK SHIRAZ ★★★

1994	6	2001	$21.00
1995	6	2001	$19.50
1996	7	2002	$21.00
1997	6	2003	N/R
1998	6	2003	N/R

MONTROSE CABERNET SAUVIGNON ★★★

before 1988		Prior	
1988	6	Now	$36.00
1989	6	Now	$34.00
1990	7	Now	$36.00
1991	7	Now	$34.00
1992	5	Now	$22.00
1993	6	2000	$25.00
1994	7	2001	$27.00
1995	6	2002	$21.00
1996	7	2002	$23.00
1997	6	2004	$18.00
1998	5	2003	N/R

MONTROSE CHARDONNAY ★★★

before 1991		Prior	
1991	7	Now	$33.00
1992	5	Now	$22.00
1993	6	Now	$24.00
1994	6	Now	$22.00
1995	7	2000	$24.00
1996	7	Now	$22.00
1997	5	2000	$14.50
1998	6	2002	$16.50

MONTROSE POETS CORNER SHIRAZ/CABERNET/FRANC ★★

before 1994		Prior	
1994	6	Now	$14.50
1995	6	Now	$13.50
1996	6	2000	$12.50
1997	5	2000	$9.75
1998	5	2000	N/R

MONTROSE POETS CORNER SEMILLON/SAUVIGNON BLANC/ CHARDONNAY ★★

before 1993		Prior	
1993	7	Now	$19.00
1994	6	Now	$15.00
1995	6	Now	$14.00
1996	6	Now	$13.00
1997	5	Now	$10.00
1998	5	2000	$9.25

Moondah Brook is the Gingin (80 km north of Perth) vineyard of the Houghton company. Winemaker: Paul Lapsley.

MOONDAH BROOK CABERNET SAUVIGNON ★★★

before 1990		Prior	
1990	6	2000	$28.00
1991	5	Now	$22.00
1992	5	Now	$20.00
1993	5	Now	$18.50
1994	6	2000	$20.00
1995	No data		
1996	5	2000	$15.00

MOONDAH BROOK CHARDONNAY ★★★

1991	6	Now	$30.00
1992	5	Now	$23.00
1993	6	2000	$26.00
1994	5	Now	$20.00
1995	5	2000	$18.50
1996	No data		
1997	5	2000	$15.50

MOONDAH BROOK CHENIN BLANC ★★★

1989	6	Now	$35.00
1990	4	Now	$21.00
1991	6	2000	$30.00
1992	6	Now	$27.00
1993	6	2000	$25.00
1994	5	Now	$19.50

1995	5	2000	$18.00
1996	No data		
1997	5	2000	$15.50

MOONDAH BROOK VERDELHO ★★

1989	6	Now	$36.00
1990	5	Now	$28.00
1991	6	2000	$31.00
1992	4	Now	$19.50
1993	6	Now	$27.00
1994	5	Now	$20.00
1995	4	Now	$15.50
1996	5	Now	$17.50
1997	5	Now	$16.50

Moorilla Estate is a small Hobart maker who painstakingly produce some very fine, rare wines. Winemaker: Alain Rousseau.

MOORILLA ESTATE CABERNET SAUVIGNON ★★★★

before 1983	Prior		
1983	5	Now	$48.00
1984	5	Now	$44.00
1985	Not made		
1986	3	Prior	
1987	3	Prior	
1988	5	Now	$33.00
1989	6	Now	$36.00
1990	6	Now	$34.00
1991	6	2000	$31.00
1992	7	2000	$34.00
1993	Not made		
1994	7	2002	$29.00
1995	4	2001	$15.00

MOORILLA ESTATE CHARDONNAY ★★★★

before 1983	Prior		
1983	7	Now	$80.00
1984	4	Now	$42.00
1985	Not made		
1986	3	Now	$27.00
1987	5	Now	$42.00
1988	5	Now	$39.00
1989	6	Now	$43.00
1990	7	Now	$46.00
1991	7	2000	$43.00
1992	7	2000	$40.00
1993	7	2000	$37.00
1994	7	2000	$34.00
1995	7	2002	$31.00
1996	5	2000	$21.00

MOORILLA ESTATE GEWURZTRAMINER ★★★★

1985	5	Now	$52.00
1986	4	Now	$39.00
1987	4	Now	$36.00
1988	5	Now	$42.00
1989	6	Now	$47.00
1990	7	Now	$50.00
1991	7	Now	$47.00
1992	6	Now	$37.00
1993	7	2000	$40.00
1994	7	2000	$37.00
1995	7	2000	$34.00
1996	5	Now	$23.00
1997	6	2000	$25.00

MOORILLA ESTATE PINOT NOIR ★★★★

before 1982		Prior	
1982	6	Now	$66.00
1983	5	Prior	
1984	7	Now	$66.00
1985	5	Prior	
1986	6	Now	$48.00
1987	7	Now	$52.00
1988	5	Now	$34.00
1989	7	Now	$45.00
1990	6	Now	$35.00
1991	7	2000	$38.00
1992	7	2002	$35.00
1993	4	Now	$18.50
1995	7	2002	$30.00
1996	7	2003	$28.00

MOORILLA ESTATE RIESLING ★★★★

1981	4	Prior	
1982	7	Now	$82.00
1983	6	Now	$64.00
1984	5	Now	$50.00
1985	5	Now	$46.00
1986	2	Prior	
1987	5	Prior	
1988	6	Now	$44.00
1989	7	Now	$47.00
1990	7	Now	$44.00
1991	7	2000	$41.00
1992	7	2002	$38.00
1993	7	2002	$35.00
1994	7	2004	$32.00
1995	6	Now	$25.00
1996	7	2001	$27.00
1997	6	2001	$22.00

Moorooduc Estate is a high quality Mornington Peninsula maker. Winemaker: Richard McIntyre.

MOOROODUC ESTATE
CABERNET SAUVIGNON ★★★★★

before 1990		Prior	
1990	5	Now	$46.00
1991	6	2001	$50.00
1992	6	2002	$47.00
1993	7	2003	$50.00
1994	7	2004	$47.00
1995	6	2004	$38.00
1996	4	2002	$23.00
1997	6	2004	$32.00
1998	6	2008	N/R

MOOROODUC ESTATE CHARDONNAY ★★★★★

before 1993		Prior	
1993	6	Now	$44.00
1994	7	2000	$48.00
1995	6	2000	$38.00
1996	6	2003	$35.00
1997	7	2003	$38.00
1998	6	2004	$30.00

MOOROODUC ESTATE PINOT NOIR ★★★★

before 1991		Prior	
1991	6	2000	$58.00
1992	5	2002	$44.00
1993	5	2000	$41.00
1994	5	2004	$38.00
1995	6	2006	$42.00
1996	6	2006	$39.00
1997	7	2008	$42.00
1998	6	2008	N/R

Morris is one of the most respected Rutherglen wineries, now under the aegis of Orlando Wyndham. Their table wines are big and powerful, and their muscats are arguably the world's best. Winemaker: David Morris.

MORRIS CABERNET SAUVIGNON ★★★

before 1982		Prior	
1982	6	Now	$50.00
1983	6	Now	$47.00
1984	5	Now	$36.00
1985	5	Now	$33.00
1986	5	Now	$31.00
1987	6	Now	$34.00
1988	6	Now	$32.00
1989	6	Now	$29.00
1990	5	2000	$23.00

1991	6	2000	$25.00
1992	6	2002	$23.00
1993	5	2002	$18.00
1994	5	2003	$16.50
1995	6	2006	$18.50
1996	5	2005	$14.50
1997	6	2006	$16.00

MORRIS CHARDONNAY ★★★

before 1987	Prior		
1987	6	Now	$33.00
1988	5	Prior	
1989	5	Prior	
1990	6	Now	$26.00
1991	5	Now	$20.00
1992	Not made		
1993	Not made		
1994	5	Now	$16.00
1995	5	2000	$15.00
1996	6	2000	$16.50
1997	6	2000	$15.50
1998	5	2000	$12.00

MORRIS DURIF ★★★★

1970	7	Now	$180.00
1971	6	Prior	
1972	6	Now	$130.00
1973	Not made		
1974	5	Prior	
1975	5	Prior	
1976	5	Prior	
1977	7	Now	$100.00
1978	6	Prior	
1979	5	Prior	
1980	6	Now	$72.00
1981	5	Now	$54.00
1982	6	Now	$60.00
1983	6	Now	$56.00
1984	5	Now	$44.00
1985	6	Now	$49.00
1986	7	Now	$52.00
1987	5	Now	$35.00
1988	5	Now	$32.00
1989	6	2000	$36.00
1990	6	2002	$33.00
1991	6	2002	$30.00
1992	6	2002	$28.00
1993	5	2002	$22.00
1994	6	2004	$24.00
1995	6	2006	$22.00
1996	5	2006	$17.50
1997	5	2008	N/R

MORRIS SEMILLON ★★★

before 1990		Prior	
1990	6	Now	$24.00
1991	Not made		
1992	Not made		
1993	Not made		
1994	6	Now	$17.50
1995	5	Now	$13.50
1996	7	2001	$17.50
1997	6	2002	$14.00
1998	6	2003	$13.00

MORRIS SHIRAZ ★★★★

1980	6	Now	$58.00
1981	5	Prior	
1982	6	Now	$50.00
1983	5	Now	$39.00
1984	5	Prior	
1985	6	Now	$40.00
1986	7	Now	$44.00
1987	5	Now	$29.00
1988	6	Now	$32.00
1989	5	Now	$24.00
1990	5	2000	$23.00
1991	5	2000	$21.00
1992	7	2002	$27.00
1993	5	2001	$18.00
1994	6	2002	$20.00
1995	5	2004	$15.50
1996	6	2004	$17.00
1997	5	2006	$13.50

Morton Estate is a small but very professional New Zealand producer of some of the country's best wines. Winemaker: Evan Ward.

MORTON ESTATE BLACK LABEL
MERLOT/CABERNET ★★★★

1989	6	Now	NZ$56.00
1990	5	Now	NZ$44.00
1991	6	Now	NZ$49.00
1992	5	Now	NZ$38.00
1993	Not made		
1994	7	Now	NZ$46.00
1995	6	Now	NZ$36.00
1996	6	2000	NZ$33.00

MORTON ESTATE BLACK LABEL
CHARDONNAY ★★★★★

before 1989		Prior	
1989	7	Now	NZ$62.00
1990	5	Now	NZ$41.00
1991	7	Now	NZ$54.00

1992	6	Now	NZ$43.00
1993	5	Now	NZ$33.00
1994	7	Now	NZ$43.00
1995	6	Now	NZ$34.00
1996	6	Now	N/R

MORTON ESTATE BLACK LABEL
PINOT NOIR ★★★★

1994	7	Now	NZ$41.00
1995	Not made		
1996	6	Now	NZ$33.00

MORTON ESTATE WHITE LABEL
CHARDONNAY ★★★

before 1991	Prior		
1991	6	Now	NZ$27.00
1992	5	Now	NZ$21.00
1993	5	Prior	
1994	7	Now	NZ$25.00
1995	6	Now	NZ$20.00
1996	7	Now	NZ$21.00
1997	6	Now	NZ$17.00

MORTON ESTATE SAUVIGNON BLANC ★★★

before 1993	Prior		
1993	6	Now	NZ$19.00
1994	6	Now	NZ$17.50
1995	6	Now	NZ$16.00
1997	6	Now	NZ$15.00
1998	6	Now	NZ$14.00

Moss Brothers *(not to be confused with its near neighbour Moss Wood) is a Margaret River vineyard.*
Winemakers: David and Jane Moss.

MOSS BROTHERS CABERNET/MERLOT ★★★

before 1992	Prior		
1992	6	2000	$33.00
1993	6	2000	$30.00
1994	7	2001	$33.00
1995	7	2002	$30.00
1996	7	2004	$28.00
1997	7	2002	$26.00

MOSS BROTHERS CHARDONNAY
★★★

before 1992	Prior		
1992	7	2000	$35.00
1993	7	2000	$32.00
1994	7	2000	$30.00
1995	7	2002	$27.00
1996	6	2001	$22.00
1997	Not made		

MOSS BROTHERS PINOT NOIR ★★★

before 1992	Prior		
1992	7	2000	$39.00
1993	7	2000	$36.00
1994	7	Now	$33.00
1995	7	Now	$31.00
1996	Not made		
1997	7	2002	$26.00

MOSS BROTHERS SEMILLON ★★★

before 1997	Prior		
1997	6	Now	$21.00
1997	7	2002	$23.00

Moss Wood is one of Australia's best wineries. The wines are deep, full and complex, with superb fruit and balance. Winemaker: Keith Mugford.

MOSS WOOD CABERNET SAUVIGNON ★★★★★

1973	4	Now	$280.00
1974	4	Now	$260.00
1975	6	Now	$360.00
1976	6	Now	$340.00
1977	6	Now	$310.00
1978	Not made		
1979	4	Now	$180.00
1980	6	Now	$250.00
1981	5	2000	$190.00
1982	4	Now	$140.00
1983	6	2000	$195.00
1984	4	Now	$120.00
1985	7	2000	$195.00
1986	6	2001	$155.00
1987	7	2002	$170.00
1988	5	2003	$110.00
1989	6	2006	$120.00
1990	7	2005	$130.00
1991	7	2006	$120.00
1992	5	2005	$82.00
1993	6	2008	$92.00
1994	7	2007	$98.00
1995	7	2009	$92.00
1996	7	2010	$84.00

MOSS WOOD CHARDONNAY ★★★★

1980	3	Prior	
1981	Not made		
1982	Not made		

1983	4	Now	$82.00
1984	5	Now	$96.00
1985	5	Now	$88.00
1986	5	Now	$82.00
1987	5	Now	$76.00
1988	5	Now	$70.00
1989	5	Now	$64.00
1990	7	2002	$84.00
1991	6	2001	$66.00
1992	6	2004	$62.00
1993	7	2005	$66.00
1994	7	2005	$62.00
1995	7	2006	$58.00
1996	7	2006	$52.00
1997	6	2007	$42.00

MOSS WOOD PINOT NOIR ★★★★

1977	3	Prior	
1978	Not made		
1979	3	Now	$76.00
1980	3	Now	$70.00
1981	6	Now	$130.00
1982	4	Now	$80.00
1983	5	Now	$92.00
1984	5	Now	$86.00
1985	6	Now	$94.00
1986	6	Now	$88.00
1987	5	Now	$68.00
1988	6	2000	$76.00
1989	4	Now	$46.00
1990	6	2002	$64.00
1991	6	2003	$60.00
1992	6	2004	$54.00
1993	6	2005	$50.00
1994	5	2000	$39.00
1995	6	2004	$44.00
1996	6	2008	$41.00

MOSS WOOD SEMILLON ★★★★

before 1987	Prior		
1987	6	2001	$58.00
1988	5	2002	$45.00
1989	4	2000	$33.00
1990	7	2005	$54.00
1991	4	2003	$29.00
1992	6	2006	$40.00
1993	7	2008	$43.00
1994	7	2000	$40.00
1995	6	2000	$31.00

1996	7	2002	$34.00
1997	No data		
1998	6	2010	$25.00

***Mountadam Vineyard** is a stylish and high quality maker at High Eden in the Eden Valley. Winemaker: Adam Wynn.*

MOUNTADAM CABERNET SAUVIGNON ★★★★★

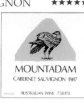

before 1984	Prior		
1984	6	Now	$78.00
1985	7	Now	$86.00
1986	6	Now	$68.00
1987	7	Prior	
1988	6	Prior	
1989	Not made		
1994	7	2000	$58.00
1995	6	2001	$46.00

MOUNTADAM CHARDONNAY ★★★★★

before 1990	Prior		
1990	6	Now	$49.00
1991	7	Now	$52.00
1992	6	Now	$42.00
1993	6	Now	$39.00
1994	7	Now	$42.00
1995	7	2001	$39.00
1996	7	2002	$36.00
1997	7	2003	$33.00

MOUNTADAM PINOT NOIR ★★★★

before 1988	Prior		
1988	7	Now	$86.00
1989	5	Prior	
1990	6	Prior	
1991	7	2000	$68.00
1992	6	Now	$54.00
1993	7	2000	$58.00
1994	6	Now	$47.00
1995	6	2001	$43.00
1996	7	2002	$47.00
1997	7	2003	$43.00

MOUNTADAM "THE RED"
(CABERNET/MERLOT) ★★★★★

1989	5	Now	$64.00
1990	6	Now	$70.00
1991	6	Now	$66.00
1992	7	Now	$70.00
1993	Not made		
1994	7	2002	$60.00
1995	6	2003	$48.00

Mount Anakie (Zambelli Wine Estates) *is a Geelong maker on the vineyard originally established by Tom Maltby, and later developed by Stephen Hickinbotham. The reds are gloriously intense. Winemaker: Otto Zambelli.*

MOUNT ANAKIE CHARDONNAY ★★★

before 1992		Prior	
1992	7	Now	$30.00
1993	7	Now	$27.00
1994	6	Now	$22.00
1995	5	Now	$17.00
1996	6	Now	$18.50
1997	6	2000	$17.50

MOUNT ANAKIE CABERNET SAUVIGNON ★★★★

1987	7	Prior	
1988	6	Now	$30.00
1989	7	Now	$32.00
1990	6	Now	$25.00
1991	5	Now	$20.00
1992	6	Now	$22.00
1993	7	Now	$24.00
1994	6	Now	$19.00
1995	5	2000	$14.50

MOUNT ANAKIE DOLCETTO ★★★

before 1992		Prior	
1992	6	Now	$19.50
1993	6	Now	$18.00
1994	5	Now	$14.00
1995	6	Now	$15.50

MOUNT ANAKIE RIESLING ★★

before 1990		Prior	
1989	6	Now	$19.00
1990	7	Prior	
1991	6	Now	$16.50
1992	7	Now	$17.50
1993	7	Now	$16.50
1994	6	Now	$13.00
1995	6	Now	$12.00
1996	6	Now	$11.00

MOUNT ANAKIE SHIRAZ ★★★★

before 1989		Prior	
1989	5	Now	$25.00
1990	7	Now	$33.00
1991	7	Now	$31.00
1992	6	Now	$24.00
1993	7	Now	$26.00
1994	5	2000	$17.50
1995	5	2000	$16.00

Mount Avoca is a Victorian producer whose range of substantial and emphatic wines is of considerable elegance. Winemaker: Matthew Barry.

MOUNT AVOCA CABERNET SAUVIGNON ★★★★

before 1988		Prior	
1988	7	Now	$44.00
1989	5	Now	$29.00
1990	6	Now	$32.00
1991	7	2001	$34.00
1992	6	2000	$27.00
1993	6	2001	$25.00
1994	6	2002	$23.00
1995	6	2003	$22.00
1996	6	2004	$20.00
1997	6	2006	N/R
1998	7	2007	N/R

MOUNT AVOCA CHARDONNAY ★★★★

before 1990		Prior	
1990	5	2000	$37.00
1991	5	Now	$34.00
1992	5	Now	$31.00
1993	5	2000	$29.00
1994	5	2001	$27.00
1995	5	2002	$25.00
1996	5	2003	$23.00
1997	6	2002	$26.00
1998	6	2004	$24.00

MOUNT AVOCA RHAPSODY (TREBBIANO/SAUVIGNON BLANC) ★★

before 1996		Prior	
1996	5	Now	$10.00
1997	6	Now	$11.00
1998	6	Now	$10.50

MOUNT AVOCA SAUVIGNON BLANC ★★★★

before 1990		Prior	
1990	6	Now	$34.00
1991	5	Now	$26.00
1992	5	Now	$24.00
1993	6	Now	$27.00
1994	6	Now	$25.00
1995	5	Now	$19.50
1996	6	Now	$21.00
1997	6	Now	$20.00
1998	7	Now	$21.00

MOUNT AVOCA SHIRAZ ★★★★

before 1988		Prior	
1988	7	Now	$45.00
1989	6	Now	$35.00
1990	6	Now	$33.00

1991	6	Now	$30.00
1992	6	Now	$28.00
1993	6	2000	$26.00
1994	6	2001	$24.00
1995	4	Now	$15.00
1996	6	2002	$20.00
1997	6	2003	$19.00
1998	7	2005	$21.00

MOUNT AVOCA TRIOSS
(SAUVIGNON BLANC/CHARDONNAY/SEMILLON) ★★

before 1996		Prior	
1996	4	Now	$8.00
1997	6	Now	$11.00
1998	7	Now	$12.00

Mount Helen vineyard in Victoria's Strathbogie Ranges produces some of the State's better wines. It is now part of Mildara Blass. Winemaker: Toni Stockhausen.

MOUNT HELEN CABERNET/MERLOT ★★★★

before 1986		Prior	
1986	6	Now	$52.00
1987	5	Now	$41.00
1988	5	Now	$38.00
1989	Not made		
1990	5	Now	$32.00
1991	4	Prior	
1992	Not made		
1993	4	Now	$20.00
1994	6	Now	$28.00
1995	6	2000	$26.00
1996	7	2003	$28.00

MOUNT HELEN CHARDONNAY ★★★★

before 1994		Prior	
1994	6	2001	$30.00
1995	7	2004	$33.00
1996	5	2006	$21.00

Mount Horrocks Wines are Clare Valley producers of some remarkably good wines. Winemaker: Stephanie Toole.

MOUNT HORROCKS CABERNET SAUVIGNON/MERLOT ★★★★

before 1990		Prior	
1990	5	Now	$34.00
1991	5	Now	$32.00
1992	5	Now	$29.00
1993	6	Now	$33.00

1994	6	2001	$30.00
1995	7	2004	$33.00
1996	5	2006	$21.00

MOUNT HORROCKS CHARDONNAY ★★★★

before 1990	Prior	
1990	5	Now	$38.00
1991	5	Now	$35.00
1992	5	Now	$33.00
1993	Not made		
1994	6	Now	$34.00
1995	6	Now	$31.00
1996	5	Now	$24.00
1997	5	Now	$22.00
1998	5	2000	$20.00

MOUNT HORROCKS CORDON CUT RIESLING
(375ml) ★★★★

before 1990	Prior	
1990	7	Now	$48.00
1991	5	Now	$32.00
1992	5	Now	$29.00
1993	6	Now	$33.00
1994	6	2000	$30.00
1995	6	2003	$28.00
1996	7	2004	$30.00
1997	6	2000	$24.00
1998	7	2001	$26.00

MOUNT HORROCKS SEMILLON(/SAUVIGNON
BLANC from 1995) ★★★★

before 1991	Prior	
1991	5	Now	$33.00
1992	6	Now	$37.00
1993	7	Now	$40.00
1994	6	2000	$31.00
1995	5	2001	$24.00
1996	6	2002	$27.00
1997	5	2005	$21.00
1998	5	2006	$19.50

MOUNT HORROCKS WATERVALE RIESLING ★★★★

before 1990	Prior	
1990	6	Now	$34.00
1991	5	Now	$26.00
1992	5	Now	$24.00
1993	6	Now	$27.00
1994	7	2000	$29.00
1995	7	2002	$27.00
1996	7	2003	$25.00
1997	7	2005	$23.00
1998	7	2007	$21.00

Mount Hurtle is the McLaren Vale winery of Geoff Merrill.
Eventually the label will be reserved for wines made solely
from fruit grown on the Mount Hurtle vineyard.
Winemaker: Geoff Merrill.

MOUNT HURTLE CABERNET SAUVIGNON ★★★★

1985	5	Now	$33.00
1986	5	Now	$30.00
1987	4	Now	$22.00
1988	Not made		
1989	Not made		
1990	6	Now	$27.00
1991	6	Now	$25.00
1992	5	Now	$19.50
1993	6	Now	$21.00
1994	6	2000	$20.00

MOUNT HURTLE SAUVIGNON BLANC ★★★

1990	7	Now	$29.00
1991	4	Now	$15.00
1992	7	Now	$24.00
1993	6	Now	$19.50
1994	6	Now	$18.00
1995	5	Now	$14.00
1996	5	Now	$13.00

Mount
HURTLE

1990
McLaren Vale
Sauvignon Blanc

MOUNT HURTLE SHIRAZ ★★★

1990	6	Now	$25.00
1991	5	Now	$19.50
1992	5	Now	$18.00
1993	6	Now	$20.00
1994	7	Now	$21.00

Mount Ida, like Mount Helen, is now owned by Mildara
Blass. The wine is vintaged in the Heathcote area.
Winemaker: Toni Stockhausen.

MOUNT IDA SHIRAZ ★★★★★

1989	4	Now	$36.00
1990	6	Now	$50.00
1991	5	Now	$38.00
1992	7	Now	$50.00
1993	Not made		
1994	7	Now	$43.00
1995	5	Now	$28.00
1996	7	2008	$37.00

Mount Langi Ghiran is a Great Western district producer
with a growing range of respected wines.
Winemaker: Trevor Mast.

MOUNT LANGI GHIRAN CABERNET SAUVIGNON BLEND ★★★★

before 1985	Prior		
1985	5	Now	$44.00
1986	7	2005	$56.00

1987	5	Now	$38.00
1988	6	Now	$42.00
1989	6	2000	$39.00
1990	7	Now	$42.00
1991	6	Now	$33.00
1992	6	Now	$31.00
1993	7	2003	$33.00
1994	7	2004	$31.00
1995	No data		
1996	7	2005	$26.00

Mount Mary is an extreme quality small vineyard in the Yarra Valley. Their wines are among Australia's best. Winemakers: John Middleton and Mario Marson.

MOUNT MARY QUINTET (CABERNETS) ★★★★★

1975	5	Now	$380.00
1976	6	Now	$420.00
1977	7	Now	$460.00
1978	7	Now	$420.00
1979	7	Now	$390.00
1980	7	Now	$360.00
1981	7	Now	$330.00
1982	6	Now	$260.00
1983	5	Now	$205.00
1984	7	Now	$260.00
1985	6	Now	$210.00
1986	7	2001	$230.00
1987	6	2000	$180.00
1988	7	2002	$195.00
1989	5	Now	$130.00
1990	7	2005	$165.00
1991	7	2006	$155.00
1992	7	2007	$140.00
1993	7	2008	$130.00
1994	7	2009	$120.00
1995	7	2010	$110.00
1996	7	2011	$105.00

MOUNT MARY CHARDONNAY ★★★★★

before 1980	Prior		
1980	6	Now	$230.00
1981	6	Now	$215.00
1982	6	Now	$200.00
1983	6	Now	$185.00
1984	7	Now	$200.00
1985	7	Now	$185.00
1986	6	Now	$145.00
1987	6	Now	$135.00
1988	7	Now	$145.00
1989	7	Now	$135.00
1990	6	Now	$105.00
1991	7	2003	$115.00
1992	7	2002	$105.00

1993	7	2000	$100.00
1994	7	2002	$92.00
1995	7	2005	$86.00
1996	7	2006	$80.00
1997	7	2006	$74.00

MOUNT MARY PINOT NOIR ★★★★★

1976	6	Now	$410.00
1977	6	Now	$380.00
1978	6	Now	$350.00
1979	5	Now	$270.00
1980	7	Now	$350.00
1981	7	Now	$320.00
1982	7	Now	$300.00
1983	6	Now	$240.00
1984	6	Now	$220.00
1985	6	Now	$205.00
1986	7	Now	$220.00
1987	7	Now	$205.00
1988	7	2000	$190.00
1989	6	2002	$150.00
1990	7	2002	$160.00
1991	7	2003	$150.00
1992	7	2002	$140.00
1993	7	2004	$130.00
1994	6	2005	$100.00
1995	7	2005	$110.00
1996	7	2006	$100.00
1997	7	2006	$96.00

MOUNT MARY TRIOLET (SAUVIGNON BLANC/SEMILLON/MUSCADELLE) ★★★★★

1986	6	Now	$82.00
1987	5	Now	$64.00
1988	6	Now	$70.00
1989	7	Now	$76.00
1990	7	Now	$70.00
1991	7	2002	$66.00
1992	7	2004	$60.00
1993	7	2005	$56.00
1994	7	2006	$52.00
1995	7	2007	$48.00
1996	7	2008	$45.00
1997	7	2007	$42.00

Mount Pleasant is a very famous Hunter Valley vineyard once owned and operated by Maurice O'Shea. For decades it has been the premier vineyard and label of McWilliams. Winemaker: Philip Ryan.

MOUNT PLEASANT CHARDONNAY ★★★

before 1993		Prior	
1993	7	Now	$17.50
1994	6	Now	$13.50

1995	6	Now	$12.50
1996	7	Now	$13.50
1997	6	2000	$11.00
1998	7	2001	N/R

MOUNT PLEASANT ELIZABETH SEMILLON ★★★

before 1986		Prior	
1986	7	Now	$27.00
1987	7	Now	$25.00
1988	5	Now	$17.00
1989	6	Now	$18.50
1990	5	Now	$14.50
1991	7	Now	$18.50
1992	6	Now	$15.00
1993	7	2000	$16.00
1994	7	2001	$15.00
1995	7	2002	N/R
1996	7	2003	N/R
1997	7	2005	N/R

MOUNT PLEASANT LOVEDALE SEMILLON ★★★★★

1984	7	2000	$41.00
1985	Not made		
1986	7	2000	$36.00
1987	Not made		
1995	7	2005	N/R
1996	7	2006	N/R

MOUNT PLEASANT MAURICE O'SHEA SHIRAZ ★★★★★

1983	7	Now	$78.00
1984	6	Now	$62.00
1985	7	2000	$66.00
1986	7	2000	$62.00
1987	7	2000	$58.00
1988	Not made		
1989	6	Now	$42.00
1990	6	Now	$39.00
1991	Not made		
1992	Not made		
1993	6	2001	$31.00
1994	7	2002	$33.00
1995	7	2003	$31.00
1996	7	2004	N/R
1997	7	2005	N/R
1998	7	2006	N/R

MOUNT PLEASANT PHILIP SHIRAZ ★★★

before 1987		Prior	
1987	7	Now	$26.00
1988	5	Prior	
1989	5	Now	$16.00
1990	5	Now	$15.00
1991	7	2000	$19.50

1992	6	2000	$15.50
1993	6	2001	$14.50
1994	6	2001	$13.00
1995	7	2002	N/R
1996	7	2003	N/R
1997	7	2004	N/R
1998	7	2005	N/R

MOUNT PLEASANT OLD PADDOCK AND OLD HILL SHIRAZ ★★★★★

1983	7	Now	$64.00
1984	6	Now	$50.00
1985	7	2000	$56.00
1986	7	2000	$50.00
1987	7	2000	$48.00
1988	Not made		
1989	6	Now	$35.00
1990	6	Now	$32.00
1991	Not made		
1992	Not made		
1993	6	2001	$25.00
1994	7	2002	$28.00
1995	7	2003	$25.00
1996	7	2004	$24.00
1997	7	2005	N/R
1998	7	2006	N/R

MOUNT PLEASANT ROSEHILL SHIRAZ ★★★★★

1984	7	2000	$60.00
1985	7	2000	$56.00
1986	Not made		
1987	7	Now	$48.00
1988	6	Now	$38.00
1989	6	Now	$35.00
1990	5	Now	$27.00
1991	7	2000	$35.00
1992	Not made		
1993	Not made		
1994	Not made		
1995	7	2003	$26.00
1996	7	2004	$24.00
1997	7	2005	N/R
1998	7	2006	N/R

Mount View Estate is a small terraced vineyard near Cessnock in the Hunter Valley. Unusually for the area, their range includes some very fine fortified wines. Winemaker: Keith Tulloch.

MOUNT VIEW ESTATE CABERNET SAUVIGNON ★★★

before 1983	Prior		
1983	7	Now	$70.00
1984	Not made		

1985	5	Prior	
1986	6	Prior	
1987	6	Prior	
1988	6	Prior	
1989	5	Prior	
1990	6	Prior	
1991	6	Now	$33.00
1992	Not made		
1993	5	Now	$23.00
1994	7	2002	$30.00
1995	Not made		
1996	5	2000	$18.50
1997	6	2002	N/R

MOUNT VIEW ESTATE CHARDONNAY ★★★

before 1993		Prior	
1993	6	Now	$22.00
1994	6	Now	$20.00
1995	5	Now	$15.50

MOUNT VIEW ESTATE SHIRAZ ★★★

before 1986		Prior	
1986	7	Now	$64.00
1987	6	Prior	
1988	Not made		
1989	Not made		
1990	6	Prior	
1991	7	Now	$43.00
1992	5	Prior	
1993	6	Now	$32.00
1994	7	2002	$34.00
1995	6	2000	$27.00
1996	5	Now	$21.00
1997	6	2003	$23.00

MOUNT VIEW ESTATE VERDELHO (LIQUEUR) ★★★★

1986	6	Now	$39.00
1987	7	Now	$42.00
1988	6	Now	$33.00
1989	6	Now	$31.00
1990	5	Now	$24.00
1991	7	2000	$31.00
1992	5	Now	$20.00
1993	6	2002	$22.00
1994	7	2004	$24.00
1995	6	2004	$19.50

MOUNT VIEW ESTATE VERDELHO (TRADITIONAL) ★★★

before 1988		Prior	
1988	7	Now	$37.00
1989	6	Prior	
1990	6	Prior	

1991	7	Now	$29.00
1992	6	Prior	
1993	7	Now	$25.00
1994	5	Now	$16.50
1995	6	Now	$18.50
1996	7	2000	$20.00
1997	7	2000	$18.50

Murrindindi Vineyards is a small maker in Victoria's High country, producing a fine Chardonnay and, bravely for such cool climate, a Bordeaux blend.
Winemaker: Alan Cuthbertson.

MURRINDINDI CABERNETS ★★★★

1984	6	Now	$49.00
1985	7	Now	$52.00
1986	5	Now	$35.00
1987	5	2001	$33.00
1988	7	2002	$42.00
1989	Not made		
1990	6	2006	$31.00
1991	Not made		
1992	7	2002	$31.00
1993	6	2005	$24.00
1994	7	2005	$27.00

MURRINDINDI CHARDONNAY ★★★★

1990	6	Now	$34.00
1991	6	Now	$32.00
1992	6	2000	$29.00
1993	5	Now	$23.00
1994	7	Now	$29.00
1995	6	Now	$23.00
1996	6	Now	$22.00

Nautilus Estate is a New Zealand label owned by Negociants New Zealand. The fruit now comes solely from the Marlborough region. Winemaker: Clive Jones.

NAUTILUS MARLBOROUGH CHARDONNAY ★★★★

before 1994		Prior	
1994	5	Now	NZ$27.00
1995	4	Now	NZ$20.00
1996	5	Now	NZ$23.00
1997	6	Now	NZ$26.00

NAUTILUS MARLBOROUGH SAUVIGNON BLANC ★★★★

before 1996		Prior	
1996	5	Now	NZ$19.50
1997	6	Now	NZ$21.00
1998	6	Now	NZ$20.00

Neudorf, *a vineyard in New Zealand's Nelson area, has since its first vintage in 1982 created some very fine wines, in particular their Chardonnay. Winemaker: Tim Finn.*

NEUDORF CHARDONNAY ★★★★★

before 1991		Prior	
1991	7	Now	NZ$66.00
1992	5	Prior	
1993	7	Now	NZ$56.00
1994	6	Now	NZ$45.00
1995	Not made		
1996	6	Now	NZ$38.00
1997	6	Now	NZ$36.00

NEUDORF PINOT NOIR ★★★★

1988	4	Prior	
1989	Not made		
1990	4	Now	NZ$40.00
1991	5	Now	NZ$46.00
1992	6	Now	NZ$50.00
1993	6	Now	NZ$47.00
1994	5	Now	NZ$36.00
1995	4	Prior	
1996	6	Now	NZ$38.00
1997	6	Now	NZ$35.00

NEUDORF RIESLING ★★★

1989	6	Prior	
1990	5	Now	NZ$26.00
1991	6	Now	NZ$29.00
1992	6	Now	NZ$26.00
1993	7	Now	NZ$29.00
1994	5	Now	NZ$19.00
1995	4	Prior	
1996	5	Now	NZ$16.50
1997	6	Now	NZ$18.00

NEUDORF SAUVIGNON BLANC

before 1994		Prior	★★★★
1994	6	Now	NZ$23.00
1995	5	Now	NZ$18.00
1996	6	Now	NZ$20.00
1997	6	Now	NZ$18.50

Nicholson River Winery *in Victoria's Gippsland area produces, among other wines, a Chardonnay whose quality in its best years is little short of supreme.*
Winemaker: Ken Eckersley.

NICHOLSON RIVER CHARDONNAY

before 1991		Prior	
1991	7	Now	$70.00
1992	6	Now	$56.00
1993	5	Prior	
1994	6	Now	$48.00

1995	6	Now	$44.00
1996	7	2000	$48.00
1997	7	2002	$44.00

NICHOLSON RIVER PINOT NOIR
★★★★★

1988	5	Now	$70.00
1989	5	Now	$64.00
1990	6	Now	$72.00
1991	5	2000	$56.00
1992	7	2000	$72.00
1993	6	2001	$58.00
1994	Not made		
1995	Not made		
1996	6	2005	$46.00
1997	5	2003	$35.00

Nobilo Wines, one of New Zealand's longest established
producers, have a sizable range of popular wines.
Winemaker: Greg Foster.

NOBILO CABERNET SAUVIGNON
(HUAPAI) ★★★

before 1985	Prior		
1985	6	Now	NZ$27.00
1986	7	Now	NZ$30.00
1987	7	Now	NZ$27.00
1988	7	Now	NZ$25.00
1989	7	Now	NZ$23.00
1990	Not made		
1991	Not made		
1992	6	Now	NZ$16.00

No data since 1992

NOBILO CHARDONNAY
(POVERTY BAY) ★★★★

before 1997	Prior		
1997	5	Now	NZ$12.50
1998	7	Now	NZ$16.00

NOBILO MULLER-THURGAU

before 1997	Prior		★★
1997	5	Now	NZ$7.75
1998	6	Now	NZ$8.50

NOBILO SAUVIGNON BLANC
(MARLBOROUGH) ★★★

before 1997	Prior		
1997	5	Now	NZ$13.50
1998	6	Now	NZ$15.00

NOBILO WHITE CLOUD ★★

| before 1998 | Prior | | |
| 1998 | 6 | Now | NZ$10.00 |

Normans Wines are substantial McLaren Vale based producers of a large, reliable range including the flagship "Chais Clarendon" wines. Winemaker: Roger Harbord.

NORMANS BOTRYTIS (375ml) ★★★★

1995	5	Now	$18.50
1996	6	2000	$20.00
1997	6	2002	$19.00

NORMANS CHAIS CLARENDON CABERNET SAUVIGNON ★★★★

before 1986	Prior		
1986	5	Now	$70.00
1987	5	Now	$64.00
1988	6	Now	$72.00
1989	5	Now	$56.00
1990	7	2000	$72.00
1991	5	Now	$48.00
1992	6	2000	$52.00
1993	Not made		
1994	6	2005	$46.00
1995	6	2006	$42.00
1996	7	2008	$46.00
1997	Not made		
1998	7	2010	N/R

NORMANS CHAIS CLARENDON CHARDONNAY ★★★★

before 1989	Prior		
1989	5	Now	$33.00
1990	7	Now	$43.00
1991	5	Now	$28.00
1992	Not made		
1993	Not made		
1994	6	Now	$27.00
1995	5	Now	$20.00
1996	5	Now	$19.00
1997	6	2000	$21.00
1998	Not made		

NORMANS CHAIS CLARENDON SHIRAZ ★★★★

before 1988	Prior		
1988	6	Now	$68.00
1989	6	Now	$62.00
1990	7	Now	$68.00
1991	Not made		
1992	6	Now	$50.00
1993	6	Now	$46.00
1994	6	Now	$43.00
1995	6	2000	$40.00
1996	7	2002	$43.00
1997	6	2003	N/R
1998	7	2005	N/R

NORMANS UNWOODED CHARDONNAY ★★★

1996	7	Now	$18.00
1997	6	Now	$14.00
1998	6	2000	$13.00

NORMANS WHITE LABEL CABERNET SAUVIGNON ★★★

before 1988		Prior	
1988	7	Now	$29.00
1989	5	Now	$19.50
1990	5	Now	$18.00
1991	6	Now	$20.00
1992	6	Now	$18.50
1993	5	Now	$14.00
1994	6	Now	$15.50
1995	6	Now	$14.50
1996	7	2002	$15.50
1997	6	2004	$12.50
1998	6	2008	N/R

NORMANS WHITE LABEL CHARDONNAY ★★★

before 1990		Prior	
1990	6	Now	$26.00
1991	5	Now	$20.00
1992	5	Now	$19.00
1993	6	Now	$21.00
1994	5	Now	$16.00
1995	6	Now	$18.00
1996	7	Now	$19.50
1997	6	Now	$15.50
1998	6	2000	$14.50

NORMANS WHITE LABEL MERLOT ★★★

1995	6	Now	$15.00
1996	7	Now	$16.50
1998	6	2000	$13.00

NORMANS WHITE LABEL PINOT NOIR ★★★

1996	5	Now	$15.00
1997	5	Now	$14.00
1998	6	2001	$15.50

Oakridge Estate is a Yarra Valley (Southern side) maker of remarkably powerful yet graceful Reserve Cabernet (produced only in outstanding years). Winemaker: Michael Zitzlaff.

OAKRIDGE ESTATE CABERNET SAUVIGNON/ MERLOT ★★★★

before 1991		Prior	
1991	6	Now	$32.00
1992	6	Now	$30.00
1993	6	Now	$27.00
1994	6	Now	$25.00

1995	6	2001	$23.00
1996	5	Now	$18.00
1997	6	2002	$20.00

OAKRIDGE ESTATE CHARDONNAY ★★★★

1993	5	Prior	
1994	6	Now	$29.00
1995	5	Now	$22.00
1996	4	Prior	
1997	7	2001	$27.00
1998	6	2002	$21.00

OAKRIDGE RESERVE CABERNET SAUVIGNON

★★★★

1986	7	2000	$100.00
1987	Not made		
1988	Not made		
1989	Not made		
1990	5	Now	$52.00
1991	7	2002	$68.00
1992	Not made		
1993	Not made		
1994	6	2002	$46.00
1995	5	2001	$35.00
1996	Not made		
1997	7	2005	$43.00

Oakvale is an historic winery in the Hunter Valley's Pokolbin area, established in 1893. Winemaker: Barry Shields.

OAKVALE CHARDONNAY ★★★

before 1994		Prior	
1994	6	Now	$21.00
1995	7	Now	$23.00
1996	6	2000	$18.50
1997	6	2001	$17.00

OAKVALE PEACH TREE SEMILLON ★★

1986	5	Prior	
1987	7	Now	$39.00
1988	7	2000	$36.00
1989	5	Now	$24.00
1990	6	2000	$27.00
1991	6	Now	$25.00
1992	6	Now	$23.00
1993	5	Now	$17.50
1994	6	Now	$19.50
1995	7	Now	$21.00
1996	6	2001	$17.00
1997	7	2002	$18.00

OAKVALE PEPPERCORN SHIRAZ ★★★

1985	6	Prior	
1986	Not made		
1987	7	Now	$48.00
1988	5	Prior	
1989	6	Now	$35.00
1990	6	Prior	
1991	7	Now	$35.00
1992	Not made		
1993	6	Now	$26.00
1994	6	Now	$24.00
1995	7	2000	$26.00
1996	6	2001	$20.00
1997	6	2001	$19.00

Okahu Estate in New Zealand's northlands has, in its short history, made some spectacular wines, none more so than the admirable Shiraz.
Winemaker: Michael Bendit.

OKAHU ESTATE CLIFTON CHARDONNAY ★★★★

1994	5	Now	NZ$36.00
1995	Not made		
1996	7	2001	NZ$44.00
1997	5	2002	NZ$29.00

OKAHU ESTATE KAZ SHIRAZ ★★★★★

1994	7	2000	NZ$60.00
1995	6	2003	NZ$48.00
1996	7	2005	NZ$52.00

OKAHU ESTATE NINETY MILE CABERNET/MERLOT ★★★★

1995	4	2000	NZ$21.00
1996	5	2000	NZ$24.00
1997	6	2005	NZ$27.00

Orlando (Orlando Wyndham) is a large producer with a comprehensive range of well respected wines.
Winemaker: Philip Laffer.

ORLANDO CENTENARY HILL BAROSSA SHIRAZ ★★★★★

1994	6	2002	$64.00
1995	5	2002	$50.00
1996	7	2006	$64.00
1997	6	2007	$52.00
1997	7	2008	$56.00

ORLANDO GRAMPS BAROSSA VALLEY GRENACHE ★★★★

1994	6	Now	$20.00
1995	4	Now	$12.50
1996	5	Now	$15.00
1997	6	2000	$16.50
1998	6	2001	N/R

ORLANDO GRAMPS BOTRYRIS SEMILLON ★★★

before 1996		Prior	
1996	7	Now	$17.50
1997	7	Now	$16.50
1998	7	Now	$15.00

ORLANDO GRAMPS CABERNET/
MERLOT ★★★★

before 1990		Prior	
1990	7	Now	$34.00
1991	6	Now	$27.00
1992	5	Now	$20.00
1993	5	Now	$19.00
1994	5	Now	$17.50
1995	6	2000	$19.50
1996	6	2002	$18.50
1997	5	2000	$14.00
1998	7	2004	N/R

ORLANDO GRAMPS
CHARDONNAY ★★★

before 1995		Prior	
1995	7	Now	$18.50
1996	7	Now	$17.00
1997	7	Now	$16.00
1998	7	Now	$15.00

ORLANDO JACARANDA RIDGE COONAWARRA
CABERNET ★★★★★

1982	7	Now	$145.00
1983	Not made		
1984	Not made		
1985	Not made		
1986	6	Now	$92.00
1987	6	Now	$84.00
1988	6	Now	$78.00
1989	5	Now	$60.00
1990	Not made		
1991	7	2000	$72.00
1992	6	2000	$58.00
1993	Not made		
1994	5	2001	$41.00
1995	Not made		
1996	7	2006	$50.00
1997	5,2006		N/R
1998	7	2008	N/R

ORLANDO JACOBS CREEK
CHABLIS ★★

before 1997		Prior	
1997	6	Now	$8.75
1998	7	Now	$9.50

ORLANDO JACOBS CREEK CHARDONNAY ★★

before 1996		Prior	
1996	7	Now	$10.00
1997	7	Now	$9.50
1998	7	Now	$9.00

ORLANDO JACOBS CREEK GRENACHE/SHIRAZ ★★

before 1997		Prior	
1997	7	Now	$10.50
1998	7	Now	$10.00

ORLANDO JACOBS CREEK RIESLING ★★

before 1995		Prior	
1995	7	Now	$11.00
1996	7	Now	$10.00
1997	7	Now	$9.50
1998	7	Now	$9.00

ORLANDO JACOBS CREEK SEMILLON/CHARDONNAY ★★

1996	6	Now	$9.75
1997	7	Now	$10.50
1998	6	Now	$8.50

ORLANDO JACOBS CREEK SHIRAZ/CABERNET ★★

before 1994		Prior	
1994	5	Now	$9.75
1995	5	Now	$9.00
1996	6	Now	$10.00
1997	6	2000	$9.25
1998	7	2002	N/R

ORLANDO LAWSONS PADTHAWAY SHIRAZ ★★★★

1985	5	Prior	
1986	6	Now	$100.00
1987	4	Prior	
1988	7	Now	$100.00
1989	6	Now	$80.00
1990	6	2000	$74.00
1991	7	2004	$80.00
1992	5	2000	$52.00
1993	6	2001	$58.00
1994	7	2006	$62.00
1995	5	2002	$42.00
1996	6	2006	N/R
1997	6	2007	N/R
1998	7	2010	N/R

ORLANDO RUSSET RIDGE CABERNET/SHIRAZ/MERLOT ★★★★

1991	6	Now	$29.00
1992	5	Now	$22.00
1993	5	Now	$21.00

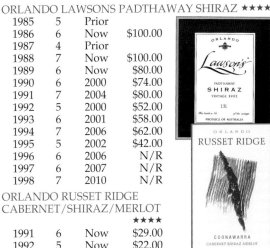

217

1994	6	2000	$23.00
1995	5	2000	$18.00
1996	7	2004	$23.00
1997	5	2001	$15.50
1998	7	2006	N/R

ORLANDO RUSSET RIDGE
CHARDONNAY ★★★

1996	6	Now	$15.50
1997	7	Now	$17.00
1998	7	Now	$15.50

ORLANDO STEINGARTEN RIESLING ★★★★

before 1987		Prior	
1987	7	Now	$44.00
1988	7	Now	$41.00
1989	6	Now	$33.00
1990	7	Now	$35.00
1991	6	Now	$28.00
1992	6	Now	$26.00
1993	Not made		
1994	7	Now	$26.00
1995	7	Now	$24.00
1996	7	Now	$22.00
1997	7	2000	$20.00
1998	7	2001	N/R

ORLANDO ST HELGA EDEN VALLEY
RIESLING ★★★★

before 1986		Prior	
1986	7	Now	$40.00
1987	6	Prior	
1988	6	Now	$29.00
1989	6	Now	$27.00
1990	7	Now	$29.00
1991	5	Prior	
1992	7	Now	$25.00
1993	6	Now	$20.00
1994	7	Now	$21.00
1995	7	Now	$20.00
1996	7	Now	$18.50
1997	7	Now	$17.00
1998	7	2000	$16.00

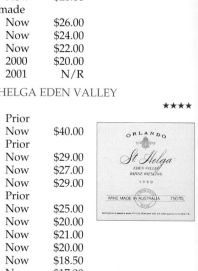

ORLANDO ST HILARY CHARDONNAY ★★★★

before 1992		Prior	
1992	7	Now	$28.00
1993	6	Now	$22.00
1994	6	Now	$21.00
1995	6	Now	$19.50
1996	7	Now	$21.00
1997	7	Now	$19.50
1998	7	2000	$18.00

ORLANDO ST HUGO COONAWARRA CABERNET SAUVIGNON ★★★★

before 1986		Prior	
1986	7	Now	$76.00
1987	5	Now	$50.00
1988	5	Now	$47.00
1989	6	Now	$52.00
1990	7	2002	$56.00
1991	6	2003	$45.00
1992	6	2005	$41.00
1993	5	2003	$32.00
1994	6	2006	$35.00
1995	Not made		
1996	5	2008	$25.00
1997	5	2005	N/R
1998	7	2010	N/R

Oyster Bay Wines is a Marlborough (New Zealand) producer owned and operated by Delegat's Wine Estates. See the note under the Delegat's entry which will explain the missing ratings. Winemaker: Not stated.

OYSTER BAY CHARDONNAY ★★★

OYSTER BAY SAUVIGNON BLANC ★★★★

Parker Estate is a Coonawarra vineyard producing Bordeaux style reds of remarkable quality. The flagship wine, Terra Rossa First Growth, is an extraordinary achievement. Winemaker: Chris Cameron.

PARKER ESTATE TERRA ROSSA FIRST GROWTH ★★★★★

1988	6	Now	$120.00
1989	5	Now	$92.00
1990	7	2002	$120.00
1991	7	2004	$110.00
1992	Not made		
1993	5	2000	$68.00
1994	6	2004	$74.00
1995	Not made		
1996	6	2007	$64.00

Palliser Estate in New Zealand's Martinborough region is a painstaking maker of a range of admirable wines made from close-planted vines. Winemaker: Allan Johnson.

PALLISER ESTATE CHARDONNAY

before 1996		Prior	★★★★
1996	5	Now	NZ$20.00
1997	6	Now	NZ$22.00
1998	6	Now	NZ$21.00

PALLISER ESTATE PINOT NOIR ★★★

1991	5	Now	NZ$39.00
1992	5	Now	NZ$36.00
1993	6	Now	NZ$40.00
1994	6	Now	NZ$37.00
1995	6	Now	NZ$34.00
1996	7	2002	NZ$37.00
1997	7	2003	NZ$35.00

PALLISER ESTATE RIESLING
★★★★

1991	5	Now	NZ$23.00
1992	5	Now	NZ$22.00
1993	6	Now	NZ$24.00
1994	5	Now	NZ$18.50
1995	5	Now	NZ$17.50
1996	7	2000	NZ$22.00
1997	6	2001	NZ$18.00
1998	7	2002	NZ$19.00

PALLISER ESTATE SAUVIGNON BLANC . ★★★★

before 1997		Prior	
1997	6	Now	NZ$21.00
1998	6	Now	NZ$20.00

C.J.Pask is a Hawkes Bay (New Zealand) maker of a range of impressive wines, including a fine Reserve Chardonnay. Winemaker: Kate Radburnd.

C.J. PASK CABERNET/MERLOT ★★★

before 1995		Prior	
1995	6	Now	NZ$23.00
1996	6	2001	NZ$21.00
1997	6	2001	NZ$20.00

C.J. PASK CABERNET SAUVIGNON ★★★★

before 1995		Prior	
1995	6	Now	NZ$23.00
1996	6	2001	NZ$21.00
1997	6	2002	NZ$20.00

C.J. PASK CHARDONNAY ★★★

before 1995		Prior	
1995	6	Now	NZ$24.00
1996	7	Now	NZ$26.00
1997	5	2000	NZ$17.50
1998	6	2001	NZ$19.50

C.J. PASK CHARDONNAY RESERVE ★★★★

before 1994		Prior	
1994	6	Now	NZ$32.00
1995	7	Now	NZ$35.00
1996	7	2000	NZ$32.00
1997	5	2001	NZ$21.00
1998	6	2001	NZ$24.00

C.J. PASK MERLOT ★★★

Year			
1995	7	Now	NZ$25.00
1996	6	Now	NZ$20.00
1997	6	2001	NZ$18.50

C.J. PASK SAUVIGNON BLANC ★★★

Year			
before 1997		Prior	
1997	6	Now	NZ$15.00
1998	6	Now	NZ$14.00

Passing Clouds is a Bendigo district maker with very individual wines of grace and power.
Winemakers: Graeme Leith and Greg Bennett.

PASSING CLOUDS "ANGEL BLEND" (CABERNETS) ★★★★

Year			
1982	6	Now	$94.00
1983	Not made		
1984	6	Now	$80.00
1985	6	Now	$74.00
1986	Not made		
1987	6	Now	$64.00
1988	Not made		
1989	Not made		
1990	6	2005	$50.00
1991	6	2006	$47.00
1992	6	2007	$44.00
1993	Not made		
1994	6	2009	$37.00
1995	6	2010	$34.00
1996	6	2000	$32.00
1997	6	2003	$30.00

PASSING CLOUDS SHIRAZ/CABERNET SAUVIGNON ★★★★

Year			
1980	6	Now	$88.00
1981	6	Now	$82.00
1982	6	Now	$76.00
1983	6	Now	$70.00
1984	6	Now	$64.00
1985	5	Now	$50.00
1986	6	Now	$56.00
1987	4	Prior	
1988	5	Prior	
1989	5	Prior	
1990	6	Prior	
1991	6	Now	$38.00
1992	6	Now	$35.00
1993	Not made		
1994	6	2000	$30.00
1995	6	2001	$28.00
1996	6	2002	$26.00
1997	6	2002	$24.00

PASSING CLOUDS PINOT NOIR ★★★★

before 1994		Prior	
1994	7	Now	$30.00
1995	6	Now	$24.00
1996	6	Now	$22.00
1997	6	Now	$20.00
1998	6	2000	$19.00

PASSING CLOUDS SHIRAZ ★★★★

1994	5	Now	$25.00
1995	Not made		
1996	6	2000	$26.00
1997	6	2002	$24.00

Pauletts Polish Hill River Wines *is a Clare area producer of finely crafted wines. Winemaker: Neil Paulett.*

PAULETTS POLISH HILL RIVER RIESLING ★★★★

before 1986		Prior	
1986	6	Now	$40.00
1987	6	Now	$37.00
1988	7	Now	$40.00
1989	5	Now	$26.00
1990	7	Now	$34.00
1991	6	Now	$27.00
1992	6	Now	$25.00
1993	7	Now	$27.00
1994	6	2000	$21.00
1995	7	2005	$23.00
1996	6	2003	$18.50
1997	6	2005	$17.00

PAULETTS POLISH HILL RIVER SHIRAZ ★★★

1984	7	Prior	
1985	4	Now	$29.00
1986	6	Now	$40.00
1987	6	Now	$37.00
1988	5	Now	$29.00
1989	7	Now	$37.00
1990	5	Now	$25.00
1991	6	Now	$27.00
1992	5	Now	$21.00
1993	6	Now	$23.00
1994	6	Now	$22.00
1995	6	2000	$20.00
1996	5	Now	$15.50

Peel Estate *is a South West Coastal (W.A.) producer of stylish and elegant wines. Winemaker: Will Nairn.*

PEEL ESTATE CABERNET SAUVIGNON ★★★★

1983	6	Now	$60.00
1984	7	2000	$64.00
1985	6	Now	$50.00

1986	5	Now	$39.00
1987	4	Now	$29.00
1988	Not made		
1989	6	2000	$38.00
1990	7	2002	$41.00
1991	5	2000	$27.00
1992	7	2002	$35.00
1993	6	2003	$27.00
1994	7	2006	$30.00
1995	6	2005	$24.00

PEEL ESTATE CHARDONNAY ★★★★

before 1989	Prior		
1989	6	Now	$35.00
1990	5	Now	$27.00
1991	6	Now	$30.00
1992	7	2000	$33.00
1993	6	2000	$26.00
1994	7	2002	$28.00
1995	6	2003	$22.00
1996	6	2004	$20.00
1997	7	2005	$22.00

PEEL ESTATE CHENIN BLANC (WOOD-AGED) ★★★★

before 1982	Prior		
1982	5	Now	$62.00
1983	5	Prior	
1984	7	Now	$74.00
1985	5	Now	$49.00
1986	7	Now	$64.00
1987	5	Now	$42.00
1988	7	Now	$54.00
1989	6	Now	$43.00
1990	5	2000	$33.00
1991	6	Now	$37.00
1992	7	2002	$40.00
1993	6	2000	$32.00
1994	7	2004	$34.00
1995	6	2005	$27.00
1996	6	2006	$25.00
1997	7	2007	$27.00

PEEL ESTATE SHIRAZ ★★★★

before 1982	Prior		
1982	5	Now	$66.00
1983	6	Now	$74.00
1984	6	Now	$68.00
1985	5	Prior	
1986	7	Now	$68.00
1987	5	Now	$45.00
1988	7	2000	$58.00

1989	6	2001	$47.00
1990	7	2004	$50.00
1991	5	2000	$33.00
1992	7	2005	$43.00
1993	6	2003	$34.00
1994	7	2006	$37.00
1995	6	2006	$29.00

Pelorus is the outstandingly fine sparkling wine made by New Zealand's Cloudy Bay operation. Winemaker: Kevin Judd.

PELORUS METHODE CHAMPENOISE ★★★★★

1987	6	Now	NZ$64.00
1988	6	Now	NZ$60.00
1989	5	Now	NZ$46.00
1990	6	Now	NZ$50.00
1991	6	Now	NZ$48.00
1992	5	Now	NZ$37.00
1993	5	Now	NZ$34.00
1994	5	Now	NZ$31.00

Penfolds is the flagship label of the huge Southcorp Wine Group. They have a richly warranted reputation, particularly for red wines. Winemaker: John Duval.

PENFOLDS ADELAIDE HILLS CHARDONNAY

★★★★

1995	6	Now	$26.00
1996	7	Now	$28.00
1997	6	2001	$22.00
1998	6	2002	$21.00

PENFOLDS ADELAIDE HILLS SEMILLON ★★★★

1995	6	Now	$24.00
1996	5	Now	$18.50
1997	7	2000	$24.00
1998	7	2002	$22.00

PENFOLDS AGED RIESLING ★★★★

1992	6	Now	$19.50
1993	6	Now	$18.00
1994	Not made		
1995	6	Now	$15.00
1996	Not made		
1997	7	2003	N/R
1998	6	2004	N/R

PENFOLDS BAROSSA VALLEY OLD VINES
SEMILLON ★★★★

1995	6	Now	$23.00
1996	5	Now	$18.00
1997	6	Now	$20.00
1998	6	Now	$18.50

PENFOLDS BAROSSA VALLEY SEMILLON/CHARDONNAY

★★★

before 1996		Prior	
1996	6	Now	$13.00
1997	6	Now	$12.00
1998	7	Now	$13.00

PENFOLDS BIN 28 KALIMNA SHIRAZ

★★★★

before 1983		Prior	
1983	7	Now	$62.00
1984	5	Prior	
1985	4	Prior	
1986	7	Now	$50.00
1987	6	Prior	
1988	6	Now	$37.00
1989	5	Prior	
1990	7	Now	$37.00
1991	7	Now	$34.00
1992	6	Now	$27.00
1993	6	2000	$25.00
1994	6	2001	$23.00
1995	5	2001	$18.00
1996	7	2003	$23.00

PENFOLDS BIN 128 COONAWARRA SHIRAZ ★★★★

before 1986		Prior	
1986	7	Now	$52.00
1987	6	Prior	
1988	6	Prior	
1989	5	Prior	
1990	6	Now	$33.00
1991	7	Now	$35.00
1992	4	Prior	
1993	7	2000	$30.00
1994	5	Now	$20.00
1995	4	Now	$15.00
1996	6	2003	$20.00

PENFOLDS BIN 389 CABERNET SAUVIGNON/SHIRAZ

★★★★

before 1982		Prior	
1982	7	Now	$92.00
1983	7	Now	$84.00
1984	4	Prior	
1985	6	Prior	
1986	6	Now	$58.00
1987	6	Now	$54.00
1988	6	Now	$50.00
1989	6	Now	$46.00

1990	7	2000	$50.00
1991	7	2001	$46.00
1992	6	Now	$36.00
1993	7	2002	$39.00
1994	6	2000	$31.00
1995	5	2001	$24.00
1996	7	2004	$31.00

PENFOLDS BIN 407 CABERNET SAUVIGNON ★★★★

1990	7	2000	$41.00
1991	7	2000	$38.00
1992	5	Now	$25.00
1993	6	2001	$28.00
1994	7	2004	$30.00
1995	4	2000	$16.00
1996	7	2005	$26.00

PENFOLDS BIN 707 CABERNET SAUVIGNON

★★★★★

1976	5	Now	$460.00
1977	5	Prior	
1978	4	Prior	
1979	5	Prior	
1980	6	Prior	
1981	Not made		
1982	7	Now	$400.00
1983	7	Now	$370.00
1984	5	Prior	
1985	6	Prior	
1986	7	Now	$290.00
1987	7	Now	$270.00
1988	6	Now	$220.00
1989	5	Now	$165.00
1990	7	2002	$220.00
1991	7	2002	$200.00
1992	5	2000	$130.00
1993	7	2005	$170.00
1994	7	2004	$160.00
1995	Not made		
1996	7	2007	$135.00

PENFOLDS CHARDONNAY
"THE VALLEYS" ★★★★

before 1994		Prior	
1994	7	Now	$22.00
1995	6	Prior	
1996	6	Now	$16.00
1997	7	Now	$17.50
1998	6	2000	$14.00

PENFOLDS GRANGE

★★★★★

Please note: Some of the older years of this wine listed below should probably be shown as "Prior". However the extreme desirability to collectors of Grange coupled with the fact that the cellaring conditions of such a wine are likely to be of a high standard, justify a "Now" classification and the concomitant value calculation. Speaking of which, however, it must be said that both the retail and the auction prices paid for Grange vintages are wildly illogical, collector-driven values which grossly inflate the prices of rarer vintages (rare often because no one bothered to keep the lesser years) and undervalue the years in which collectors acquired and kept good quantities of the wines.

1951	5	Now	$5960.00
1952	6	Now	$6620.00
1953	7	Now	$7160.00
1954	3	Now	$2840.00
1955	7	Now	$6140.00
1956	6	Now	$4860.00
1957	4	Now	$3000.00
1958	3	Now	$2080.00
1959	4	Now	$2580.00
1960	5	Now	$2980.00
1961	4	Now	$2200.00
1962	6	Now	$3060.00
1963	5	Now	$2360.00
1964	4	Now	$1740.00
1965	7	Now	$2840.00
1966	6	Now	$2240.00
1967	5	Now	$1740.00
1968	4	Now	$1280.00
1969	4	Now	$1180.00
1970	6	Now	$1660.00
1971	7	Now	$1780.00
1972	5	Now	$1180.00
1973	5	Now	$1080.00
1974	5	Now	$1000.00
1975	6	Now	$1120.00
1976	7	Now	$1220.00
1977	6	Now	$960.00
1978	5	Now	$740.00
1979	5	Now	$680.00
1980	6	Now	$760.00
1981	6	Now	$700.00
1982	6	Now	$640.00
1983	7	2000	$700.00
1984	5	Now	$470.00
1985	5	Now	$430.00
1986	7	2000	$560.00
1987	6	2000	$440.00
1988	6	2000	$410.00
1989	5	Now	$320.00
1990	7	2005	$410.00

1991	7	2006	$380.00
1992	5	2002	$250.00
1993	6	2005	$280.00
1994	6	2006	$260.00

PENFOLDS KOONUNGA HILL CHARDONNAY ★★

before 1996		Prior	
1996	7	Now	$14.50
1997	6	Now	$11.50
1998	6	Now	$10.50

PENFOLDS KOONUNGA HILL SEMILLON/SAUVIGNON BLANC ★

1995	6	Prior	
1996	6	Now	$13.00
1997	5	Now	$10.00
1998	6	Now	$11.00

PENFOLDS KOONUNGA HILL SHIRAZ/CABERNET ★★

1990	7	Now	$23.00
1991	7	Now	$21.00
1992	5	Now	$14.00
1993	6	Now	$15.50
1994	5	Now	$12.00
1995	6	Now	$13.50
1996	7	2001	$14.50
1997	6	2001	$11.50

PENFOLDS MAGILL ESTATE SHIRAZ ★★★★

before 1985		Prior	
1985	5	Now	$90.00
1986	5	Now	$84.00
1987	5	Now	$78.00
1988	6	Now	$86.00
1989	5	Now	$66.00
1990	7	Now	$86.00
1991	7	2000	$80.00
1992	5	2000	$52.00
1993	5	2001	$49.00
1994	6	2002	$54.00
1995	7	2005	$58.00
1996	6	2004	$46.00

PENFOLDS OLD VINES BAROSSA VALLEY RED ★★★

1992	7	2000	$32.00
1993	6	Now	$25.00
1994	6	2001	$24.00
1995	6	2002	$22.00
1996	7	2003	$24.00

PENFOLDS RAWSONS RETREAT RED ★

1995	5	Now	$10.50
1996	6	Now	$12.00
1997	5	Now	$9.25

PENFOLDS RAWSONS RETREAT
SEMILLON/CHARDONNAY ★★

1996	5	Now	$10.00
1997	6	Now	$11.00
1998	6	Now	$10.50

PENFOLDS ST HENRI ★★★★

before 1980		Prior	
1980	6	Now	$120.00
1981	5	Prior	
1982	6	Now	$100.00
1983	6	Now	$94.00
1984	5	Now	$72.00
1985	6	Now	$80.00
1986	7	Now	$88.00
1987	5	Now	$58.00
1988	5	Now	$54.00
1989	5	Now	$50.00
1990	7	2000	$64.00
1991	6	2001	$50.00
1992	5	2001	$39.00
1993	6	2003	$44.00
1994	5	2003	$34.00
1995	6	2004	$37.00

PENFOLDS "THE CLARE ESTATE"
CHARDONNAY ★★★

before 1996		Prior	
1996	6	2001	$13.50
1997	7	Now	$15.00
1998		Not made	

PENFOLDS "THE CLARE ESTATE" RED BLEND ★★★

before 1990		Prior	
1990	6	Now	$22.00
1991	7	Now	$23.00
1992	5	Now	$15.50
1993	6	Now	$17.50
1994	6	Now	$16.00
1995	6	Now	$15.00
1996	6	Now	$14.00
1997		Not made	

Penley Estate is a recently established 67 hectare vineyard in Coonawarra producing four fine reds and an admirable sparkling wine. Winemaker: Kym Tolley.

PENLEY ESTATE CABERNET SAUVIGNON ★★★★★

1989	6	Now	$82.00
1990	7	2001	$88.00
1991	7	2006	$82.00
1992	6	2004	$64.00

1993	7	2007	$70.00
1994	7	2008	$64.00
1995	6	2007	$50.00
1996	6	2008	$48.00

PENLEY ESTATE METHODE CHAMPENOISE ★★★★★

1989	4	Now	$23.00
1990	6	Now	$32.00
1991	7	2001	$34.00

PENLEY ESTATE PHOENIX (CABERNET SAUVIGNON) ★★★★

1995	5	2000	$19.00
1996	6	2002	$21.00
1997	7	2003	$23.00

PENLEY ESTATE SHIRAZ ★★★★

before 1992	Prior		
1992	5	Now	$25.00
1993	5	Now	$23.00
1994	4	Now	$17.50
1995	Not made		
1996	6	2000	$22.00
1997	6	2001	$21.00

PENLEY ESTATE SHIRAZ/CABERNET ★★★★

1989	4	Prior	
1990	5	Now	$38.00
1991	6	Now	$42.00
1992	6	2000	$39.00
1993	6	2001	$36.00
1994	6	2001	$33.00
1995	6	2003	$31.00
1996	6	2004	$28.00

Petaluma is a label under which some fine wines are released
grapes coming from the producer's vineyards in Clare,
Piccadilly Valley and Coonawarra, but all vinified at the
Petaluma winery at Piccadilly in the Mount Lofty Ranges.
(Please note: some of these winemaker's ratings may appear
surprisingly low. This is purely because this winemaker prefer
to use more of the range of 1 to 7 in comparing his wines with
themselves in other years. Would that more others would do
the same.) Winemaker: Brian Croser.

PETALUMA CHARDONNAY

before 1984	Prior	★★★★★	
1984	3	Now	$50.00
1985	3	Now	$48.00
1986	4	Now	$58.00
1987	4	Now	$54.00
1988	4	Now	$50.00
1989	4	Now	$47.00

1990	5	Now	$54.00
1991	5	Now	$50.00
1992	7	Now	$64.00
1993	4	Now	$34.00
1994	4	Now	$32.00
1995	6	2002	$44.00
1996	6	2004	$41.00
1997	7	2005	$44.00

PETALUMA COONAWARRA REDS ★★★★★

1979	4	Now	$140.00
1980	3	Now	$100.00
1981	3	Now	$92.00
1982	4	Now	$110.00
1983	Not made		
1984	2	Prior	
1985	3	Prior	
1986	5	Now	$100.00
1987	5	Now	$96.00
1988	6	2000	$105.00
1989	Not made		
1990	6	2005	$92.00
1991	5	2005	$70.00
1992	7	2010	$92.00
1993	5	2005	$60.00
1994	6	2010	$68.00
1995	6	2010	$62.00
1996	4	2005	$39.00
1997	5	2005	$45.00

PETALUMA
1987 COONAWARRA
750ml
PRODUCE OF AUSTRALIA BOTTLED AT PICCADILLY SA

PETALUMA RIESLING ★★★★★

before 1980		Prior	
1980	7	Now	$105.00
1981	4	Now	$56.00
1982	4	Now	$52.00
1983	2	Prior	
1984	4	Now	$45.00
1985	5	Now	$52.00
1986	5	Now	$48.00
1987	6	Now	$54.00
1988	4	Now	$33.00
1989	3	Now	$23.00
1990	4	Now	$28.00
1991	4	Now	$26.00
1992	6	2002	$36.00
1993	5	2000	$28.00
1994	5	2000	$26.00
1995	4	2000	$19.00
1996	7	2005	$31.00
1997	5	2005	$20.00

PETALUMA
1998 RIESLING
750ml
PRODUCE OF AUSTRALIA BOTTLED AT PICCADILLY SA

Peter Lehmann Wines is a greatly respected Barossa winemaker with a reliable range of underpriced fine wines. Winemakers: Andrew Wigan, Peter Scholz, Ian Hongell and Leonie Lange.

PETER LEHMANN CABERNET SAUVIGNON ★★★★

before 1984		Prior	
1984	6	Now	$52.00
1985	5	Prior	
1986	6	Now	$45.00
1987	7	Now	$49.00
1988	6	Now	$39.00
1989	6	Now	$36.00
1990	7	2000	$39.00
1991	6	2001	$30.00
1992	7	2002	$33.00
1993	7	2004	$31.00
1994	6	2003	$24.00
1995	5	2002	$18.50
1996	7	2006	$24.00
1996	5	2002	$16.00

PETER LEHMANN CHARDONNAY ★★★★

before 1991		Prior	
1991	7	Now	$27.00
1992	6	Prior	
1993	6	Now	$20.00
1994	6	2000	$19.00
1995	5	2000	$14.50
1996	5	2001	$13.50
1997	6	2002	$15.00
1998	7	2008	$16.00

PETER LEHMANN CLANCY'S (SHIRAZ BLEND) ★★★★

before 1990		Prior	
1990	6	Now	$22.00
1991	7	2000	$24.00
1992	7	2001	$22.00
1993	6	2002	$17.50
1994	6	2003	$16.50
1995	5	2002	$12.50
1996	7	2004	$16.50
1997	7	2005	$15.00

PETER LEHMANN MENTOR (CABERNET/MALBEC/SHIRAZ/MERLOT) ★★★★

1991	6	2000	$40.00
1992	7	2001	$43.00
1993	7	2002	$40.00
1994	6	2004	$32.00

PETER LEHMANN NOBLE (BOTRYTIS) SEMILLON (375ml)

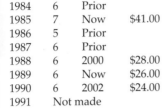

★★★★

Year			Price
1981	5	Prior	
1982	7	Now	$52.00
1983	Not made		
1984	6	Prior	
1985	7	Now	$41.00
1986	5	Prior	
1987	6	Prior	
1988	6	2000	$28.00
1989	6	Now	$26.00
1990	6	2002	$24.00
1991	Not made		
1992	7	2004	$24.00
1993	Not made		
1994	6	2004	$17.50
1995	5	2005	$13.50
1996	6	2006	$15.00
1997	5	2006	$11.50

PETER LEHMANN RIESLING

★★★★

Year			Price
before 1991		Prior	
1991	6	Now	$19.50
1992	5	Now	$15.00
1993	7	2000	$19.50
1994	6	2000	$15.50
1995	6	2002	$14.50
1996	6	2006	$13.00
1997	7	2007	$14.50
1998	7	2008	$13.00

PETER LEHMANN SEMILLON ★★★

Year			Price
before 1992		Prior	
1992	6	Now	$17.50
1993	6	Now	$16.00
1994	7	2002	$17.50
1995	7	2003	$16.00
1996	6	2003	$13.00
1997	6	2004	$12.00
1998	7	2005	$13.00

PETER LEHMANN SHIRAZ ★★★

Year			Price
before 1992		Prior	
1992	7	Now	$28.00
1993	7	2000	$26.00
1994	7	2001	$24.00
1995	6	2000	$19.00
1996	7	2003	$21.00
1997	7	2005	$19.00

PETER LEHMANN STONEWELL SHIRAZ ★★★★★

1987	6	Prior	
1988	6	Now	$78.00
1989	7	2000	$84.00
1990	7	2001	$78.00
1991	7	2002	$72.00
1992	6	2003	$58.00
1993	7	2004	$62.00
1994	7	2005	$58.00

Pewsey Vale is a very fine vineyard in the cooler heights (480 metres) of the Eden Valley. The owners are S. Smith and Sons of Yalumba fame. Winemaker: Louisa Rose.

PEWSEY VALE CABERNET SAUVIGNON ★★★

before 1990		Prior	
1990	6	Now	$25.00
1991	5	Now	$19.50
1992	6	Now	$21.00
1993	5	Now	$16.50
1994	6	Now	$18.50
1995	5	Now	$14.50
1996	6	2001	$16.00

PEWSEY VALE RIESLING ★★★★

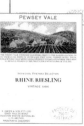

before 1992		Prior	
1992	6	Now	$17.50
1993	5	Now	$13.50
1994	6	Now	$15.00
1995	5	Now	$11.50
1996	6	Now	$13.00
1997	7	2002	$14.00
1998	6	2003	$11.00

Pfeiffer Wines is a North East Victorian fortified wine specialist, but produces as well a small range of attractive and inexpensive table wines. Cellar door sales only. Winemaker: Chris Pfeiffer.

PFEIFFER AUSLESE TOKAY (375ml) ★★★★

1985	5	Now	$35.00
1986	5	Now	$32.00
1987	5	Now	$30.00
1988	7	2000	$39.00
1989	6	Now	$31.00
1990	6	Now	$28.00
1991	5	Now	$22.00
1992	5	Now	$20.00
1993	6	2000	$22.00
1994	6	Now	$21.00
1995	6	Now	$19.50
1996	5	2000	$15.00
1997	5	2002	$14.00
1998	6	2005	$15.50

PFEIFFER CABERNET SAUVIGNON ★★★

1985	3	Prior	
1986	6	Now	$38.00
1987	5	Now	$29.00
1988	6	Now	$32.00
1989	6	Now	$30.00
1990	5	Now	$23.00
1991	7	2002	$30.00
1992	7	2005	$28.00
1993	6	2005	$22.00
1994	6	2005	$20.00
1995	6	2006	$19.00
1996	7	2008	$20.00
1997	6	2008	$16.00

PFEIFFER CHARDONNAY ★★★

1985	5	Now	$34.00
1986	4	Prior	
1987	4	Now	$23.00
1988	7	2000	$38.00
1989	4	Now	$20.00
1990	5	2000	$23.00
1991	5	2001	$22.00
1992	6	2004	$24.00
1993	6	2004	$22.00
1994	7	2000	$24.00
1995	6	2006	$19.00
1996	7	2010	$20.00
1997	7	2010	$19.00
1998	6	2010	$15.00

PFEIFFER PINOT NOIR ★★★

1985	5	Now	$35.00
1986	5	2000	$32.00
1987	4	Prior	
1988	7	2000	$39.00
1989	5	Now	$26.00
1990	6	Now	$29.00
1991	6	2000	$26.00
1992	7	2002	$29.00
1993	Not made		
1994	7	2006	$24.00
1995	5	2005	$16.00
1996	5	2006	$15.00
1997	6	2008	$16.50

Pibbin is a very small (2 Ha) Adelaide Hills vineyard specialising in Pinot Noir. Winemaker: Roger Salkeld.

PIBBIN PINOT NOIR ★★★★

1991	5	Prior	
1992	6	Now	$36.00
1993	6	Now	$34.00
1994	6	Now	$31.00
1995	6	Now	$29.00
1996	6	2000	$27.00
1997	7	2004	$29.00

Pierro Vineyards *is a Margaret River maker with 10 hectares of vines. The range includes a superb Chardonnay. Winemaker: Michael Peterkin.*

PIERRO CHARDONNAY ★★★★★

1985	4	Prior	
1986	6	Now	$110.00
1987	5	Now	$86.00
1988	5	Prior	
1989	6	Now	$88.00
1990	6	Now	$82.00
1991	5	Now	$62.00
1992	5	Now	$58.00
1993	6	Now	$64.00
1994	6	Now	$60.00
1995	5	Now	$46.00
1996	6	2000	$52.00
1997	6	2001	$48.00

PIERRO PINOT NOIR ★★★★

before 1990		Prior	
1990	5	Now	$52.00
1991	Not made		
1992	5	Now	$45.00
1993	5	Now	$41.00
1994	5	Now	$38.00
1995	6	Now	$42.00
1996	6	Now	$39.00
1997	6	2000	$36.00

PIERRO SEMILLON/SAUVIGNON BLANC ★★★★

before 1992		Prior	
1992	6	Now	$35.00
1993	6	Now	$32.00
1994	5	1996	$25.00
1995	5	Now	$23.00
1996	5	Now	$21.00
1997	6	2000	$24.00

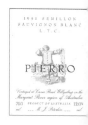

Pike's Wines *is a Clare area vineyard making limited quantities of very fine wines. Winemaker: Neil Pike.*

PIKE'S CABERNET SAUVIGNON ★★★★

1984	5	Now	$49.00
1985	6	Now	$54.00
1986	6	Now	$50.00
1987	6	Now	$47.00
1988	5	Now	$36.00
1989	6	Now	$40.00

1990	7	Now	$43.00
1991	7	Now	$40.00
1992	6	2000	$32.00
1993	5	2000	$24.00
1994	6	2001	$27.00
1995	6	2001	$25.00
1996	7	2002	$27.00
1997	6	2002	$22.00

PIKE'S RIESLING ★★★★

1985	6	Now	$40.00
1986	6	Now	$37.00
1987	6	Now	$34.00
1988	5	Now	$26.00
1989	5	Now	$24.00
1990	7	2000	$32.00
1991	6	Now	$25.00
1992	6	2001	$23.00
1993	6	2001	$22.00
1994	5	2002	$17.00
1995	7	2003	$22.00
1996	5	2003	$14.50
1997	7	2004	$18.50
1998	7	2006	$17.50

PIKE'S POLISH HILL RIVER SAUVIGNON BLANC ★★★

before 1995		Prior	
1995	5	Now	$17.00
1996	5	Now	$15.50
1997	6	Now	$17.50
1998	6	Now	$16.00

PIKE'S POLISH HILL RIVER SHIRAZ ★★★★

1987	6	Now	$46.00
1988	6	Now	$42.00
1989	5	Now	$32.00
1990	7	2000	$42.00
1991	7	2001	$39.00
1992	5	2004	$26.00
1993	6	2003	$29.00
1994	7	2004	$31.00
1995	6	2005	$24.00
1996	7	2006	$26.00
1997	6	2005	$21.00

Pipers Brook Vineyard is a viticulturally exemplary vineyard in the Launceston area. The wines are among the country's finest. Winemaker: Dr Andrew Pirie.

PIPERS BROOK VINEYARD CABERNET SAUVIGNON "OPIMIAN" ★★★★★

1981	6	Now	$120.00
1982	7	Now	$130.00
1983	5	Now	$86.00

237

1984	5	Now	$80.00
1985	4	Now	$60.00
1986	5	Prior	
1987	4	Prior	
1988	6	2005	$70.00
1989	5	Now	$54.00
1990	Not made		
1991	6	Now	$56.00
1992	6	Now	$52.00
1993	Not made		
1994	Not made		
1995	7	2005	$48.00
1996	Not made		
1997	6	2006	$35.00

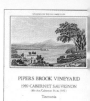

PIPERS BROOK VINEYARD
1989 CABERNET SAUVIGNON
(Merlot/Cabernet Franc 19%)
Tasmania

PIPERS BROOK VINEYARD CHARDONNAY ★★★★

before 1984	Prior		
1984	7	2000	$94.00
1985	5	Prior	
1986	7	2001	$80.00
1987	5	Now	$52.00
1988	5	Prior	
1989	5	Now	$46.00
1990	5	Now	$42.00
1991	7	2005	$54.00
1992	7	2005	$50.00
1993	6	Now	$40.00
1994	6	2000	$37.00
1995	7	Now	$40.00
1996	5	2005	$27.00
1997	7	2003	$35.00

PIPERS BROOK VINEYARD
1990 CHARDONNAY
Tasmania

PIPERS BROOK VINEYARD GEWURZTRAMINER

★★★★

1987	6	Now	$47.00
1988	7	Now	$50.00
1989	5	Now	$33.00
1990	6	Now	$37.00
1991	7	Now	$40.00
1992	6	Now	$32.00
1993	6	Now	$29.00
1994	Not made		
1995	7	2005	$29.00
1996	6	2000	$23.00
1997	7	2000	$25.00

PIPERS BROOK VINEYARD
PELLION PINOT NOIR) ★★★★★

before 1988	Prior		
1988	6	Now	$56.00
1989	Not made		
1990	6	Now	$48.00

PIPERS BROOK VINEYARD
1988 PINOT NOIR
Tasmania

1991	6	Now	$45.00
1992	7	Now	$48.00
1993	3	Prior	
1994	7	2000	$41.00
1995	6	2000	$33.00
1996	6	2005	$30.00

PIPERS BROOK VINEYARD RIESLING ★★★★

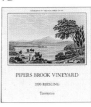

before 1986		Prior	
1986	5	Now	$50.00
1987	5	Now	$46.00
1988	5	Now	$43.00
1989	6	Now	$47.00
1990	6	Now	$44.00
1991	7	Now	$47.00
1992	7	2002	$44.00
1993	7	Now	$41.00
1994	7	2005	$38.00
1995	7	2000	$35.00
1996	6	2002	$27.00
1997	7	2010	$30.00

PIPERS BROOK VINEYARD SUMMIT
CHARDONNAY ★★★★★

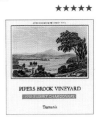

1990	5	Now	$96.00
1991	7	2008	$125.00
1992	7	2005	$115.00
1993	Not made		
1994	7	2005	$100.00
1995	Not made		
1996	Not made		
1997	7	2010	$78.00

Plantagenet *is the longest established vineyard in the Mount Barker area of Western Australia. Winemaker: Gavin Berry.*

PLANTAGENET CABERNET SAUVIGNON
(MOUNT BARKER) ★★★★

before 1981		Prior	
1981	6	Now	$86.00
1982	Not made		
1983	6	Now	$72.00
1984	5	Now	$56.00
1985	7	Now	$72.00
1986	7	Now	$68.00
1987	5	Now	$45.00
1988	7	2000	$58.00
1989	6	2000	$46.00
1990	6	2000	$43.00
1991	7	2005	$46.00
1992	6	2006	$36.00
1993	7	2008	$39.00

1994	7	2010	$36.00
1995	7	2005	$34.00
1996	7	2009	$31.00

PLANTAGENET CHARDONNAY
(MT BARKER) ★★★★

before 1987		Prior	
1987	6	Now	$48.00
1988	6	Now	$45.00
1989	6	Now	$41.00
1990	7	Now	$45.00
1991	7	Now	$41.00
1992	7	Now	$38.00
1993	7	Now	$35.00
1994	6	2000	$28.00
1995	6	2002	$26.00
1996	6	2003	$24.00
1997	6	2002	$22.00

PLANTAGENET CHARDONNAY
(OMRAH) ★★★

before 1993		Prior	
1993	6	Now	$24.00
1994	5	Now	$18.50
1995	7	Now	$24.00
1996	6	Now	$19.00
1997	6	Now	$17.50
1998	7	Now	$19.00

PLANTAGENET MERLOT/
CABERNET (OMRAH) ★★★

1994	5	Prior	
1995	6	Now	$21.00
1996	7	Now	$22.00
1997	7	Now	$21.00

PLANTAGENET RIESLING (MOUNT BARKER) ★★★★

before 1988		Prior	
1988	6	Now	$34.00
1989	7	Now	$36.00
1990	6	Now	$29.00
1991	6	Now	$27.00
1992	6	Now	$25.00
1993	7	Now	$27.00
1994	6	Now	$21.00
1995	7	Now	$23.00
1996	6	2000	$18.00
1997	7	2000	$19.50
1998	7	2002	$18.00

PLANTAGENET SHIRAZ (MOUNT BARKER) ★★★★

before 1983		Prior	
1983	7	Now	$92.00
1984	6	Now	$72.00

1985	6	Now	$68.00
1986	7	Now	$72.00
1987	6	Now	$58.00
1988	6	Now	$54.00
1989	6	Now	$50.00
1990	7	2000	$54.00
1991	7	2001	$50.00
1992	Not made		
1993	7	2003	$43.00
1994	7	2004	$39.00
1995	7	2005	$36.00
1996	7	2008	$34.00
1997	7	2009	$31.00

Poole's Rock is a 5 hectare vineyard at Broke in the Hunter Valley owned by Harbridge Fine Wines who also own the neighbouring Cockfighter's Ghost vineyard.
Winemaker: Phil Ryan.

POOLE'S ROCK CHARDONNAY

			★★★★
1996	5	Now	$20.00
1997	6	2000	$22.00
1998	7	2001	$24.00

Preece is the label under which Mitchelton Wines release two well-distributed and reliable wines which honour the great winemaker Colin Preece, who was consultant in the establishment of the Mitchelton vineyards.
Winemaker: Don Lewis.

PREECE CABERNET SAUVIGNON ★★★★

before 1991		Prior	
1991	5	Now	$21.00
1992	5	Now	$20.00
1993	5	Now	$18.50
1994	5	2000	$17.00
1995	6	2003	$19.00
1996	6	2005	$17.50

PREECE CHARDONNAY ★★★★

before 1991		Prior	
1991	6	Now	$26.00
1992	6	Now	$24.00
1993	5	Now	$19.00
1994	5	Now	$17.50
1995	6	Now	$19.50
1996	6	2000	$18.00
1997	6	2001	$16.50

Primo Estate is a family-owned Adelaide Plains producer with a brilliant and innovative winemaker with extreme quality aspirations. Winemaker: Joe Grilli.

PRIMO ESTATE COLOMBARD ★★★

before 1994		Prior	
1994	6	Now	$16.00
1995	7	Now	$17.50
1996	5	Now	$11.50
1997	7	Now	$15.00
1998	5	Now	$10.00

PRIMO ESTATE JOSEPH "LA MAGIA" BOTRYTIS RIESLING (375ml) ★★★★

1981	6	Now	$98.00
1982	5	Now	$76.00
1983	2	Now	$28.00
1984	5	Now	$64.00
1985	5	Now	$60.00
1986	Not made		
1987	Not made		
1988	Not made		
1989	5	Now	$44.00
1990	Not made		
1991	6	Now	$45.00
1992	Not made		
1993	6	Now	$39.00
1994	6	Now	$36.00
1995	5	Now	$28.00
1996	6	2001	$31.00

PRIMO ESTATE JOSEPH CABERNET/MERLOT ★★★★

1986	5	Now	$74.00
1987	5	2000	$68.00
1988	5	Now	$64.00
1989	5	2000	$58.00
1990	6	2000	$66.00
1991	5	2000	$50.00
1992	6	2002	$56.00
1993	6	2005	$52.00
1994	5	2006	$40.00
1995	6	2006	$45.00
1996	6	2009	$41.00

Prince Albert is a very small Geelong area vineyard planted solely to Pinot Noir. Winemaker: Bruce Hyett.

PRINCE ALBERT PINOT NOIR ★★★★

1978	7	Now	$145.00
1979	3	Prior	
1980	Not made		
1981	3	Now	$49.00

1982	7	Now	$105.00
1983	5	Now	$70.00
1984	6	Now	$78.00
1985	6	Now	$72.00
1986	6	Now	$66.00
1987	5	Now	$52.00
1988	5	Now	$48.00
1989	6	Now	$52.00
1990	6	Now	$49.00
1991	6	Now	$46.00
1992	7	Now	$49.00
1993	6	Now	$39.00
1994	6	Now	$36.00
1995	7	2000	$39.00
1996	6	2002	$31.00
1997	7	2002	$33.00

Pyrenees Wines - see *Warrenmang.*

Redbank *is a very fine Victorian maker of tight, powerful
and long- lived red wines. Winemaker: Neill Robb.*

REDBANK CABERNET ★★★★★

1984	6	Now	$145.00
1985	7	Now	$155.00
1986	7	2000	$145.00
1987	5	2000	$96.00
1988	7	2005	$120.00
1989	5	2002	$82.00
1990	6	2006	$92.00
1991	7	2010	$98.00
1992	6	2012	$78.00
1993	Not made		
1994	Not made		
1995	7	2020	$72.00
1996	Not made		

REDBANK LONG PADDOCK ★★★★

1985	6	Now	$28.00
1986	7	Now	$30.00
1987	6	Now	$24.00
1988	7	Now	$26.00
1989	6	Now	$20.00
1990	7	Now	$22.00
1991	6	Now	$17.50
1992	6	Now	$16.50
1993	6	Now	$15.00
1994	6	Now	$14.00
1995	6	Now	$13.00
1996	7	2000	$14.00
1997	7	2001	$13.00

REDBANK SALLY'S PADDOCK ★★★★★

1979	6	Now	$150.00
1980	7	Now	$165.00
1981	7	2010	$150.00
1982	6	2000	$120.00
1983	7	Now	$130.00
1984	6	Now	$100.00
1985	6	2000	$96.00
1986	7	2003	$100.00
1987	5	2001	$68.00
1988	7	2001	$90.00
1989	6	Now	$70.00
1990	7	2010	$76.00
1991	7	2020	$70.00
1992	6	2007	$56.00
1993	6	2008	$52.00
1994	6	2005	$48.00
1995	7	2009	$52.00
1996	7	2010	$48.00
1997	7	2015	$45.00
1998	7	2016	N/R

Redbank
Sally's Paddock
1983
Produced and bottled on the property
Redbank Valley Vineyards
Redbank, Victoria.
Australian Wine   11.2%   750 ml

Redbrook - see Evans and Tate Margaret River wines.

Redgate is a Margaret River producer owned and operated by the Ullinger family. Winemaker: Andrew Forsell.

REDGATE CABERNET FRANC ★★★★

1992	4	Now	$27.00
1993	5	Now	$31.00
1994	6	Now	$34.00
1995	7	2005	$37.00
1996	6	2006	$30.00

REDGATE CABERNET SAUVIGNON ★★★★

before 1985		Prior	
1985	6	Now	$60.00
1986	6	Now	$54.00
1987	6	Now	$50.00
1988	7	Now	$54.00
1989	5	Now	$37.00
1990	6	Now	$41.00
1991	6	2000	$38.00
1992	6	Now	$35.00
1993	5	2000	$27.00
1994	6	2004	$30.00
1995	7	2002	$32.00

REDGATE
of
MARGARET RIVER
Cabernet Sauvignon
1995
Grown, Produced and Bottled by
Redgate Wines Pty Ltd
Boodjidup Road, Margaret River
Western Australia
13% VOL.   PRODUCE OF AUSTRALIA   75cl

REDGATE CHARDONNAY ★★★★

1991	6	Now	$39.00
1992	7	Now	$43.00
1993	6	Now	$34.00

REDGATE
of
MARGARET RIVER
Chardonnay
1992
Redgate Wines Pty Ltd, Boodjidup Road
Margaret River, Western Australia
750ml PRODUCE OF AUSTRALIA ALC / VOL

1994	Not made		
1995	6	2000	$29.00
1996	6	2001	$27.00

REDGATE SAUVIGNON BLANC RESERVE ★★★

before 1992	Prior		
1992	6	Now	$29.00
1993	6	Now	$27.00
1994	Not made		
1995	6	Now	$23.00
1996	6	2000	$21.00
1997	6	2000	$20.00

Red Hill Estate is a recently established Mornington Peninsula vineyard producing a most agreeable Methode Champenoise as well as some finely crafted Burgundian styles. Winemaker: Jenny Bright.

RED HILL ESTATE CHARDONNAY ★★★★

1993	5	Now	$24.00
1994	6	Now	$27.00
1995	6	2002	$25.00
1996	6	2000	$23.00
1997	7	Now	$25.00

RED HILL ESTATE METHODE CHAMPENOISE ★★★★

1991	6	Now	$37.00
1992	5	Now	$29.00
1993	5	Now	$26.00
1994	6	Now	$29.00
1995	6	Now	$27.00
1996	7	Now	$30.00

RED HILL ESTATE PINOT NOIR ★★★★

1992	4	Now	$29.00
1993	4	Prior	
1994	4	Now	$25.00
1995	Not made		
1996	6	Now	$32.00
1997	7	2000	$35.00

Redman is one of the most respected names amongst the catalogue of established Coonawarra producers. Winemaker: Bruce Redman.

REDMAN CABERNET SAUVIGNON ★★★★

1975	6	Prior	
1976	7	Now	$110.00
1977	6	Prior	
1978	6	Prior	
1979	6	Now	$78.00
1980	7	Now	$84.00
1981	6	Now	$66.00

1982	6	Now	$62.00
1983	4	Prior	
1984	7	Now	$62.00
1985	5	Now	$41.00
1986	6	Now	$45.00
1987	7	Now	$49.00
1988	7	Now	$45.00
1989	5	2000	$30.00
1990	7	2002	$39.00
1991	6	2003	$31.00
1992	7	2003	$33.00
1993	7	2003	$31.00
1994	6	2004	$24.00
1995	5	2005	$19.00
1996	6	2006	$21.00
1997	6	2007	$19.50

REDMAN CABERNET/MERLOT ★★★★

1990	6	2000	$38.00
1991	6	2002	$35.00
1992	6	2003	$33.00
1993	7	2005	$35.00
1994	6	2005	$28.00
1995	6	2005	$26.00
1996	6	2006	$24.00

REDMAN SHIRAZ ★★★

1975	4	Prior	
1976	7	Now	$98.00
1977	5	Prior	
1978	4	Prior	
1979	4	Prior	
1980	6	Now	$62.00
1981	6	Now	$58.00
1982	6	Now	$52.00
1983	4	Prior	
1984	7	Now	$52.00
1985	5	Now	$35.00
1986	6	Now	$39.00
1987	5	Now	$30.00
1988	7	Now	$39.00
1989	6	Now	$31.00
1990	7	Now	$33.00
1991	6	2000	$26.00
1992	6	2000	$24.00
1993	7	2001	$26.00
1994	6	2002	$21.00
1995	4	2000	$13.00
1996	6	2004	$18.00
1997	6	2005	$16.50

Renmano is an old Riverland label now owned and operated by BRL Hardy.
Winemakers: Ann-Marie Wasley and Fiona Donald.

RENMANO CHAIRMAN'S SELECTION CABERNET ★★

before 1990	Prior		
1990	6	Now	$15.00
1991	6	Now	$14.00
1992	6	Now	$13.00
1993	5	Now	$10.00
1994	6	Now	$11.00

RENMANO CHAIRMAN'S SELECTION CHARDONNAY ★★

before 1991	Prior		
1991	7	Now	$18.50
1992	7	Now	$17.00
1993	5	Now	$11.50
1994	5	Now	$10.50
1995	6	Now	$11.50
1996	6	Now	$11.00

RENMANO CHAIRMAN'S SELECTION SHIRAZ ★★

1988	6	Now	$17.00
1989	6	Now	$16.00
1990	6	Now	$14.50
1991	7	Now	$16.00
1992	6	Now	$12.50
1993	5	Now	$9.75
1994	6	Now	$11.00

Reynella - see Chateau Reynella.

Reynolds Yarraman is near Muswellbrook in the Upper Hunter Valley. The wines are vinified in a rebuilt 1837 sandstone winery. Winemaker: Jon Reynolds.

REYNOLDS CABERNET SAUVIGNON (ORANGE) ★★★

1994	5	Now	$26.00
1995	6	Now	$29.00
1996	6	2000	$27.00
1997	7	2001	$29.00

REYNOLDS CHARDONNAY ★★★

1989	6	Now	$32.00
1990	Not made		
1991	6	Now	$27.00
1992	5	Now	$21.00
1993	5	Now	$19.50
1994	5	Now	$18.00
1995	5	Now	$16.50
1996	6	Now	$18.50
1997	6	2000	$17.00

REYNOLDS CHARDONNAY (ORANGE) ★★★

1995	6	Now	$22.00
1996	6	Now	$20.00
1996	6	Now	$19.00

REYNOLDS MERLOT/ CABERNET (HUNTER/ORANGE) ★★★★

1988	7	Now	$38.00
1989	6	Now	$30.00
1990	Not made		
1991	5	Now	$21.00
1992	5	Now	$19.50
1993	5	Now	$18.00
1994	6	Now	$20.00
1995	6	Now	$19.00
1996	7	Now	$20.00
1997	6	2000	$16.00

REYNOLDS SEMILLON ★★★★

1989	6	Now	$26.00
1990	Not made		
1991	7	Now	$26.00
1992	7	Now	$24.00
1993	6	Now	$19.50
1994	5	Now	$15.00
1995	5	2001	$13.50
1996	7	2002	$18.00
1997	7	2003	$16.50

REYNOLDS SHIRAZ ★★★

1993	5	Now	$22.00
1994	6	Now	$25.00
1995	7	Now	$27.00
1996	6	Now	$21.00
1997	6	Now	$19.50
1998	7	2000	$21.00

Ribbon Vale Estate, *a very long, very narrow vineyard at Margaret River, has a small range of emphatic wines. Winemaker: Mike Davies.*

RIBBON VALE CABERNET/MERLOT ★★★

1986	5	Now	$34.00
1987	5	Now	$31.00
1988	6	Now	$35.00
1989	Not made		
1990	6	Now	$30.00
1991	6	Now	$27.00
1992	Not made		
1993	7	Now	$27.00
1994	7	Now	$25.00
1995	7	Now	$24.00

RIBBON VALE MERLOT ★★★

before 1991		Prior	
1991	6	Now	$28.00
1992	5	Now	$22.00
1993	6	Now	$24.00
1994	7	Now	$26.00
1995	6	Now	$21.00

RIBBON VALE SAUVIGNON BLANC ★★★

before 1993		Prior	
1993	7	Now	$28.00
1994	6	Now	$22.00
1995	6	Now	$20.00
1996	7	Now	$22.00
1997	7	Now	$20.00

RIBBON VALE SEMILLON ★★★★

before 1993		Prior	
1993	6	Now	$24.00
1994	6	Now	$22.00
1995	5	Now	$17.50
1996	6	2001	$19.50
1997	7	2002	$21.00

RIBBON VALE WOOD MATURED SEMILLON ★★★★

1988	5	Now	$31.00
1989	5	Now	$28.00
1990	5	Now	$26.00
1991	Not made		
1992	6	Now	$27.00
1993	Not made		
1994	6	Now	$23.00
1995	6	Now	$21.00
1996	7	Now	$23.00
1997	6	2000	$18.50

Richard Hamilton is a growing McLaren Vale label owned by the Hamilton wine Group with 50 hectares under vine. Winemaker: Ralph Fowler.

RICHARD HAMILTON CABERNET SAUVIGNON "HUT BLOCK" ★★★★

before 1986		Prior	
1986	5	Now	$47.00
1987	4	Prior	
1988	4	Prior	
1989	Not made		
1990	6	Now	$42.00
1991	6	Now	$39.00
1992	5	Now	$30.00
1993	5	Now	$27.00
1994	6	2001	$31.00

1995	5	2000	$23.00
1996	7	2002	$31.00
1997	6	2003	$24.00

RICHARD HAMILTON CHARDONNAY ★★★★

before 1986		Prior	
1986	6	Now	$52.00
1987	5	Prior	
1988	3	Prior	
1989	4	Prior	
1990	5	Prior	
1991	6	Now	$36.00
1992	4	Now	$22.00
1993	5	Now	$25.00
1994	6	Now	$28.00
1995	6	2000	$26.00
1996	7	2002	$28.00
1997	6	2001	$22.00

RICHARD HAMILTON GRENACHE/SHIRAZ
"BURTON'S VINEYARD" ★★★★★

1991	5	Now	$60.00
1992	4	Now	$44.00
1993	5	Now	$50.00
1994	6	2001	$56.00
1995	6	2000	$52.00
1996	7	2003	$56.00

RICHARD HAMILTON OLD VINE
SHIRAZ ★★★★★

1990	6	Now	$68.00
1991	6	Now	$64.00
1992	5	Now	$49.00
1993	6	Now	$54.00
1994	7	2002	$58.00
1995	6	2001	$47.00
1996	7	2003	$50.00

Richmond Grove is a Barossa Valley based operation within the giant Orlando Wyndham group.
Winemaker: John Vickery.

RICHMOND GROVE BAROSSA RIESLING ★★★★★

1994	7	Now	$16.50
1995	6	Now	$13.00
1996	7	2001	$14.00
1997	7	2001	$13.00
1998	7	2002	$12.00

RICHMOND GROVE BAROSSA
SEMILLON ★★★★

1995	5	Now	$12.00
1996	7	Now	$15.50
1997	6	Now	$12.00
1998	7	2001	$13.00

250

RICHMOND GROVE BAROSSA SHIRAZ ★★★

1993	6	Now	$17.50
1994	7	2000	$19.00
1995	7	2000	$17.50
1996	7	2002	$16.50

RICHMOND GROVE CABERNET / MERLOT ★★★

1989	4	Now	$11.50
1990	4	Now	$10.50
1991	7	Now	$17.50
1992	6	Now	$13.50
1993	6	Now	$12.50
1994	6	Now	$11.50
1995	7	Now	$12.50
1996	7	2001	$11.50

RICHMOND GROVE COONAWARRA CABERNET SAUVIGNON ★★★

1992	6	Now	$20.00
1993	6	Now	$18.50
1994	7	2000	$20.00
1995	6	2001	$16.00
1996	7	2002	$17.50

RICHMOND GROVE COWRA CHARDONNAY ★★

1992	6	Now	$11.50
1993	6	Now	$10.50
1994	6	Now	$10.00
1995	7	Now	$10.50
1996	6	Now	$8.50
1997	7	Now	$9.25
1998	7	2000	$8.50

RICHMOND GROVE COWRA VERDELHO ★★

1992	5	Now	$9.25
1993	6	Now	$10.00
1994	7	Now	$11.00
1995	6	Now	$8.75
1996	7	Now	$9.50
1998	7	2000	$8.75

RICHMOND GROVE FRENCH CASK CHARDONNAY ★★★

1988	3	Now	$11.50
1989	4	Now	$14.00
1990	5	Now	$16.50
1991	6	Now	$18.50
1992	5	Now	$14.00
1993	6	Now	$15.50
1994	7	Now	$17.00
1995	5	Now	$11.00

1996	6	Now	$12.50
1997	7	2002	$13.50
1998	7	2001	$12.50

RICHMOND GROVE HUNTER VALLEY
SEMILLON/CHARDONNAY ★★

1987	4	Now	$14.50
1988	4	Now	$13.50
1989	3	Now	$9.25
1990	4	Now	$11.50
1991	4	Now	$10.50
1992	4	Now	$9.75
1993	5	Now	$11.50
1994	6	Now	$12.50
1995	7	Now	$13.50
1996	6	Now	$11.00
1997	7	Now	$11.50
1998	7	2000	$11.00

RICHMOND GROVE OAK MATURED CHABLIS ★★

1989	4	Now	$11.00
1990	5	Now	$12.50
1991	6	Now	$14.00
1992	6	Now	$13.00
1993	6	Now	$12.00
1994	7	Now	$13.00
1995	5	Now	$8.75
1996	6	Now	$9.75
1997	6	Now	$9.00
1998	6	2000	$8.25

RICHMOND GROVE WATERVALE
RIESLING ★★★★★

1994	6	Now	$14.00
1995	7	2000	$15.50
1996	7	2001	$14.00
1997	7	2002	$13.00
1998	7	2003	$12.00

Riddoch Estate *is part of the Wingara Group who also own Katnook, Deakin Estate and Sunnycliff. Since 1990 all Riddoch wines have been from Coonawarra fruit. Winemaker: Wayne Stehbens.*

RIDDOCH CABERNET SAUVIGNON
(/MERLOT) ★★★★

1982	6	Now	$43.00
1983	5	Now	$33.00
1984	5	Now	$31.00
1985	5	Now	$29.00
1986	6	Now	$32.00

1987	5	Now	$24.00
1988	6	Now	$27.00
1989	5	Now	$21.00
1990	6	Now	$23.00
1991	5	Now	$18.00
1992	6	Now	$20.00
1993	5	Now	$15.50

RIDDOCH CABERNET/SHIRAZ ★★★

1982	6	Now	$58.00
1983	5	Now	$44.00
1984	5	Now	$41.00
1985	5	Now	$38.00
1986	6	Now	$42.00
1987	5	Now	$32.00
1988	6	Now	$36.00
1989	5	Now	$28.00
1990	6	Now	$31.00
1991	5	Now	$24.00
1992	6	Now	$26.00
1993	5	Now	$20.00
1994	6	2001	$23.00
1995	5	2001	$17.50
1996	6	2002	$19.50

RIDDOCH CHARDONNAY ★★★★

1983	4	Prior	
1984	5	Now	$37.00
1985	5	Now	$34.00
1986	6	Now	$38.00
1987	5	Now	$29.00
1988	5	Now	$27.00
1989	5	Now	$25.00
1990	6	Now	$28.00
1991	5	Now	$21.00
1992	6	Now	$24.00
1993	6	Now	$22.00
1994	6	Now	$20.00
1995	5	Now	$16.00
1996	6	Now	$17.50

RIDDOCH SHIRAZ ★★★★

1990	5	Now	$24.00
1991	6	Now	$27.00
1992	6	Now	$25.00
1993	5	Now	$19.50
1994	6	Bow	$19.50
1995	5	Now	$17.00
1996	7	2000	$22.00

Robard and Butler source their grapes from around the world. It is the New Zealand wines which interest us here, all marketed by Corbans Wines, who own the label. Winemaker: Daniel Alcorso.

ROBARD AND BUTLER CHARDONNAY ★★★

before 1990	Prior		
1990	7	Now	NZ$25.00
1991	7	Now	NZ$23.00
1992	6	Now	NZ$18.50
1993	Not made		
1994	Not made		
1995	7	Now	NZ$17.00
1996	6	2000	NZ$13.50
1997	4	Now	NZ$8.25
1998	6	2000	NZ$11.50

ROBARD AND BUTLER RIESLING ★★★

before 1992	Prior		
1992	5	Now	NZ$19.00
1993	6	Now	NZ$20.00
1994	6	Now	NZ$19.00
1995	6	Now	NZ$18.00

No longer made.

The Robson Vineyard - see Murray Robson Wines.

The Rochford Winery is a very small producer in Victoria's Macedon region. Winemaker: David Creed.

ROCHFORD CABERNET SAUVIGNON ★★★★

1987	3	Prior	
1988	4	Now	$42.00
1989	5	Now	$48.00
1990	5	Now	$45.00
1991	6	Now	$50.00
1992	5	Now	$38.00
1993	5	Now	$35.00
1994	5	2000	$33.00
1995	6	2001	$37.00
1996	5	2002	$28.00

ROCHFORD CHARDONNAY ★★★★

1995	5	2001	$26.00
1996	5	2000	$24.00
1997	6	2002	$27.00

ROCHFORD PINOT NOIR ★★★★

1989	3	Now	$37.00
1990	5	Now	$56.00
1991	3	Now	$31.00
1992	6	Now	$58.00
1993	6	Now	$54.00

1994	7	2003	$58.00
1995	5	2000	$39.00
1996	6	2004	$43.00
1997	6	2005	$40.00

Rockford Wines *are Barossa Valley makers of a range of improbably generous wines from unirrigated vineyards. The makers apparently prefer not to supply vintage ratings. Winemaker: Robert O'Callaghan.*

| ROCKFORD BASKET PRESS SHIRAZ | ★★★★ |
| ROCKFORD CABERNET SAUVIGNON | ★★★★ |

Romany Rye - see Eppalock Ridge.

Rosemount *is a moderately large Upper Hunter producer of a large and eminently successful range of wines. Their Chardonnays are particularly popular. Winemaker: Philip Shaw.*

ROSEMOUNT BALMORAL
SYRAH ★★★★★

1991	7	2010	$82.00
1992	7	2015	$76.00
1993	6	2010	$60.00
1994	7	2015	$64.00
1995	7	2020	$60.00
1996	7	2025	$56.00

ROSEMOUNT ESTATE CABERNET SAUVIGNON
(DIAMOND LABEL) ★★★

before 1990	Prior	
1990	7	2001	$31.00
1991	6	2001	$24.00
1992	6	2002	$23.00
1993	5	2001	$17.50
1994	6	2002	$19.50
1995	6	2006	$18.00
1996	6	2007	$16.50
1997	7	2020	$18.00

ROSEMOUNT ESTATE CHARDONNAY
(DIAMOND LABEL) ★★★

1986	6	Now	$39.00
1987	7	Now	$42.00
1988	6	Now	$34.00
1989	5	Now	$26.00
1990	6	2000	$29.00
1991	6	2001	$27.00
1992	6	2000	$25.00
1993	6	2000	$23.00
1994	6	2005	$21.00
1995	5	2000	$16.50

1996	7	2006	$21.00
1997	6	2006	$17.00
1998	7	2007	$18.00

ROSEMOUNT ESTATE SHIRAZ
(DIAMOND LABEL) ★★★

1986	6	Now	$37.00
1987	6	Now	$34.00
1988	5	Now	$26.00
1989	5	Now	$24.00
1990	6	Now	$27.00
1991	6	Now	$25.00
1992	6	2000	$23.00
1993	7	2001	$25.00
1994	6	2001	$20.00
1995	5	2002	$15.50
1996	7	2005	$20.00
1997	6	2007	$16.00
1998	7	2009	N/R

ROSEMOUNT GIANTS CREEK
(HUNTER VALLEY CHARDONNAY) ★★★★

1987	7	2002	$56.00
1988	6	2002	$45.00
1989	6	2001	$42.00
1990	6	2005	$39.00
1991	5	2000	$30.00
1992	5	2001	$27.00
1993	6	2004	$30.00
1994	7	2010	$33.00
1995	6	2020	$26.00
1996	7	2015	$28.00

ROSEMOUNT GSM
(GRENACHE/SHIRAZ/MOURVEDRE) ★★★★

1994	7	2000	$36.00
1995	6	2000	$29.00
1996	7	2002	$31.00

ROSEMOUNT ORANGE VINEYARD
CABERNET SAUVIGNON ★★★

1993	6	2000	$24.00
1994	6	2002	$22.00
1995	7	2005	$24.00

ROSEMOUNT ORANGE VINEYARD
CHARDONNAY ★★★

1992	6	Prior	
1993	6	2007	$25.00
1994	6	2008	$24.00
1995	7	2009	$25.00
1996	7	2012	$24.00

ROSEMOUNT ROXBURGH CHARDONNAY ★★★★★

1982	7	2005	$195.00
1983	6	Prior	
1984	7	2001	$165.00
1985	6	2002	$130.00
1986	6	2002	$120.00
1987	7	2010	$130.00
1988	4	2002	$70.00
1989	5	2002	$82.00
1990	7	2006	$105.00
1991	6	2007	$84.00
1992	6	2009	$78.00
1993	6	2009	$72.00
1994	5	2000	$56.00
1995	5	2005	$50.00
1996	7	2010	$66.00
1997	No data		
1998	7	2008	$56.00

ROSEMOUNT SHOW RESERVE CHARDONNAY

★★★★

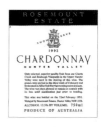

1980	6	Prior	
1981	7	2001	$105.00
1982	7	2008	$100.00
1983	5	Prior	
1984	6	2004	$74.00
1985	7	2000	$80.00
1986	6	2000	$62.00
1987	7	2012	$68.00
1988	6	2002	$54.00
1989	6	2003	$50.00
1990	5	2004	$38.00
1991	6	2001	$43.00
1992	6	2007	$40.00
1993	7	2005	$43.00
1994	5	2002	$28.00
1995	5	2006	$26.00
1996	7	2010	$34.00
1997	7	2015	$31.00

ROSEMOUNT SHOW RESERVE COONAWARRA CABERNET SAUVIGNON ★★★★★

1981	5	Now	$86.00
1982	7	2002	$110.00
1983	5	Now	$74.00
1984	5	Prior	
1985	7	2004	$88.00
1986	6	2005	$70.00
1987	5	2006	$54.00

1988	6	2006	$60.00
1989	7	2010	$64.00
1990	7	2002	$60.00
1991	7	2009	$56.00
1992	6	2011	$44.00
1993	5	2004	$34.00
1994	7	2015	$44.00
1995	5	205	$29.00
1996	6	2015	$33.00

ROSEMOUNT SHOW RESERVE HUNTER VALLEY SEMILLON ★★★★

1981	7	Now	$86.00
1982	7	2003	$80.00
1983	Not made		
1984	Not made		
1985	Not made		
1986	7	2001	$58.00
1987	7	2001	$54.00
1988	5	2000	$36.00
1989	7	2004	$46.00
1990	6	2006	$37.00
1991	6	2011	$34.00
1992	Not made		
1993	Not made		
1994	Not made		
1995	5	2010	$21.00
1996	7	2016	$27.00

ROSEMOUNT SHOW RESERVE MCLAREN VALE SHIRAZ ★★★★

1989	6	2008	$40.00
1990	5	2010	$31.00
1991	7	2015	$40.00
1992	Not made		
1993	Not made		
1994	7	2010	$32.00
1995	6	2008	$25.00
1996	7	2015	$27.00

ROSEMOUNT TRADITIONAL (CABERNET/MERLOT/PETIT VERDOT) ★★★★

1988	6	2002	$46.00
1989	5	2000	$35.00
1990	6	2002	$39.00
1991	5	2000	$30.00
1992	7	2006	$39.00
1993	6	2006	$31.00
1994	6	2012	$29.00
1995	6	2005	$27.00
1996	7	2010	$29.00

The Rothbury Estate, begun as a purist Pokolbin producer of consistently reliable wines, expanded to be owners of Baileys, Saltram and St Huberts. They are now part of Mildara Blass. Winemaker: Adam Eggins.

The ROTHBURY ESTATE BROKENBACK CHARDONNAY

★★★★

before 1988	Prior		
1988	5	Now	$29.00
1989	6	Now	$33.00
1990	5	Now	$25.00
1991	6	Now	$28.00
1992	7	2000	$30.00
1993	6	Now	$24.00
1994	7	2000	$26.00
1995	Not made		
1996	6	2001	$19.00
1997	6	2000	$18.00

The ROTHBURY ESTATE BROKENBACK SEMILLON

★★★★

before 1984	Prior		
1984	7	Now	$62.00
1985	4	Now	$33.00
1986	7	Now	$54.00
1987	5	Now	$36.00
1988	4	Now	$26.00
1989	6	2000	$37.00
1990	6	2010	$34.00
1991	5	2000	$26.00
1992	7	2010	$34.00
1993	5	2000	$22.00
1994	6	2020	$25.00
1995	5	2000	$19.50
1996	6	2002	$21.00
1997	7	2005	$23.00
1998	7	2005	$21.00

The ROTHBURY ESTATE BROKENBACK SHIRAZ

★★★★

before 1983	Prior		
1983	7	Now	$68.00
1984	4	Prior	
1985	6	Prior	
1986	7	2000	$54.00
1987	7	2000	$50.00
1988	5	Now	$33.00
1989	5	Now	$31.00
1990	5	Now	$29.00
1991	7	2010	$37.00

1992	No data		
1993	5	2000	$23.00
1994	6	2005	$25.00
1995	7	2005	$27.00
1996	7	2005	$25.00

The ROTHBURY ESTATE COWRA CHARDONNAY ★★★

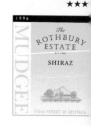

before 1993	Prior		
1993	5	Now	$16.00
1994	6	2000	$18.00
1995	5	Now	$14.00
1996	6	Now	$15.50
1997	7	2000	$16.50
1998	6	2001	$13.00

The ROTHBURY ESTATE SHIRAZ ★★★

before 1987	Prior		
1987	5	Now	$25.00
1988	4	Now	$18.50
1989	5	Now	$21.00
1990	4	Now	$16.00
1991	7	2010	$26.00
1992	Not made		
1993	5	2000	$16.00
1994	6	2005	$17.50
1995	7	2005	$19.00
1996	6	2004	$15.00
1997	6	2001	$14.00

Rotherhythe is a small producer in Tasmania's Tamar Valley. Winemaker: Steve Hyde.

ROTHERHYTHE CABERNET SAUVIGNON ★★★

1986	5	Now	$43.00
1987	Not made		
1988	6	Now	$44.00
1989	5	Now	$34.00
1990	6	Now	$38.00
1991	6	Now	$35.00
1992	7	Now	$38.00
1993	6	Now	$30.00
1994	6	2001	$28.00
1995	5	Now	$21.00

ROTHERHYTHE PINOT NOIR ★★★★

before 1988	Prior		
1988	5	Now	$44.00
1989	6	Now	$49.00
1990	5	Now	$37.00
1991	6	Now	$42.00
1992	6	Now	$39.00

1993	5	Now	$30.00
1994	7	2000	$39.00
1995	6	2000	$31.00

Rouge Homme is a long established and respected Coonawarra based maker owned by Southcorp. Vinemaker: Paul Gordon.

ROUGE HOMME CABERNET SAUVIGNON ★★★

before 1984		Prior	
1984	6	Now	$40.00
1985	7	Now	$43.00
1986	7	Now	$40.00
1987	5	Now	$26.00
1988	6	Prior	
1989	5	Prior	
1990	7	Now	$29.00
1991	7	Now	$27.00
1992	6	Now	$21.00
1993	6	Now	$20.00
1994	7	Now	$21.00
1995	6	2000	$17.00
1996	7	2002	$18.50
1997	7	2006	N/R
1998	7	2007	N/R

ROUGE HOMME PINOT NOIR ★★★

1983	6	Now	$54.00
1984	4	Prior	
1985	6	Now	$46.00
1986	5	Now	$35.00
1987	5	Now	$33.00
1988	5	Now	$30.00
1989	5	Now	$28.00
1990	5	Now	$26.00
1991	6	Now	$29.00
1992	5	Now	$22.00
1993	6	Now	$25.00
1994	7	Now	$27.00
1995	6	Now	$21.00
1996	6	Now	$19.50
1997	6	2000	$18.00

ROUGE HOMME RICHARDSON'S WHITE BLOCK CHARDONNAY ★★★

before 1989		Prior	
1989	5	Now	$18.50
1990	6	Now	$21.00
1991	6	Now	$19.50
1992	5	Now	$15.00
1993	6	Now	$16.50

1994	6	Now	$15.00
1995	6	Now	$14.00
1996	7	Now	$15.00

ROUGE HOMME RICHARDSON'S RED (CABERNET/MERLOT/MALBEC/FRANC) ★★★

1992	5	Now	$17.50
1993	7	2000	$23.00
1994	7	2002	$21.00
1995	6	2001	$16.50
1996	7	2003	$18.00
1997	7	2003	N/R

ROUGE HOMME SHIRAZ/CABERNET ★★★

1980	7	Now	$60.00
1981	5	Prior	
1982	5	Now	$37.00
1983	Not made		
1984	5	Now	$31.00
1985	6	Now	$35.00
1986	6	Now	$32.00
1987	5	Now	$25.00
1988	5	Now	$23.00
1989	4	Prior	
1990	7	Now	$27.00
1991	7	Now	$25.00
1992	6	Now	$20.00
1993	6	2000	$19.00
1994	7	2000	$20.00
1995	6	2001	$16.00
1996	7	2003	$17.50
1997	7	2003	$16.00
1998	7	2004	N/R

St Hallett is an old Barossa Valley producer whose rebuilt vineyards and new winery equipment have achieved for it an esteemed position as one of the valley's best makers. Winemaker: Stuart Blackwell.

ST HALLETT CABERNET/MERLOT ★★★★

before 1991	Prior		
1991	6	Now	$26.00
1992	7	Now	$28.00
1993	6	Now	$22.00
1994	5	Now	$17.00
1995	5	Now	$16.00
1996	7	2002	$21.00
1997	6	2000	N/R

ST HALLETT CHARDONNAY ★★★

before 1988	Prior		
1988	6	Now	$40.00
1989	6	Now	$37.00

1990	6	Now	$34.00
1991	6	Now	$31.00
1992	5	Now	$24.00
1993	6	Now	$27.00
1994	6	2000	$25.00
1995	5	2000	$19.00
1996	6	2003	$21.00
1997	6	2004	$20.00
1998	6	2005	$18.50

ST HALLETT OLD BLOCK SHIRAZ ★★★★★

1980	3	Prior	
1981	Not made		
1982	5	Now	$90.00
1983	6	Now	$100.00
1984	6	Now	$92.00
1985	6	Now	$86.00
1986	7	Now	$92.00
1987	5	Now	$60.00
1988	6	Now	$68.00
1989	5	Now	$52.00
1990	6	Now	$58.00
1991	7	2002	$62.00
1992	5	2000	$41.00
1993	6	2004	$46.00
1994	6	2005	$43.00
1995	6	2005	$39.00
1996	7	2010	$43.00
1997	6	2010	N/R
1998	7	2015	N/R

St Huberts (owned by Mildara Blass) is a small vineyard in the Yarra Valley renowned for the quality of its Cabernet fruit. Winemaker: Fiona Purnell.

ST HUBERTS CABERNET SAUVIGNON ★★★★

before 1979	Prior		
1979	7	Now	$92.00
1980	6	Now	$74.00
1981	6	Now	$68.00
1982	7	Now	$74.00
1983	Not made		
1984	6	Now	$54.00
1985	5	Now	$42.00
1986	5	Now	$39.00
1987	Not made		
1988	6	Now	$40.00
1989	Not made		
1990	7	Now	$40.00
1991	6	2004	$31.00
1992	6	2005	$29.00

1993	6	2006	$27.00
1994	7	2008	$29.00
1995	5	2006	$19.50
1996	6	2006	$21.00

ST HUBERTS CHARDONNAY ★★★★

before 1987		Prior	
1987	6	Now	$39.00
1988	6	Now	$36.00
1989	5	Now	$28.00
1990	7	Now	$36.00
1991	5	Now	$24.00
1992	6	Now	$26.00
1993	6	Now	$24.00
1994	7	Now	$26.00
1995	7	2000	$24.00
1996	6	2001	$19.50

ST HUBERTS PINOT NOIR ★★★★

before 1989		Prior	
1989	7	Now	$52.00
1990	7	Now	$48.00
1991	5	Now	$31.00
1992	5	Now	$29.00
1993	5	Now	$27.00
1994	5	Now	$25.00
1995	6	Now	$28.00
1996	6	2000	$26.00
1997	6	2002	$24.00
1998	7	2003	$26.00

St Leonards, part of All Saints Estate, is the label under
which the best of the Estate's wines are released.
Winemaker: Peter Brown.

ST LEONARDS CARLYLE CHARDONNAY ★★★★

1992	6	2000	$27.00
1993	Not made		
1996	6	2001	$23.00
1997	6	2001	$22.00

ST LEONARDS WAHGUNYAH
SHIRAZ ★★★★★

1994	7	2003	$40.00
1995	7	2005	$37.00
1996	7	2004	$35.00

St Mary's is a Penola (near Coonawarra) vineyard and
winery. Winemaker: Barry Mulligan.

ST MARY'S CHARDONNAY

1994	5	Prior	★★★
1995	5	Now	$15.50
1996	6	2000	$17.50
1997	6	2002	$16.00

ST MARY'S HOUSE BLOCK
CABERNET SAUVIGNON ★★★

1990	6	Now	$40.00
1991	6	2000	$37.00
1992	5	2000	$29.00
1993	5	2000	$26.00
1994	6	2003	$29.00
1995	Not made		
1996	5	2002	$21.00
1997	6	2005	$23.00

ST MARY'S RIESLING ★★★

| before 1996 | Prior | | |
| 1996 | 6 | 2001 | $12.00 |

ST MARY'S SHIRAZ ★★★

1993	5	2000	$25.00
1994	6	2006	$28.00
1995	Not made		
1996	5	2003	$20.00
1997	Not made		

St Nesbit is a New Zealand (South Auckland) maker producing a very fine dry red from Cabernet Sauvignon, Cabernet Franc and Merlot.
Winemaker: Tony Molloy.

ST NESBIT ★★★★★

1984	6	Now	NZ$98.00
1985	6	Now	NZ$90.00
1986	5	Prior	
1987	7	Now	NZ$90.00
1988	5	Now	NZ$60.00
1989	7	2005	NZ$78.00
1990	7	2005	NZ$72.00
1991	7	2005	NZ$66.00
1992	Not made		
1993	Not made		
No data since 1993			

Saint Clair Estate were poineers to the Marlborough wine industry in New Zealand, planting one of the first private vineyards in the valley in 1978. Winemaker: Kim Crawford.

SAINT CLAIR CHARDONNAY
(MARLBOROUGH) ★★★

1994	6	Now	N/R
1995	5	Prior	
1996	6	Now	N/R
1997	6	Now	N/R

SAINT CLAIR RIESLING ★★★

before 1996	Prior		
1996	6	Now	N/R
1997	6	Now	N/R

SAINT CLAIR SAUVIGNON BLANC ★★★

before 1996		Prior	
1996	6	Now	NZ$16.00
1997	6	Now	NZ$15.00

Salitage is an impressive maker from the Pemberton region of Western Australia. The name is derived from the first two letters of each of the names of the Horgan family's four children - Sarah, Lisa, Tamara and Gerard.
Winemaker: Patrick Coutts.

SALITAGE CABERNET BLEND ★★★★

1995	5	2002	$34.00
1996	5	2004	$32.00
1997	Not made		

SALITAGE CHARDONNAY ★★★★

1993	5	Now	$39.00
1994	6	Now	$43.00
1995	4	Now	$26.00
1996	5	2001	$31.00
1997	6	2002	$34.00

SALITAGE PINOT NOIR ★★★★★

1993	5	Now	$48.00
1994	5	2000	$44.00
1995	4	2000	$33.00
1996	5	Now	$38.00
1997	5	2002	$35.00

Salisbury is the label under which the lower priced range of varietal wines are released by Alambie Wines of Irymple in North Western Victoria.
Winemaker: Bob Shields.

Sally's Paddock - see Redbank

Saltram, an historic name in Australian wine, has been perhaps a little torpid for a decade or so. The operation is now owned by Mildara Blass, we can expect a higher profile to be shown. The famous "Mamre Brook" label has now spli into two wines - a Cabernet and a Shiraz.
Winemaker: Nigel Dolan.

SALTRAM MAMRE BROOK
BAROSSA VALLEY CABERNET ★★★

1996	7	2004	$20.00
1997	6	2004	$16.50

SALTRAM MAMRE BROOK BAROSSA VALLEY SHIRAZ

★★★

1996	7	2003	$20.00
1997	6	2003	$16.50

SALTRAM MAMRE BROOK CABERNET SAUVIGNON/SHIRAZ

★★★

1980	5	Now	$44.00
1981	5	Now	$41.00
1982	6	Now	$46.00
1983	6	Now	$42.00
1984	6	Now	$39.00
1985	7	Now	$42.00
1986	7	Now	$39.00
1987	7	Now	$36.00
1988	5	Now	$24.00
1989	7	Now	$31.00
1990	5	Now	$20.00
1991		Not made	
1992		Not made	
1993	6	Now	$19.50
1994	6	Now	$18.00
1995	6	2000	$17.00

Not made as a blend after 1995.

SALTRAM MAMRE BROOK CHARDONNAY

★★★

before 1988		Prior	
1988	7	Now	$38.00
1989	7	Now	$35.00
1990	7	Now	$33.00
1991		No data	
1992		No data	
1993	7	Now	$26.00
1994	7	Now	$24.00
1995	6	2000	$19.00
1996	7	2001	$20.00
1997	5	Now	$13.50
1998	7	2001	$17.50

SALTRAM NUMBER ONE SHIRAZ

★★★★★

1994	7	2004	$42.00
1995	6	2005	$34.00
1996	7	2008	$36.00

Sandalford is one of the Swan Valley's bigger producers. They also own a vineyard at Margaret River, which produces their best wines. Winemaker: Bill Crappsley.

SANDALFORD CAVERSHAM ESTATE CABERNET/SHIRAZ

★★

before 1994		Prior	
1994	6	2000	$16.00
1995	5	Prior	
1996	6	2001	$14.00
1997	5	2000	$10.50

267

SANDALFORD CAVERSHAM ESTATE VERDELHO ★★

before 1995		Prior	
1995	5	2000	$12.50
1996	6	2000	$13.50
1997	6	2001	$12.50
1998	7	2004	$14.00

SANDALFORD 1840 COLLECTION CABERNET/MERLOT ★★★

before 1996		Prior	
1996	7	2001	$18.00
1997	6	2000	$14.00

SANDALFORD 1840 COLLECTION CHARDONNAY ★★

1994	4	Prior	
1995	7	2005	$23.00
1996	5	2000	$15.00
1997	6	2005	$16.50

SANDALFORD 1840 COLLECTION SEMILLON/SAUVIGNON BLANC

before 1995		Prior	★★
1995	5	2000	$13.50
1996	6	2000	$15.00

SANDALFORD MOUNT BARKER./MARGARET RIVER CABERNET SAUVIGNON ★★★

before 1993		Prior	
1993	5	Now	$24.00
1994	6	2000	$27.00
1995	6	2001	$25.00
1996	6	2002	$23.00

SANDALFORD MOUNT BARKER./ MARGARET RIVER CHARDONNAY

1992	5	Prior	★★★★
1993	6	2004	$26.00
1994	6	2002	$24.00
1995	7	2004	$26.00
1996	6	2004	$21.00
1997	7	2007	$22.00

SANDALFORD MOUNT BARKER/ MARGARET RIVER RIESLING ★★★

before 1994		Prior	
1994	6	2000	$23.00
1995	6	2005	$21.00
1996	7	2006	$23.00
1997	5	2001	$15.50
1998	5	2002	$14.00

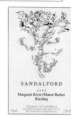

SANDALFORD MARGARET RIVER (/MOUNT BARKER) SHIRAZ ★★★★

before 1993		Prior	
1993	5	2000	$20.00
1994	6	2004	$22.00
1995	7	2005	$24.00
1996	6	2004	$19.00

SANDALFORD MARGARET RIVER VERDELHO ★★★

before 1995		Prior	
1995	5	Now	$19.50
1996	7	2004	$25.00
1997	6	2005	$20.00
1998	6	2006	$19.00

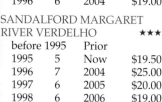

Sandstone Wines is the label established by Margaret River based winemaking consultants Mike and Jan Davies. Winemakers: Jan and Mike Davies.

SANDSTONE CABERNET SAUVIGNON ★★★

1988	6	Prior	
1989	6	2001	$32.00
1990	6	2000	$30.00
1991	7	2001	$32.00
1992	7	2002	$30.00
1993	7	2003	$27.00
1994	5	Prior	
1995	6	2005	$20.00
1996	7	2005	$22.00

SANDSTONE SEMILLON ★★★★

before 1990		Prior	
1990	5	Now	$32.00
1991	5	2000	$30.00
1992	6	2000	$33.00
1993	6	2000	$30.00
1994	6	2000	$28.00
1995	7	2001	$30.00
1996	6	2002	$24.00
1997	7	2003	$26.00

Scarpantoni Estates are McLaren Flat producers with a good range of sensitively made wines.
Winemakers: Domenico Scarpantoni and Michael Filippo.

SCARPANTONI BLOCK 3 SHIRAZ ★★★

1980	5	Now	$48.00
1981	4	Now	$35.00
1982	5	Prior	
1983	5	Prior	
1984	4	Prior	
1985	5	Now	$33.00
1986	4	Prior	

1987	5	Now	$28.00
1988	6	2003	$31.00
1989	5	2000	$24.00
1990	7	2005	$31.00
1991	6	2005	$24.00
1992	6	2006	$23.00
1993	5	2005	$17.50
1994	6	2007	$19.50
1995	5	2007	$15.00
1996	7	2011	$19.50

SCARPANTONI CABERNET SAUVIGNON ★★★

before 1983		Prior	
1983	5	Now	$35.00
1984	5	Now	$32.00
1985	5	Now	$30.00
1986	6	2000	$33.00
1987	5	Now	$26.00
1988	6	2000	$28.00
1989	5	Now	$22.00
1990	6	2003	$24.00
1992	6	2003	$22.00
1993	5	2005	$17.50
1994	7	2006	$22.00
1995	6	2005	$18.00
1996	7	2006	$19.50

SCARPANTONI CHARDONNAY ★★★

before 1991		Prior	
1991	4	Now	$14.00
1992	5	Now	$16.00
1993	4	Now	$12.00
1994	4	Now	$11.00
1995	6	Now	$15.50
1996	7	Now	$16.50

SCARPANTONI SAUVIGNON BLANC ★★

before 1995		Prior	
1995	6	Now	$11.50
1996	7	Now	$12.50

Schinus, formerly "Schinus Molle", is the second label of
Dromana Estate, the wines often containing fruit not
necessarily from the Mornington Peninsula.
Winemaker: Garry Crittenden.

SCHINUS CABERNET ★★★

1987	5	Now	$22.00
1988	5	Now	$21.00
1989	5	Now	$19.50
1990	6	Now	$21.00
1991	7	Now	$23.00

1992	5	Now	$15.50
1993	5	Now	$14.00
1994	7	2000	$18.50

SCHINUS CHARDONNAY ★★★

1988	5	Now	$23.00
1989	5	Now	$21.00
1990	6	Now	$24.00
1991	6	Now	$22.00
1992	6	Now	$20.00
1993	5	Now	$15.50
1994	5	Now	$14.50
1995	6	Now	$16.00

SCHINUS SAUVIGNON BLANC ★★★

before 1992		Prior	
1992	7	Now	$21.00
1993	6	Now	$16.50
1994	6	Now	$15.50
1995	6	Now	$14.00

Scotchmans Hill on the Bellarine Peninsula (Geelong area) is a 24 hectare vineyard planted with Cabernet Franc, Chardonnay, Riesling and Pinot Noir. Winemaker: Robin Brockett.

SCOTCHMANS HILL CABERNET/MERLOT ★★★★

1990	6	Now	$37.00
1991	6	Now	$34.00
1992	6	Now	$31.00
1993	7	Now	$34.00
1994	6	2000	$27.00
1995	7	2001	$29.00
1996	5	2001	$19.50

SCOTCHMANS HILL CHARDONNAY ★★★★

1988	6	Now	$38.00
1989	5	Now	$29.00
1990	6	Now	$33.00
1991	7	Now	$35.00
1992	7	Now	$33.00
1993	6	Now	$26.00
1994	7	Now	$28.00
1995	6	Now	$22.00
1996	5	Now	$17.00
1997	7	2000	$22.00

SCOTCHMANS HILL PINOT NOIR ★★★★

1990	6	Now	$32.00
1991	7	Now	$34.00
1992	7	Now	$32.00
1993	5	Now	$21.00
1994	7	Now	$27.00
1995	7	Now	$25.00
1996	6	Now	$20.00
1997	6	2000	$18.50

SCOTCHMANS HILL RIESLING ★★★★

1989	7	Now	$24.00
1990	5	Now	$15.50
1991	7	Now	$20.00
1992	7	Now	$19.00
1993	Not made		
1994	6	Now	$14.00
1995	Not made		

SCOTCHMANS HILL
SAUVIGNON BLANC ★★★

1993	6	Now	$20.00
1994	7	Now	$22.00
1995	6	Now	$17.00
1996	7	Now	$18.50
1997	6	Now	$15.00

Seaview (part of the Southcorp group) owns a clutch of McLaren Vale vineyards producing a markedly popular range of wines. Winemaker: Steve Chapman.

SEAVIEW CABERNET SAUVIGNON ★★★

before 1990	Prior		
1990	6	Now	$22.00
1991	7	Now	$24.00
1992	6	Now	$19.00
1993	7	Now	$20.00
1994	6	Now	$16.50
1995	6	Now	$15.00
1996	7	2001	$16.50
1997	6	2001	$13.00

SEAVIEW CHARDONNAY ★★

before 1995	Prior		
1995	6	Now	$15.00
1996	6	Now	$13.50
1997	6	Now	$12.50
1998	6	Now	$12.00

SEAVIEW CHARDONNAY BRUT ★★★

1992	7	Prior	
1993	7	Now	$15.50
1994	6	Now	$12.50

SEAVIEW EDWARDS AND
CHAFFEY CHARDONNAY ★★★★

1994	6	Now	$31.00
1995	6	Now	$29.00
1996	7	2000	$31.00
1997	7	2001	$29.00
1998	6	202	$23.00

SEAVIEW EDWARDS AND CHAFFEY CABERNET SAUVIGNON ★★★★

1992	7	2000	$49.00
1993	Not made		
1994	6	2001	$36.00
1995	Not made		
1996	6	2003	$31.00

SEAVIEW EDWARDS AND CHAFFEY SHIRAZ ★★★★★

1992	7	2000	$52.00
1993	Not made		
1994	6	2001	$39.00
1995	6	2003	$36.00
1996	6	2004	$33.00

SEAVIEW PINOT NOIR/CHARDONNAY BRUT ★★★

1991	6	Prior	
1992	7	Now	$19.00
1993	7	Now	$17.50
1994	7	Now	$16.50

SEAVIEW RIESLING ★★★

1993	6	Now	$15.50
1994	6	Now	$14.00
1995	Not made		
1996	7	Now	$14.00
1997	Not made		
1998	6	2000	$10.50

SEAVIEW SAUVIGNON BLANC ★★

1992	7	Now	$23.00
1993	6	Now	$18.50
1994	6	Now	$17.00
1995	Not made		
1996	6	Now	$14.50
1997	6	Now	$13.50
1998	6	Now	$12.50

SEAVIEW SEMILLON/SAUVIGNON BLANC ★★

before 1996	Prior		
1996	6	Now	$13.50
1997	6	Now	$12.50
1998	5	Now	$9.50

SEAVIEW SHIRAZ ★★★

1993	6	Now	$17.50
1994	7	Now	$19.00
1995	6	Now	$15.00
1996	7	2000	$16.50
1997	6	2001	$13.00

SEAVIEW VERDELHO ★★

1994	6	Now	$15.50
1995	6	Now	$14.50
1996	6	Now	$13.00
1997	Not made		
1998	7	2000	$13.00

Seppelt, now part of Southcorp Wines, is a large Adelaide based company with vineyards in three states: Barossa Valley, Padthaway and Adelaide Hills in South Australia, Great Western and Drumborg in Victoria and Barooga and Tumbarumba in New South Wales. Wines span the gamut from volume-selling to limited edition. Winemaker: Ian McKenzie.

SEPPELT BLACK LABEL (TERRAIN SERIES) CABERNET SAUVIGNON ★★

before 1991	Prior		
1991	6	Now	$16.50
1992	5	Now	$12.50
1993	5	Now	$11.50
1994	6	Now	$13.00
1995	6	Now	$12.00
1997	7	Now	$13.00

SEPPELT CHALAMBAR SHIRAZ ★★★

1991	7	2000	$29.00
1992	6	2000	$23.00
1993	7	2005	$24.00
1994	7	2010	$23.00
1995	7	2010	$21.00
1996	7	2010	$19.50
1997	7	2010	$18.00

SEPPELT CORELLA RIDGE CHARDONNAY ★★★

before 1995	Prior		
1995	6	Now	$14.50
1996	7	Now	$15.50
1997	7	2000	$14.50

SEPPELT DORRIEN CABERNET SAUVIGNON ★★★★

before 1980	Prior		
1980	7	Now	$140.00
1981	6	Prior	
1982	6	Now	$105.00
1983	Not made		
1984	6	Now	$90.00
1985	Not made		
1986	5	Now	$64.00
1987	6	Now	$72.00
1988	7	Now	$78.00
1989	6	Now	$62.00

1990	7	Now	$66.00
1991	7	Now	$62.00
1992	6	Now	$49.00
1993	7	Now	$52.00
1994	7	2000	$49.00

SEPPELT HARPERS RANGE CABERNET SAUVIGNON

★★★

1991	7	2000	$29.00
1992	6	2000	$23.00
1993	5	Now	$17.50
1994	7	2000	$23.00
1995	6	2002	$18.00
1996	7	2003	$19.50

SEPPELT SALINGER METHODE
CHAMPENOISE

★★★★

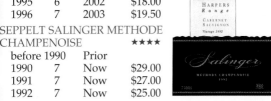

before 1990		Prior	
1990	7	Now	$29.00
1991	7	Now	$27.00
1992	7	Now	$25.00

SEPPELT SHEOAK SPRING RIESLING

★★★

before 1996		Prior	
1996	7	Now	$18.00
1997	6	Now	$14.50
1998	6	Now	$13.00

SEPPELT SUNDAY CREEK
PINOT NOIR

★★★★

1992	6	Now	$23.00
1993	6	Now	$21.00
1994	6	Now	$19.50
1995	7	Now	$21.00
1996	7	Now	$19.50
1997	7	Now	$18.00

Sevenhill is a Jesuit winery established in the Clare Valley in 1851, and renowned for some magnificent long-lived reds. Winemakers: Brother John May and John Monten.

SEVENHILL CABERNET SAUVIGNON

★★★★

1995	7	2007	$28.00
1996	6	2006	$22.00
1997	6	2007	$20.00

SEVENHILL DRY RED

★★★

before 1995		Prior	
1995	5	Now	$15.00
1996	6	2000	$17.00
1997	6	2001	$15.50

SEVENHILL RIESLING

★★★★

before 1995		Prior	
1995	6	Now	$20.00
1996	5	Now	$15.50
1997	6	2000	$17.50
1998	5	2000	$13.50

SEVENHILL SHIRAZ ★★★★

1989	6	Now	$37.00
1990	5	2000	$28.00
1991	5	Prior	
1992	6	2001	$29.00
1993	6	Now	$27.00
1994	6	2000	$25.00
1995	7	2006	$27.00
1996	5	2004	$18.00
1997	5	2004	$16.50

SEVENHILL ST IGNATIUS ★★★★★

1990	6	2000	$39.00
1991	5	Now	$30.00
1992	6	2000	$33.00
1993	5	2001	$26.00
1994	6	2002	$28.00
1995	5	2003	$22.00
1996	7	2005	$28.00
1997	6	2006	$22.00

Seville Estate is a leading Yarra Valley small vineyard whose wines are difficult to find but well worth the effort. Winemaker: Peter McMahon.

SEVILLE ESTATE CABERNET SAUVIGNON ★★★★

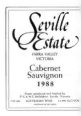

before 1984		Prior	
1984	7	Now	$66.00
1985	6	Now	$52.00
1986	7	Now	$56.00
1987	5	Now	$37.00
1988	6	Now	$42.00
1989	6	Now	$39.00
1990	6	Now	$36.00
1991	7	Now	$39.00
1992	7	2000	$36.00
1993	6	2000	$28.00
1994	7	2001	$31.00
1995	6	2002	$24.00
1996	Not made		

SEVILLE ESTATE CHARDONNAY ★★★★★

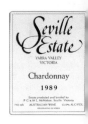

before 1986		Prior	
1986	6	Now	$50.00
1987	6	Now	$47.00
1988	6	Now	$44.00
1989	6	Now	$40.00
1990	7	Now	$44.00
1991	7	Now	$40.00
1992	7	Now	$37.00
1993	6	Now	$30.00
1994	7	Now	$32.00
1995	7	Now	$30.00
1996	7	Now	$27.00

SEVILLE ESTATE PINOT NOIR ★★★★

before 1987		Prior	
1987	6	Now	$48.00
1988	7	Now	$52.00
1989	6	Now	$41.00
1990	Not made		
1991	7	Now	$41.00
1992	6	Now	$32.00
1993	6	Now	$30.00
1994	7	Now	$32.00
1995	6	2000	$26.00
1996	7	2002	$28.00

SEVILLE ESTATE RIESLING BOTRYTIS AFFECTED (375ml) ★★★★

1979	6	Now	$72.00
1980	7	2000	$78.00
1981	5	Now	$52.00
1982	6	Now	$58.00
1983	3	Now	$26.00
1984	6	Now	$49.00
1985	6	Now	$46.00
1986	Not made		
1987	6	Now	$39.00
1988	Not made		
1989	Not made		
1990	Not made		
1991	7	2000	$34.00
1992	7	2001	$31.00
1993	7	2002	$29.00
Not made after 1993			

SEVILLE ESTATE SHIRAZ ★★★★

before 1983		Prior	
1983	6	Now	$70.00
1984	Not made		
1985	6	Now	$60.00
1986	7	Now	$64.00
1987	6	Now	$50.00
1988	7	Now	$56.00
1989	6	Now	$44.00
1990	7	Now	$48.00
1991	7	Now	$44.00
1992	7	Now	$41.00
1993	7	Now	$38.00
1994	6	Now	$30.00
1995	6	2000	$28.00
1996	6	2002	$26.00

Shantell Vineyard is a Yarra Valley maker whose releases to date have included some very agreeable wines, the Cabernet in particular being impressive. Winemakers: Shan and Turid Shanmugam.

SHANTELL CABERNET SAUVIGNON ★★★★

1988	6	Now	$45.00
1989	4	Now	$28.00
1990	6	2002	$38.00
1991	6	Now	$36.00
1992	5	2000	$27.00
1993	6	2002	$30.00
1994	5	Now	$23.00
1995	No data		
1996	5	2001	$20.00

SHANTELL CHARDONNAY ★★★

1988	6	Now	$36.00
1989	5	Now	$28.00
1990	7	Now	$36.00
1991	6	Now	$28.00
1992	6	Now	$26.00
1993	6	Now	$24.00
1994	6	Now	$22.00
1995	7	2001	$24.00
1996	6	2001	$19.50

SHANTELL PINOT NOIR ★★★

1988	6	Now	$43.00
1989	4	Prior	
1990	7	Now	$43.00
1991	5	Now	$28.00
1992	5	Now	$26.00
1993	5	Now	$24.00
1994	4	Now	$18.00
1995	5	Now	$21.00
1996	5	2000	$19.50

Shaw & Smith is a stylish and perfectionist winemaking partnership between Martin Shaw and Michael Hill Smith MW. The renown earned by their releases to date goes well beyond the shores of this continent. Winemaker: Martin Shaw.

SHAW & SMITH RESERVE CHARDONNAY ★★★★★

before 1992		Prior	
1992	6	Now	$47.00
1993	4	Prior	
1994	5	Now	$33.00
1995	4	Now	$24.00
1996	5	Now	$28.00
1997	5	Now	$26.00

SHAW & SMITH UNOAKED CHARDONNAY ★★★★

before 1996		Prior	
1996	5	Now	$18.50
1997	5	Now	$17.00
1998	5	Now	$16.00

SHAW & SMITH SAUVIGNON BLANC ★★★★★

before 1997		Prior	
1997	5	Now	$16.50
1998	6	Now	$18.50

Shottesbrooke Vineyards are McLaren Vale producers of some stylish, well-constructed wines.
Winemaker: Nick Holmes.

SHOTTESBROOKE CABERNET/MERLOT ★★★★

1984	7	Now	$58.00
1985	6	Now	$46.00
1986	6	Now	$42.00
1987	5	Prior	
1988	7	Now	$42.00
1989	6	Now	$33.00
1990	6	Now	$31.00
1991	6	Now	$29.00
1992	7	2000	$31.00
1993	5	2002	$20.00
1994	6	2003	$23.00
1995	7	2005	$24.00

Skillogalee Vineyards are Clare Valley producers whose very low market profile belies the fine quality of their wines.
Winemaker: Dave Palmer.

SKILLOGALEE CABERNETS ★★★

1980	6	Now	$82.00
1981	5	Now	$64.00
1982	5	Now	$58.00
1983	4	Prior	
1984	6	Now	$60.00
1985	4	Prior	
1986	5	Now	$43.00
1987	6	Now	$48.00
1988	5	Now	$37.00
1989	5	Now	$34.00
1990	7	2000	$45.00
1991	6	Now	$35.00
1992	5	Now	$27.00
1993	6	Now	$30.00
1994	6	2002	$28.00
1995	5	2002	$21.00
1996	6	2004	$24.00

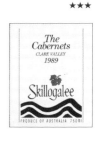

SKILLOGALEE RIESLING

★★★★

1977	6	Prior	
1978	7	Now	$82.00
1979	6	Prior	
1980	6	Prior	
1981	6	Prior	
1982	6	Prior	
1983	6	Prior	
1984	6	Now	$44.00
1985	5	Prior	
1986	6	Prior	
1987	6	Now	$35.00
1988	4	Prior	
1989	6	Now	$30.00
1990	7	Now	$32.00
1991	7	Now	$30.00
1992	6	Now	$24.00
1993	7	2000	$26.00
1994	7	2003	$24.00
1995	7	2004	$22.00
1996	6	2001	$17.50
1997	7	2002	$19.00

SKILLOGALEE SHIRAZ

★★★★

1980	6	Now	$52.00
1981	4	Prior	
1982	5	Now	$37.00
1983	5	Now	$35.00
1984	6	Now	$38.00
1985	5	Now	$30.00
1986	5	Now	$27.00
1987	7	Now	$36.00
1988	6	Now	$28.00
1989	6	Now	$26.00
1990	7	Now	$28.00
1991	6	Now	$22.00
1992	5	Now	$17.50
1993	6	Now	$19.00
1994	7	2001	$21.00
1995	6	2001	$16.50

Spring Vale *is a new vineyard on Tasmania's East Coast, producing a superb Pinot Noir. Winemaker: Andrew Hood.*

SPRING VALE PINOT NOIR

★★★★★

before 1992		Prior	
1992	6	Now	$47.00
1993	6	Now	$44.00

1994	7	2000	$47.00
1995	6	2000	$37.00
1996	5	Now	$29.00
1997	7	2005	$37.00
1998	6	2006	$30.00

tanley - see Leasingham.

tanton and Killeen make good honest Rutherglen wines *orthy* of considerable respect. Winemaker: Chris Killeen.

TANTON & KILLEEN
ABERNET SAUVIGNON ★★★

before 1991	Prior		
1991	5	Now	$22.00
1992	7	2000	$28.00
1993	Not made		
1994	Not made		
1995	6	2000	$19.00
1996	6	2000	$18.00
1997	Not made		
1998	6	2002	N/R

TANTON AND KILLEEN MOODEMERE DURIF
★★★★

before 1987	Prior		
1987	7	Now	$54.00
1988	5	Now	$36.00
1989	Not made		
1990	6	Now	$37.00
1991	5	Now	$29.00
1992	7	2002	$37.00
1993	Not made		
1994	6	2004	$27.00
1995	6	2005	$25.00
1996	6	2000	$23.00
1997	6	2003	$22.00
1998	6	2005	N/R

TANTON AND KILLEEN MOODEMERE
HIRAZ ★★★★

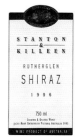

before 1991	Prior		
1991	5	Now	$20.00
1992	7	Now	$26.00
1993	6	Now	$21.00
1994	Not made		
1995	5	Now	$15.00
1996	5	Now	$14.00
1997	6	2005	$15.50
1998	6	2005	N/R

STANTON AND KILLEEN VINTAGE PORT ★★★

1971	5	Now	$110.00
1972	7	Now	$140.00
1973	3	Prior	
1974	4	Prior	
1975	7	Now	$110.00
1976	6	Now	$90.00
1977	6	Now	$82.00
1978	5	Now	$64.00
1979	5	Now	$58.00
1980	5	2000	$54.00
1981	3	2000	$30.00
1982	6	2000	$56.00
1983	7	2005	$60.00
1984	5	Now	$40.00
1985	6	Now	$45.00
1986	7	2005	$48.00
1987	5	2000	$32.00
1988	7	2005	$41.00
1989	4	Now	$22.00
1990	7	2010	$35.00
1991	6	2006	$28.00
1992	7	2010	$30.00
1993	7	2010	$28.00
1994	5	2008	N/R
1995	6	2010	N/R
1996	4	2016	N/R
1997	7	2017	N/R
1998	6	2015	N/R

Stoneleigh Vineyard in New Zealand's Marlborough area, at the northern tip of the South Island, is owned and operate by the Corbans company. Winemaker: Michael Kluczko.

STONELEIGH CABERNET SAUVIGNON ★★

before 1989	Prior		
1989	7	Now	NZ$37.00
1990	6	Now	NZ$29.00
1991	7	Now	NZ$32.00
1992	5	Now	NZ$21.00
1993	5	Now	NZ$19.50
1994	7	2000	NZ$25.00
1995	Not made		
1996	7	2002	NZ$21.00
1997	6	2001	NZ$17.00
1998	7	2002	NZ$18.50

STONELEIGH CHARDONNAY
★★★

before 1990	Prior		
1990	6	Now	NZ$29.00
1991	7	Now	NZ$31.00
1992	5	Now	NZ$20.00
1993	6	Now	NZ$23.00
1994	7	2000	NZ$25.00
1995	6	Now	NZ$19.50

1996	7	2002	NZ$21.00
1997	7	2000	NZ$19.50
1998	7	2001	NZ$18.00

STONELEIGH RIESLING ★★★★★

before 1988		Prior	
1988	5	Now	NZ$25.00
1989	7	Now	NZ$32.00
1990	7	Now	NZ$30.00
1991	7	Now	NZ$28.00
1992	5	Now	NZ$18.50
1993	6	Now	NZ$20.00
1994	7	2002	NZ$22.00
1995	5	2002	NZ$14.50
1996	7	2005	NZ$19.00
1997	7	2005	NZ$17.50
1998	7	2006	NZ$16.50

STONELEIGH SAUVIGNON BLANC

before 1995		Prior	★★★★
1995	5	Now	NZ$14.50
1996	7	Now	NZ$18.50
1997	7	Now	NZ$17.00
1998	7	Now	NZ$16.00

Stoney Vineyard in Tasmania's Coal River Valley is a perfectionist operation producing some superb wines, the best of which are released as "Domaine A" (q.v.).
Winemaker: Peter Althaus.

STONEY VINEYARD AURORA ★★★★

1994	7	Now	$32.00
1995	6	Now	$25.00
1996	Not made		
1997	7	Now	$25.00
1998	7	Now	$23.00

STONEY VINEYARD CABERNET SAUVIGNON ★★★★

1993	5	Now	$27.00
1994	7	2000	$36.00
1995	6	Now	$28.00
1996	4	Now	$17.50
1997	Not made		
1998	7	2003	$26.00

STONEY VINEYARD PINOT NOIR ★★★★

| 1995 | 4 | Now | $27.00 |
| 1995 | 7 | 2002 | $44.00 |

STONEY VINEYARD SAUVIGNON BLANC ★★★★

1993	6	Now	$41.00
1994	7	Now	$45.00
1995	6	Now	$35.00

1996	5	2000	$27.00
1997	7	2004	$35.00
1998	7	Now	$33.00

Stonier Wines is the largest of the Mornington Peninsula vineyards and perhaps the best exemplar of the area's extreme promise. As well as the premium Reserve wines there is a range of lower priced wines. Winemaker: Tod Dexter.

STONIER CABERNET ★★★★

1990	6	Prior	
1991	5	Now	$20.00
1992	6	Now	$22.00
1993	7	Now	$24.00
1994	6	Now	$19.00
1995	6	Now	$18.00

STONIER CHARDONNAY ★★★★

before 1993		Prior	
1993	6	Now	$30.00
1994	6	Now	$27.00
1995	5	Now	$21.00
1996	5	Now	$19.50
1997	6	2000	$22.00
1998	6	2001	$20.00

STONIER PINOT NOIR ★★★★

1990	4	Prior	
1991	6	Now	$41.00
1992	6	Now	$38.00
1993	6	Now	$35.00
1994	6	Now	$33.00
1995	7	Now	$35.00
1996	3	Prior	
1997	7	2000	$30.00
1998	6	2001	$24.00

STONIER RESERVE
CABERNET SAUVIGNON ★★★★★
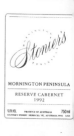

before 1988		Prior	
1988	6	Now	$88.00
1989	2	Prior	
1990	5	Prior	
1991	5	Now	$58.00
1992	5	Now	$54.00
1993	6	Now	$60.00
1994	6	Now	$54.00
1995	5	2000	$42.00
1996	Not made		
1997	7	2002	$50.00
1998	6	2003	N/R

STONIER RESERVE CHARDONNAY ★★★★★

before 1993		Prior	
1993	6	Now	$50.00
1994	6	Now	$46.00
1995	6	2000	$42.00
1996	6	2001	$39.00
1997	7	2002	$42.00
1998	7	2003	$39.00

STONIER RESERVE PINOT NOIR

before 1991		Prior	★★★★★
1991	7	Now	$74.00
1992	6	Now	$58.00
1993	7	Now	$62.00
1994	6	Now	$50.00
1995	7	2000	$54.00
1996	Not made		
1997	7	2002	$46.00
1998	6	2003	N/R

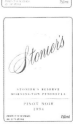

Stonyridge are winegrowers on New Zealand's Waiheke Island east of Auckland who annually produce a painstakingly assembled Cabernet of extreme quality. Winemaker: Stephen White.

STONYRIDGE LAROSE CABERNETS ★★★★★

before 1987		Prior	
1987	7	2000	NZ$220.00
1988	5	Prior	
1989	6	Now	NZ$160.00
1990	7	2000	NZ$175.00
1991	6	Now	NZ$140.00
1992	Not made		
1993	7	2004	NZ$140.00
1994	7	2008	NZ$130.00
1995	5	2001	NZ$86.00
1996	7	2007	NZ$110.00
1997	7	2005	NZ$100.00

Sutherland Wines are Pokolbin growers whose high quality fruit persuaded them to become makers. The wines are substantial and full-blooded. Winemaker: Neil Sutherland.

SUTHERLAND WINES CHARDONNAY ★★★★

before 1994		Prior	
1994	6	Now	$21.00
1995	6	Now	$20.00
1996	5	Now	$15.50
1997	6	Now	N/R

SUTHERLAND WINES CHENIN BLANC ★★★

before 1993		Prior	
1993	5	Now	$18.50
1994	5	Now	$17.00

1995	4	Now	$12.50
1996	5	Now	$15.00
1997	6	Now	N/R

SUTHERLAND WINES SEMILLON ★★★

before 1988	Prior		
1988	6	Now	$28.00
1989	7	Now	$30.00
1990	5	Prior	
1991	5	Prior	
1992	Not made		
1993	5	Now	$16.00
1994	5	Now	$14.50
1995	5	Now	$13.50

SUTHERLAND WINES SHIRAZ

before 1992	Prior	★★★	
1992	5	Now	$21.00
1993	6	Now	$23.00
1994	6	Now	$21.00
1995	6	Now	$20.00
1996	5	Now	$15.50

Taltarni is a Central Victorian medium-sized company producing high quality wines, much of which is exported to England and the U. S. Winemaker: Chris Markell.

TALTARNI CABERNET SAUVIGNON ★★★★

1977	6	Now	$105.00
1978	6	Now	$98.00
1979	6	Now	$90.00
1980	5	Now	$70.00
1981	6	Now	$78.00
1982	6	Now	$72.00
1983	5	Now	$54.00
1984	6	Now	$62.00
1985	5	Now	$47.00
1986	6	Now	$52.00
1987	6	Now	$49.00
1988	7	Now	$52.00
1989	6	Now	$42.00
1990	7	Now	$45.00
1991	7	2000	$42.00
1992	6	Now	$33.00
1993	5	2002	$25.00
1994	7	2003	$33.00
1995	6	2004	$26.00
1996	6	2004	$24.00
1997	7	2006	N/R
1998	7	2005	N/R

TALTARNI FUME BLANC ★★★★

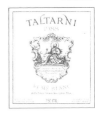

before 1996		Prior	
1996	7	Now	$20.00
1997	6	Now	$16.00

TALTARNI MERLOT(/CABERNET FRANC) ★★★★

1984	5	Now	$58.00
1985	5	Now	$54.00
1986	6	Now	$60.00
1987	Not made		
1988	6	2000	$50.00
1989	6	Now	$47.00
1990	7	Now	$50.00
1991	7	Now	$47.00
1992	6	Now	$38.00
1993	6	Now	$35.00
1994	6	2000	$32.00
1995	6	2000	$30.00
1996	6	2000	$28.00
1997	6	2005	N/R

TALTARNI SHIRAZ ★★★★

1977	6	Now	$110.00
1978	6	Now	$105.00
1979	5	Now	$82.00
1980	6	Now	$90.00
1981	6	Now	$84.00
1982	6	Now	$78.00
1983	5	Now	$60.00
1984	6	Now	$66.00
1985	6	Now	$62.00
1986	6	Now	$56.00
1987	6	Now	$52.00
1988	7	Now	$56.00
1989	6	Now	$45.00
1990	6	Now	$42.00
1991	7	Now	$45.00
1992	6	Now	$36.00
1993	6	Now	$33.00
1994	7	2000	$36.00
1995	6	2000	$28.00
1996	6	2002	$26.00
1997	6	2004	N/R

Tamburlaine is a Hunter Valley producer whose wines have grown in both quantity and quality over the last eight years. Wine sales are exclusively from the cellar door. Winemaker: Mark Davidson.

TAMBURLAINE MERLOT/CABERNET ★★★★

1986	4	Now	$34.00
1987	6	Now	$47.00
1988	6	Now	$44.00

1989	7	Now	$47.00
1990	6	Now	$37.00
1991	6	Now	$35.00
1992	Not made		
1993	6	2001	$30.00
1994	5	2002	$23.00
1995	7	2003	$30.00
1996	7	2004	$27.00
1997	7	2005	$25.00
1998	7	2006	$23.00

TAMBURLAINE CHARDONNAY "THE CHAPEL" ★★★★

1986	7	Now	$52.00
1987	5	Now	$35.00
1988	6	Now	$39.00
1989	7	Now	$42.00
1990	6	Now	$33.00
1991	7	Now	$36.00
1992	6	Now	$29.00
1993	7	2000	$31.00
1994	7	2001	$29.00
1995	7	2002	$26.00
1996	6	2003	$21.00
1997	7	2004	$23.00
1998	7	2005	$21.00

TAMBURLAINE SEMILLON ★★★

1986	4	Now	$27.00
1987	6	Now	$38.00
1988	5	Now	$29.00
1989	6	Now	$32.00
1990	5	Now	$25.00
1991	6	2000	$28.00
1992	5	2002	$21.00
1993	7	2003	$28.00
1994	6	2004	$22.00
1995	6	2005	$20.00
1996	6	2006	$19.00
1997	7	2006	$20.00
1998	7	2007	$19.00

TAMBURLAINE "THE CHAPEL" RESERVE RED ★★★★

1986	6	Now	$52.00
1987	6	Now	$49.00
1988	6	Now	$46.00
1989	7	Now	$49.00
1990	5	Now	$33.00
1991	6	2000	$36.00
1992	Not made		

1993	6	2002	$31.00
1994	6	2003	$29.00
1995	5	2004	$22.00
1996	7	2005	$29.00
1997	7	2007	$26.00
1998	7	2008	$24.00

TAMBURLAINE VERDELHO ★★★

1991	6	Now	$25.00
1992	7	Now	$27.00
1993	6	2000	$22.00
1994	7	2001	$23.00
1995	6	2002	$18.50
1996	7	2003	$20.00
1997	5	2003	$13.50
1998	7	2005	$17.50

Tapestry is the label applied to wines made at the old
Merrivale winery in McLaren Vale. The operation is owned
by Brian Light. Winemaker: Brian Light.

TAPESTRY CABERNET SAUVIGNON ★★★

1993	5	2000	$19.50
1994	6	2000	$21.00
1995	5	2001	$16.50

TAPESTRY SHIRAZ ★★★

1993	5	2000	$18.50
1994	6	2001	$20.00
1995	6	2001	$19.00

Tarrawarra is a high prestige Yarra Valley producer with a
notable but individually styled Chardonnay.
Winemaker: Clare Hatton.

TARRAWARRA CHARDONNAY ★★★★

1986	4	Now	$68.00
1987	6	Now	$94.00
1988	7	Now	$100.00
1989	5	Now	$66.00
1990	6	Now	$74.00
1991	6	Now	$68.00
1992	6	Now	$64.00
1993	5	Now	$49.00
1994	6	Now	$54.00
1995	6	2002	$50.00
1996	7	2003	$54.00
1997	6	2005	$43.00
1998	7	2005	$47.00

TARRAWARRA PINOT NOIR ★★★★

1988	6	Now	$82.00
1989	5	Now	$64.00
1990	6	Now	$70.00

1991	6	Now	$66.00
1992	7	2000	$70.00
1993	5	Now	$47.00
1994	6	2000	$52.00
1995	7	2005	$56.00
1996	7	2002	$52.00
1997	6	2002	$41.00
1998	7	2003	$45.00

Taylors of Clare are medium-sized makers of a small range of popular and reliable wines. Winemakers: Susan Mickan and Kelvin Buderick.

TAYLORS CABERNET SAUVIGNON ★★★

before 1986	Prior		
1986	6	Now	$43.00
1987	6	Now	$39.00
1988	5	Now	$30.00
1989	6	Now	$34.00
1990	6	Now	$31.00
1991	5	Now	$24.00
1992	7	Now	$31.00
1993	6	Now	$25.00
1994	7	Now	$27.00
1995	4	Now	$14.00
1996	6	Now	$19.50
1997	6	2002	$18.50

TAYLORS CHARDONNAY ★★★

before 1996	Prior		
1996	7	Now	$20.00
1997	6	2001	$16.50

TAYLORS CLARE RIESLING ★★

before 1994	Prior		
1994	6	Now	$19.00
1995	Not made		
1996	7	2001	$19.00
1997	7	2002	$17.50
1998	7	2005	$16.50

TAYLORS PINOT NOIR ★★★

before 1996	Prior		
1996	6	Now	$18.50
1997	6	Now	$17.00
1998	6	2000	$16.00

TAYLORS SHIRAZ ★★★

before 1986	Prior		
1986	6	Now	$45.00
1987	4	Now	$27.00
1988	5	Now	$32.00
1989	6	Now	$35.00

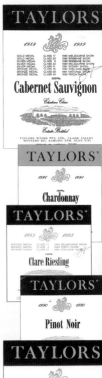

1990	7	Now	$38.00
1991	5	Now	$25.00
1992	4	Now	$18.50
1993	6	Now	$26.00
1994	7	Now	$28.00
1995	7	Now	$26.00
1996	4	Now	$13.50
1997	6	2002	$19.00

Te Mata Estate, *one of the most respected specialist producers in New Zealand, unfortunately prefers not to submit winemaker ratings. Winemaker: Peter Cowley.*

TE MATA AWATEA (CABERNETS) ★★★★

TE MATA CAPE CREST SAUVIGNON BLANC ★★★★

TE MATA CASTLE HILL SAUVIGNON BLANC ★★★★

TE MATA COLERAINE
CABERNET/MERLOT ★★★★★

TE MATA ELSTON CHARDONNAY ★★★★

Thistle Hill Vineyard *is an extremely impressive Mudgee maker with a limited range of the noble varieties. The wines are all notably generous, with both power and elegance in the fruit. Winemaker: David Robertson.*

THISTLE HILL CABERNET SAUVIGNON ★★★★★

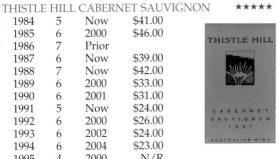

1984	5	Now	$41.00
1985	6	2000	$46.00
1986	7	Prior	
1987	6	Now	$39.00
1988	7	Now	$42.00
1989	6	2000	$33.00
1990	6	2001	$31.00
1991	5	Now	$24.00
1992	6	2000	$26.00
1993	6	2002	$24.00
1994	6	2004	$23.00
1995	4	2000	N/R
1996	6	2004	N/R
1997	5	2004	N/R
1998	5	2006	N/R

THISTLE HILL CHARDONNAY ★★★★

1984	6	Now	$60.00
1985	5	Prior	
1986	6	Now	$50.00
1987	5	Prior	
1988	6	Now	$44.00
1989	5	Now	$34.00
1990	6	Now	$38.00
1991	5	Now	$29.00
1992	6	2000	$32.00
1993	6	2001	$30.00

1994	6	Now	$27.00
1995	4	Now	$17.00
1996	5	2001	$20.00
1997	6	2000	$22.00
1998	4	2001	N/R

THISTLE HILL PINOT NOIR ★★★★★

1985	6	Now	$74.00
1986	6	Prior	
1987	5	Prior	
1988	6	Now	$58.00
1989	6	Now	$54.00
1990	7	2000	$58.00
1991	5	Now	$38.00
1992	5	Now	$36.00
1993	5	2000	$33.00
1994	7	2001	$43.00
1995	5	2001	$28.00
1996	5	2002	$26.00
1997	5	2003	$24.00
1998	4	2003	N/R

THISTLE HILL RIESLING ★★★★

1989	5	Prior	
1990	6	2000	$30.00
1991	5	Now	$23.00
1992	5	Now	$21.00
1993	6	2000	$24.00
1994	6	2000	$22.00
1995	5	2000	$17.00
1996	5	2001	$16.00
1997	4	2001	$11.50
1998	4	2002	$10.50

Tim Adams Wines is a winemaking operation in the Clare Valley, using fruit sourced from local growers. These generously flavoured wines are unfortunately not rated by the winemaker for this edition, so star rankings only are given. Winemaker: Tim Adams.

TIM ADAMS ABERFELDY SHIRAZ ★★★★

TIM ADAMS CABERNET ★★★★

TIM ADAMS FERGUS GRENACHE ★★★

TIM ADAMS SEMILLON ★★★★

Tingle-Wood Wines is a small maker in the Denmark area. Winemaker: John Wade.

TINGLE-WOOD YELLOW TINGLE (RIESLING) ★★★

1988	5	Now	$25.00
1989	6	Now	$28.00
1990	7	Now	$31.00

1991	7	Now	$28.00
1992	Not made		
1993	7	Now	$24.00
1994	Not made		
1995	No data		
1996	No data		
1997	5	Now	$12.50

Tisdall Wines produce a range of reliable and inexpensive wines of agreeable quality. Winemaker: Toni Stockhausen.

TISDALL CABERNET/MERLOT ★★

before 1991	Prior		
1991	7	Now	$26.00
1992	5	Now	$17.00
1993	4	Now	$12.50
1994	5	Now	$14.50
1995	6	Now	$16.00
1996	6	Now	$15.00

TISDALL CHARDONNAY ★★

before 1988	Prior		
1988	3	Now	$16.50
1989	4	Now	$20.00
1990	5	Now	$24.00
1991	4	Now	$17.50
1992	5	Now	$20.00
1993	4	Now	$15.00
1994	6	Now	$21.00
1995	4	Now	$13.00
1996	5	Now	$15.00
1997	6	Now	$16.50

Tollana, owned by Southcorp, is a traditional Eden Valley label with a range of popular wines. Recently Adelaide Hills fruit is also sourced. Winemaker: Neville Falkenberg.

TOLLANA BOTRYTIS RIESLING (375ml) ★★★

before 1994	Prior		
1994	5	Now	$15.50
1995	7	Now	$20.00
1996	6	Now	$16.00
1997	6	Now	$15.00
1998	6	2002	N/R

TOLLANA CABERNET SAUVIGNON BIN 222 ★★★

before 1990	Prior		
1990	6	Now	$34.00
1991	7	Now	$37.00
1992	5	Now	$24.00
1993	7	Now	$31.00
1994	5	Now	$20.00
1995	5	2000	$19.00
1996	7	2002	$25.00
1997	6	2001	$20.00

TOLLANA EDEN VALLEY CHARDONNAY ★★★

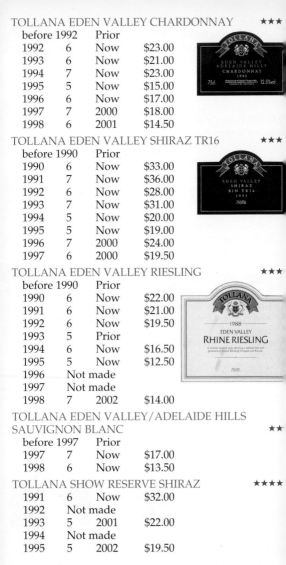

before 1992		Prior	
1992	6	Now	$23.00
1993	6	Now	$21.00
1994	7	Now	$23.00
1995	5	Now	$15.00
1996	6	Now	$17.00
1997	7	2000	$18.00
1998	6	2001	$14.50

TOLLANA EDEN VALLEY SHIRAZ TR16 ★★★

before 1990		Prior	
1990	6	Now	$33.00
1991	7	Now	$36.00
1992	6	Now	$28.00
1993	7	Now	$31.00
1994	5	Now	$20.00
1995	5	Now	$19.00
1996	7	2000	$24.00
1997	6	2000	$19.50

TOLLANA EDEN VALLEY RIESLING ★★★

before 1990		Prior	
1990	6	Now	$22.00
1991	6	Now	$21.00
1992	6	Now	$19.50
1993	5	Prior	
1994	6	Now	$16.50
1995	5	Now	$12.50
1996	Not made		
1997	Not made		
1998	7	2002	$14.00

TOLLANA EDEN VALLEY/ADELAIDE HILLS SAUVIGNON BLANC ★★

before 1997		Prior	
1997	7	Now	$17.00
1998	6	Now	$13.50

TOLLANA SHOW RESERVE SHIRAZ ★★★★

1991	6	Now	$32.00
1992	Not made		
1993	5	2001	$22.00
1994	Not made		
1995	5	2002	$19.50

Trentham Estate is just across the Murray from Mildura, but produces wines of much higher quality than expectable from the area. Winemaker: Tony Murphy.

TRENTHAM ESTATE CABERNET/MERLOT ★★

before 1990		Prior	
1990	6	Now	$26.00
1991	5	Prior	
1992	6	Now	$22.00

1993	5	Now	$17.00
1994	5	Now	$16.00
1995	6	Now	$17.50
1996	6	Now	$16.00
1997	5	2000	$12.50

TRENTHAM ESTATE CHARDONNAY ★★★

before 1992	Prior		
1992	7	Now	$28.00
1993	5	Now	$18.50
1994	5	Now	$17.50
1995	4	Now	$12.50
1996	5	Now	$15.00
1997	6	Now	$16.50
1998	6	2000	$15.00

TRENTHAM ESTATE MERLOT ★★★

before 1993	Prior		
1993	5	Now	$18.00
1994	4	Now	$13.50
1995	6	Now	$18.50
1996	6	Now	$17.00
1997	5	2000	$13.00

TRENTHAM ESTATE SHIRAZ ★★★

1991	7	Now	$27.00
1992	7	Now	$25.00
1993	4	Now	$13.50
1994	6	Now	$18.50
1995	6	2000	$17.50
1996	5	2000	$13.50
1997	4	2000	$10.00

Tulloch is a famous maker in the Hunter Valley now owned by Southcorp but operating as an individual company. Winemaker: Patrick Auld.

TULLOCH HECTOR OF GLEN ELGIN DRY RED ★★★★

before 1987	Prior		
1987	6	Now	$50.00
1988	Not made		
1989	5	Now	$37.00
1990	Not made		
1991	6	Now	$38.00
1992	Not made		
1993	Not made		
1994	6	Now	$30.00
1995	6	2000	$28.00
1996	6	2005	$26.00
1997	7	2007	N/R

TULLOCH UNOAKED CHARDONNAY ★★★

before 1995	Prior	
1995	5	Now	$16.00
1996	6	Now	$18.00
1997	5	Now	$14.00
1998	Not made	

TULLOCH VERDELHO ★★★

before 1995	Prior	
1995	5	Now	$13.50
1996	5	Now	$12.50
1997	6	Now	$14.00
1998	6	Now	$13.00

Tunnel Hill is the second label of the Yarra Valley's Tarrawarra. The wines are both reasonably priced and of good quality. Winemaker: Clare Hatton.

TUNNEL HILL CHARDONNAY ★★★

before 1994	Prior	
1994	6	Now	$26.00
1995	4	Now	$16.00
1996	4	Now	$14.50
1997	Not made	
1998	6	2000	$19.00

TUNNEL HILL PINOT NOIR ★★★★

before 1991	Prior	
1991	5	Now	$31.00
1992	6	Now	$35.00
1993	4	Now	$21.00
1994	6	Now	$30.00
1995	4	Now	$18.50
1996	5	Now	$21.00
1997	6	2000	$24.00
1998	7	2001	$26.00

Tyrrells is a thriving Pokolbin family-owned company with a dedicated following. Winemaker: Andrew Spinaze.

TYRRELLS CHARDONNAY VAT 47 ★★★★★

1972	4	Prior	
1973	7	Now	$330.00
1974	5	Prior	
1975	5	Prior	
1976	6	Now	$225.00
1977	7	Now	$240.00
1978	5	Prior	
1979	7	Now	$210.00
1980	7	Now	$190.00
1981	5	Prior	
1982	6	Now	$140.00
1983	6	Prior	

1984	7	Now	$140.00
1985	6	Now	$110.00
1986	7	Now	$120.00
1987	6	Now	$96.00
1988	6	Prior	
1989	7	Now	$96.00
1990	6	2000	$76.00
1991	7	2000	$82.00
1992	6	2002	$66.00
1993	6	2000	$60.00
1994	6	2001	$56.00
1995	7	2003	$60.00
1996	6	2003	$48.00
1997	5	2003	$37.00
1998	5	2004	$34.00

TYRRELLS DRY RED VAT 5 (SHIRAZ) ★★★

before 1975		Prior	
1975	7	Now	$150.00
1976	5	Prior	
1977	6	Now	$110.00
1978	5	Prior	
1979	6	Prior	
1980	6	Now	$88.00
1981	5	Now	$68.00
1982	5	Prior	
1983	6	Now	$70.00
1984	5	Prior	
1985	7	Now	$70.00
1986	5	Now	$46.00
1987	6	Now	$52.00
1988	5	Prior	
1989	6	Now	$44.00
1990	5	Now	$34.00
1991	7	2001	$44.00
1992	5	Now	$29.00
1993	5	2000	$27.00
1994	5	2001	$25.00
1995	7	2005	$32.00
1996	6	2005	$26.00
1997	6	2007	$24.00
1998	6	2007	N/R

YRRELLS DRY RED VAT 9 (SHIRAZ) ★★★★★

before 1975		Prior	
1975	7	Now	$220.00
1976	6	Prior	
1977	7	Now	$190.00
1978	5	Prior	
1979	7	Now	$160.00
1980	6	Now	$130.00

1981	5	Now	$100.00
1982	5	Prior	
1983	6	Now	$100.00
1984	5	Prior	
1985	7	Now	$100.00
1986	5	Now	$68.00
1987	7	Now	$88.00
1988	6	Prior	
1989	6	2000	$64.00
1990	5	Now	$50.00
1991	7	2001	$64.00
1992	7	2000	$60.00
1993	5	2000	$39.00
1994	5	2002	$36.00
1995	6	2005	$41.00
1996	6	2005	$38.00
1997	6	2007	$35.00
1998	6	2007	N/R

TYRRELLS HUNTER/COONAWARRA
SHIRAZ/CABERNET VAT 8 ★★★★

1990	5	Now	$47.00
1991	7	Now	$60.00
1992	5	Now	$40.00
1993	7	2001	$52.00
1994	6	2002	$41.00
1995	6	2005	$38.00
1996	6	2006	$35.00
1997	5	2004	N/R
1998	6	2006	N/R

TYRRELLS HUNTER RIVER
SEMILLON VAT 1 ★★★★

before 1972		Prior	
1972	7	Now	$195.00
1973	6	Now	$155.00
1974	7	Prior	
1975	6	Prior	
1976	7	Now	$140.00
1977	6	Now	$110.00
1978	5	Now	$88.00
1979	5	Now	$82.00
1980	4	Now	$60.00
1981	5	Prior	
1982	5	Now	$64.00
1983	6	Now	$72.00
1984	5	Now	$56.00
1985	5	Now	$50.00
1986	7	Now	$66.00
1987	6	Now	$52.00
1988	5	Now	$41.00

1989	7	Now	$52.00
1990	6	Now	$42.00
1991	7	Now	$45.00
1992	6	2000	$36.00
1993	6	2000	$33.00
1994	7	2004	N/R
1995	5	2003	N/R
1996	6	2006	N/R
1997	6	2007	N/R

TYRRELLS MOON MOUNTAIN CHARDONNAY ★★★★

1995	5	2000	$26.00
1996	7	Now	$34.00
1997	6	2000	$27.00
1998	5	2000	$20.00

TYRRELLS PINOT NOIR VAT 6 ★★★★★

1974	5	Prior	
1975	5	Now	$170.00
1976	7	Now	$220.00
1977	4	Prior	
1978	4	Prior	
1979	5	Now	$125.00
1980	6	Now	$140.00
1981	7	Now	$150.00
1982	5	Now	$100.00
1983	6	Now	$110.00
1984	5	Now	$86.00
1985	6	Now	$96.00
1986	6	Now	$88.00
1987	6	Now	$82.00
1988	5	Now	$64.00
1989	7	2000	$82.00
1990	6	Now	$64.00
1991	7	2000	$70.00
1992	7	2002	$64.00
1993	6	2002	$52.00
1994	5	2002	$40.00
1995	Not made		
1996	6	2004	$41.00
1997	7	2008	N/R

Vasse Felix is a very fine Margaret River maker with a small range of convincing wines including a sumptuously elegant Cabernet and one of the finest Shiraz wines in the country. Winemaker: Clive Otto.

VASSE FELIX CABERNET SAUVIGNON ★★★★★

before 1985		Prior	
1985	7	Now	$88.00
1986	6	Now	$70.00

1987	4	Prior	
1988	6	Now	$60.00
1989	5	Now	$46.00
1990	6	Now	$52.00
1991	7	Now	$56.00
1992	6	Now	$44.00
1993	5	Now	$34.00
1994	6	Now	$38.00
1995	7	2001	$41.00
1996	6	2000	$32.00
1997	6	2002	$30.00

VASSE FELIX CLASSIC DRY WHITE ★★★★

before 1992		Prior	
1992	4	Now	$19.00
1993	6	Now	$26.00
1994	5	Now	$20.00
1995	7	Now	$27.00
1996	6	Now	$21.00
1997	5	Now	$16.50
1998	7	Now	$21.00

VASSE FELIX SHIRAZ ★★★★★

before 1988		Prior	
1988	7	Now	$74.00
1989	Not made		
1990	6	Now	$54.00
1991	7	Now	$58.00
1992	4	Prior	
1993	6	Now	$43.00
1994	7	Now	$46.00
1995	6	Now	$37.00
1996	7	2000	$40.00
1997	6	2001	$31.00

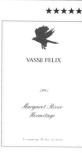

Vidal is a winery operation owned by Villa Maria (New Zealand), the wines being unvaryingly from Hawkes Bay fruit. As with Villa Maria, the Reserve wines are the best and the Estate wines the lesser label.
Winemaker: Rod McDonald.

VIDAL ESTATE CABERNET/MERLOT ★★★

before 1991		Prior	
1991	5	Now	NZ$23.00
1992	4	Now	NZ$17.50
1993	4	Now	NZ$16.00
1994	5	Now	NZ$18.50
1995	7	Now	NZ$24.00
1996	6	Now	NZ$19.50
1997	5	2000	NZ$15.00

VIDAL ESTATE CHARDONNAY

before 1995		Prior	★★★
1995	6	Now	NZ$17.50
1996	6	Now	NZ$16.00
1997	6	Now	NZ$15.00
1998	7	Now	NZ$16.00

VIDAL ESTATE LIGHTLY OAKED SAUVIGNON BLANC (FORMERLY FUME) ★★★

before 1994	Prior		
1994	6	Now	NZ$19.50
1995	No data		
1996	No data		
1997	6	Now	NZ$15.50
1998	6	Now	NZ$14.50

VIDAL ESTATE PINOT NOIR
★★★

1993	6	Now	NZ$33.00
1994	5	Now	NZ$25.00
1995	Not made		
1996	5	2000	NZ$21.00
1997	5	2000	NZ$20.00
1998	5	2002	NZ$18.50

VIDAL RESERVE CABERNET SAUVIGNON ★★★★

1989	5	Now	NZ$50.00
1990	6	Now	NZ$56.00
1991	6	Now	NZ$52.00
1992	Not made		
1993	Not made		
1994	5	Now	NZ$34.00
1995	7	Now	NZ$44.00
1996	Not made		
1997	6	2005	NZ$32.00

VIDAL RESERVE CABERNET/MERLOT ★★★★

1987	7	Now	NZ$76.00
1988	Not made		
1989	6	Now	NZ$54.00
1990	7	Now	NZ$60.00
1991	5	Now	NZ$39.00
1992	6	Now	NZ$44.00
1993	Not made		
1994	Not made		
1995	Not made		
1996	6	2000	NZ$32.00

VIDAL RESERVE CHARDONNAY ★★★★

before 1990	Prior		
1990	6	Now	NZ$54.00
1991	6	Now	NZ$50.00
1992	5	Now	NZ$39.00
1993	5	Now	NZ$36.00
1994	6	Now	NZ$40.00
1995	6	Now	NZ$37.00
1996	7	Now	NZ$40.00
1997	6	2000	NZ$31.00
1998	6	2004	NZ$29.00

VIDAL RESERVE FUME BLANC

			★★★★
before 1991		Prior	
1991	5	Now	NZ$20.00
1992	5	Now	NZ$19.00
1993	6	Now	NZ$21.00
1994	7	Now	NZ$23.00

Not made since 1994.

VIDAL RESERVE GEWURZTRAMINER

			★★★★
before 1991		Prior	
1991	7	Now	NZ$26.00
1992	6	Now	NZ$20.00
1993	Not made		
1994	6	Now	NZ$17.50
1995	7	Now	NZ$19.00

Not made since 1995

VIDAL RESERVE NOBLE SEMILLON

			★★★★
1993	Not made		
1994	5	2000	NZ$41.00
1995	Not made		
1996	7	2005	NZ$50.00
1997	6	2001	NZ$40.00

Villa Maria, once one of New Zealand's more rustic makers has undergone an extreme quality change to be at the forefront of the country's fine wine producers. The Private Bin series is their commercial range; the Reserve wines (made only when the quality justifies the label) are their best. Between these sits their Cellar Selction range. Winemaker: Michelle Richardson.

VILLA MARIA PRIVATE BIN CABERNET SAUVIGNON/ MERLOT

			★★★
before 1995		Prior	
1995	4	Now	NZ$17.50
1996	5	Now	NZ$20.00
1997	4	Now	NZ$15.00

VILLA MARIA PRIVATE BIN CHARDONNAY

			★★★
before 1996		Prior	
1996	5	Now	NZ$16.00
1997	6	Now	NZ$18.00
1998	6	Now	NZ$16.50

VILLA MARIA PRIVATE BIN GEWURZTRAMINER

			★★
1995	3	Now	NZ$11.50
1996	6	Now	NZ$21.00
1997	6	Now	NZ$19.50
1998	6	Now	NZ$18.00

VILLA MARIA PRIVATE BIN
RIESLING ★★

1994	4	Now	NZ$14.00
1995	5	Now	NZ$16.00
1996	7	Now	NZ$21.00
1997	7	Now	NZ$19.50
1998	7	Now	NZ$18.00

VILLA MARIA PRIVATE BIN
SAUVIGNON BLANC ★★★

before 1996		Prior	
1996	5	Now	NZ$15.50
1997	7	Now	NZ$20.00
1998	6	Now	NZ$16.00

VILLA MARIA RESERVE
CABERNET/ MERLOT ★★★★

before 1994		Prior	
1994	5	Now	NZ$30.00
1995	7	Now	N/R
1996	7	Now	N/R
1997	6	Now	N/R

VILLA MARIA RESERVE CHARDONNAY ★★★★

before 1991		Prior	
1991	5	Now	NZ$42.00
1992	4	Now	NZ$31.00
1993	5	Now	NZ$36.00
1994	4	Now	NZ$27.00
1995	4	Now	NZ$25.00
1996	7	Now	NZ$40.00
1997	6	Now	NZ$32.00

VILLA MARIA RESERVE
SAUVIGNON BLANC ★★★★

before 1994		Prior	
1994	5	Now	NZ$18.00
1995	Not made		
1996	7	Now	NZ$22.00
1997	No data		
1998	No data		

Virgin Hills is a high country, cool climate vineyard near Kyneton in Victoria. Winemaker: Martin Williams.

VIRGIN HILLS (DRY RED) ★★★★★

1974	7	Now	$215.00
1975	6	2000	$170.00
1976	6	Prior	
1977	3	Prior	
1978	6	Now	$135.00
1979	6	Now	$125.00
1980	6	2002	$115.00
1981	5	Now	$90.00
1982	7	2003	$115.00
1983	7	2005	$105.00

1984	4	Now	$56.00
1985	7	2005	$92.00
1986	4	Now	$49.00
1987	3	Now	$34.00
1988	7	2008	$72.00
1989	Not made		
1990	6	2002	$54.00
1991	7	2008	$58.00
1992	7	2010	$54.00
1993	6	2004	$43.00
1994	7	2004	$46.00
1995	6	2010	$36.00

Wairau River is a new vineyard in New Zealand's Blenheim area producing a remarkably good Sauvignon Blanc. Winemaker: John Belsham.

WAIRAU RIVER SAUVIGNON BLANC ★★★★

before 1994		Prior	
1994	6	Now	NZ$26.00
1995	4	Now	NZ$16.00
1996	6	Now	NZ$22.00
1997	6	Now	NZ$20.00

Wantirna Estate is a Yarra Valley vineyard of extremely small size and extremely high quality. Winemakers: Reg and Maryann Egan.

WANTIRNA ESTATE CABERNET
SAUVIGNON/MERLOT ★★★★

before 1986		Prior	
1986	7	Now	$92.00
1987	6	Now	$72.00
1988	7	Now	$78.00
1989	6	Now	$62.00
1990	6	Now	$58.00
1991	7	2000	$62.00
1992	7	2001	$58.00
1993	6	2003	$46.00
1994	7	2000	$49.00
1995	7	2004	$46.00
1996	6	2005	$36.00
1997	6	2006	N/R
1998	7	2008	N/R

WANTIRNA ESTATE CHARDONNAY ★★★★

before 1990		Prior	
1991	Not made		
1992	Not made		
1993	6	Prior	
1994	7	Now	$50.00
1995	7	Now	$46.00
1996	7	Now	$43.00
1997	6	2000	$34.00
1998	7	2000	N/R

WANTIRNA ESTATE PINOT NOIR ★★★★★

before 1991		Prior	
1991	6	Now	$58.00
1992	7	Now	$62.00
1993	6	Now	$50.00
1994	6	Now	$46.00
1995	7	2000	$50.00
1996	7	2001	$46.00
1997	7	2004	$43.00
1998	6	2000	N/R

Warramate is a small, low key Yarra Valley vineyard with hand-crafted wines. Winemakers: Jack and David Church.

WARRAMATE CABERNET SAUVIGNON ★★★★

before 1986		Prior	
1986	6	Now	$50.00
1987	6	Now	$47.00
1988	7	Now	$50.00
1989	6	Now	$40.00
1990	6	Now	$37.00
1991	7	Now	$40.00
1992	6	2000	$32.00
1993	6	2001	$30.00
1994	6	2002	$27.00
1995	7	2002	$30.00
1996	6	2003	$23.00

WARRAMATE RIESLING ★★★★

before 1991		Prior	
1991	7	Now	$28.00
1992	5	Now	$18.50
1993	7	Now	$24.00
1994	7	Now	$22.00
1995	7	Now	$20.00
1996	7	2000	$19.00
1997	7	2000	$17.50
1998	7	2002	$16.50

WARRAMATE SHIRAZ ★★★★

before 1986		Prior	
1986	6	Now	$50.00
1987	6	Now	$47.00
1988	6	Now	$44.00
1989	7	Now	$47.00
1990	6	Now	$37.00
1991	6	Now	$35.00
1992	7	Now	$37.00
1993	6	2000	$30.00
1994	6	2002	$27.00
1995	7	2001	$30.00
1996	6	2002	$23.00

Warrenmang is a ten hectare vineyard in the Moonambel district of Central Victoria. Winemaker: Simon Clayfield.

WARRENMANG CHARDONNAY ★★★★

before 1996		Prior	
1996	6	Now	$22.00

WARRENMANG GRAND PYRENEES ★★★★

before 1992		Prior	
1992	6	2000	$31.00
1993	6	2002	$29.00
1994	7	2002	$31.00
1995	5	Now	$20.00

WARRENMANG SHIRAZ ★★★★

before 1993		Prior	
1993	6	Now	$29.00
1994	7	2000	$31.00
1995	6	2000	$24.00
1996	6	2002	$23.00

Water Wheel Vineyards have completely changed their wine styles since new owners took over. The following ratings apply to the new wines. Winemaker: Bill Trevaskis.

WATER WHEEL CABERNET SAUVIGNON ★★★★

before 1993		Prior	
1993	7	Now	$22.00
1994	6	Now	$17.50
1995	6	2001	$16.00
1996	7	2001	$17.50
1997	7	2002	$16.00

WATER WHEEL CHARDONNAY ★★★

before 1995		Prior	
1995	5	Now	$13.50
1996	6	Now	$15.00
1997	7	Now	$16.00
1998	7	2000	$15.00

WATER WHEEL SHIRAZ ★★★

before 1993		Prior	
1993	7	Now	$22.00
1994	6	Now	$17.50
1995	6	2001	$16.00
1996	7	2001	$17.50
1997	7	2002	$16.00

Vendouree (formerly Birks Wendouree) is a Clare Valley maker of some of the most powerful, long living red wines Australia has produced. Since 1980 the style has changed to present a much greater elegance, without sacrificing the depth of these remarkable wines. Unfortunately the proprietors do not believe in rating their own wines, so the wines are simply named and "star ranked" as follows. Winemaker: Tony Brady.

VENDOUREE CABERNET SAUVIGNON	★★★★
VENDOUREE SHIRAZ	★★★★

Vignalls Wines in the Albany region of Western Australia produce wines of marked elegance and power including a justly renowned Pinot Noir. Winemaker: Bill Wignall.

VIGNALLS CHARDONNAY ★★★★

before 1988	Prior	
1988	6	Now	$40.00
1989	6	Now	$37.00
1990	6	Now	$34.00
1991	6	Now	$32.00
1992	6	Now	$29.00
1993	6	Now	$27.00
1994	6	Now	$25.00
1995	6	Now	$23.00
1996	6	Now	$22.00

VIGNALLS PINOT NOIR ★★★★★

1985	5	Now	$52.00
1986	5	Now	$49.00
1987	6	Now	$54.00
1988	6	Now	$50.00
1989	6	Now	$47.00
1990	6	Prior	
1991	6	Prior	
1992	6	Now	$37.00
1993	6	Now	$34.00
1994	4	Prior	
1995	6	Now	$29.00
1996	6	Now	$27.00

VIGNALLS SAUVIGNON BLANC

★★★★

before 1993	Prior	
1993	7	Now	$25.00
1994	5	Now	$16.50
1995	7	Now	$21.00
1996	7	Now	$20.00
1997	6	Now	$15.50

Wildwood is a small maker in Victoria's Macedon region. The wines to date are of impressive style and elegance. Winemaker: Wayne Stott.

WILDWOOD CABERNETS ★★★★

before 1990		Prior	
1990	6	Now	$32.00
1991	7	Now	$35.00
1992	5	Now	$23.00
1993	7	2000	$30.00
1994	6	2001	$23.00
1995	4	2000	$14.50
1996	6	2003	$20.00

WILDWOOD CHARDONNAY ★★★★

before 1993		Prior	
1993	7	2000	$37.00
1994	5	Now	$24.00
1995	5	Now	$22.00
1996	5	2000	$21.00
1997	6	2001	$23.00
1998	5	2002	$18.00

WILDWOOD MERLOT/CABERNET FRANC ★★★★★

1991	7	Now	$48.00
1992	7	Now	$45.00
1993	7	Now	$41.00
1994	6	2001	$33.00
1995	5	2001	$25.00
1996	6	2003	$28.00

WILDWOOD PINOT NOIR ★★★★

before 1994		Prior	
1994	6	Now	$36.00
1995	4	Now	$22.00
1996	6	2000	$31.00
1997	5	2002	$24.00
1998	7	2002	$31.00

WILDWOOD SHIRAZ ★★★

before 1993		Prior	
1993	7	2001	$36.00
1994	Not made		
1995	5	2000	$22.00
1996	6	2001	$25.00

Willespie are Margaret River producers of a range of densely flavoured and convincing wines. Winemaker: Michael Lemmes.

WILLESPIE CABERNET SAUVIGNON ★★★★

before 1984		Prior	
1984	5	Now	$52.00
1985	5	Now	$49.00
1986	5	2001	$45.00

1987	7	2005	$58.00
1988	6	Now	$47.00
1989	7	Now	$50.00
1990	7	Now	$47.00
1991	7	Now	$43.00
1992	6	Now	$34.00
1993	7	2000	$37.00
1994	7	2001	$34.00
1995	7	2002	$32.00
1996	6	2003	N/R

WILLESPIE SAUVIGNON BLANC ★★★★

1989	4	Prior	
1990	6	Now	$37.00
1991	7	Now	$39.00
1992	6	Now	$31.00
1993	7	Now	$34.00
1994	6	Now	$27.00
1995	7	Now	$29.00
1996	6	Now	$23.00
1997	7	Now	$25.00
1998	7	Now	$23.00

WILLESPIE SEMILLON/SAUVIGNON BLANC ★★★★

1993	7	Now	$29.00
1994	6	Now	$23.00
1995	7	Now	$25.00
1996	7	Now	$23.00
1997	7	Now	$21.00

WILLESPIE VERDELHO ★★★★

before 1990		Prior	
1990	7	Now	$38.00
1991	7	Now	$35.00
1992	6	Now	$27.00
1993	7	Now	$30.00
1994	6	Now	$23.00
1995	7	Now	$25.00
1996	6	Now	$20.00
1997	7	2000	$22.00

*Willow Creek is a new Mornington Peninsula producer
with 15 hectares of Chardonnay, Cabernet and Pinot Noir.
Winemaker: Kim Hart.*

WILLOW CREEK PINOT NOIR ★★★

1994	7	Now	$32.00
1995	7	Now	$30.00
1996	6	2001	$24.00
1997	7	2003	$25.00

WILLOW CREEK TULUM CHARDONNAY ★★★★

1993	6	Now	$27.00
1994	7	Now	$29.00
1995	7	Now	$27.00
1996	Not made		
1997	Not made		

WILLOW CREEK UNOAKED
CHARDONNAY ★★★★

1994	5	Now	$16.50
1995	6	Now	$18.50
1996	6	Now	$17.00
1997	7	Now	$18.50

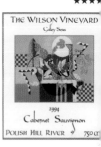

The Wilson Vineyard is a Polish Hill River region (Clare Valley) producer who has done a great deal to promote the high quality of the area. Winemaker: John Wilson.

The WILSON VINEYARD
CABERNET SAUVIGNON ★★★★

1982	4	Prior	
1983	Not made		
1984	5	Now	$43.00
1985	7	Now	$56.00
1986	7	Now	$52.00
1987	6	Now	$41.00
1988	7	2005	$44.00
1989	4	Now	$23.00
1990	6	2005	$32.00
1991	5	Now	$25.00
1992	6	2005	$28.00
1993	Not made		
1994	7	2008	$28.00
1995	5	2003	$18.50
1996	6	2005	$20.00
1997	6	2005	$19.00
1998	6	2010	N/R

The WILSON VINEYARD
CHARDONNAY ★★★

1994	5	Now	$15.00
1995	6	Now	$17.00
1996	7	Now	$18.00
1997	6	Now	$14.50
1998	6	2001	$13.50

The WILSON VINEYARD
HIPPOCRENE (SPARKLING RED) ★★★★

1990	6	2005	$30.00
1991	6	2005	$28.00
1992	5	Now	$22.00
1993	6	Now	$24.00
1994	6	2002	$22.00

The WILSON VINEYARD RIESLING ★★★★

1985	7	2000	$40.00
1986	6	Now	$32.00
1987	6	Now	$30.00
1988	7	2002	$32.00
1989	6	Now	$25.00
1990	6	2005	$23.00
1991	7	2005	$25.00
1992	7	2005	$23.00
1993	5	Now	$15.50
1994	6	2010	$17.50
1995	7	2010	$18.50
1996	7	2010	$17.50
1997	7	2010	$16.00

The WILSON VINEYARD ZINFANDEL (375 ml) ★★★

1986	5	Now	$33.00
1987	4	Prior	
1988	6	Now	$34.00
1989	Not made		
1990	6	Now	$29.00
1991	6	Now	$27.00
1992	Not made		
1993	Not made		
1994	6	Now	$21.00
1995	Not made		
1996	Not made		
1997	6	2000	$17.00

Windy Ridge Vineyard and Winery in South Gippsland is *the southernmost vineyard on the Australian mainland. Its owner would also probably lay claim to it's being the windiest. Winemaker: Graeme Wilson.*

WINDY RIDGE CABERNET/MALBEC ★★★★

1988	3	Now	$28.00
1989	5	Prior	
1990	7	2000	$56.00
1991	6	2001	$45.00
1992	Not made		
1993	Not made		
1994	6	2004	$35.00
1995	7	2005	$38.00
1996	4	2004	$20.00
1997	7	2007	N/R
1998	6	2008	N/R

WINDY RIDGE PINOT NOIR ★★★★★

1988	5	Prior	
1989	6	2000	$64.00
1990	5	Prior	

1991	5	Prior	
1992	Not made		
1993	Not made		
1994	6	2000	$43.00
1995	7	2002	$47.00
1996	5	2003	N/R
1997	6	2004	N/R
1998	7	2007	N/R

Winstead *is a tiny (1.2 ha) vineyard in Tasmania's Bagdad region. The wines are admirable. Winemaker: Andrew Hood.*

WINSTEAD PINOT NOIR ★★★★

1994	7	2002	$41.00
1995	6	2000	$32.00
1996	5	Now	$25.00
1997	6	2002	$28.00

WINSTEAD RIESLING ★★★★★

1994	6	Now	$27.00
1995	7	2000	$29.00
1996	5	Now	$19.00
1997	6	2002	$21.00
1998	6	2002	$20.00

Wirra Wirra *is a McLaren Vale producer of a range of very stylish and elegant wines. Winemaker: Ben Riggs.*

WIRRA WIRRA "THE ANGELUS"
CABERNET SAUVIGNON ★★★★★

before 1984	Prior		
1984	6	Now	$68.00
1985	5	Now	$52.00
1986	Not made		
1987	5	Now	$45.00
1988	5	Now	$41.00
1989	5	2000	$38.00
1990	6	2002	$42.00
1991	6	2003	$39.00
1992	6	2005	$36.00
1993	6	2005	$34.00
1994	6	2004	$31.00
1995	5	2004	$24.00

WIRRA WIRRA CHARDONNAY ★★★★

before 1990	Prior		
1990	6	Now	$32.00
1991	7	Now	$35.00
1992	6	Now	$27.00
1993	5	Now	$21.00
1994	5	2004	$19.50
1995	6	2004	$22.00
1996	6	2004	$20.00

WIRRA WIRRA CHURCH BLOCK ★★★★

before 1982		Prior	
1982	6	Now	$52.00
1983	5	Prior	
1984	5	Now	$37.00
1985	5	Now	$34.00
1986	7	Now	$45.00
1987	5	Now	$29.00
1988	6	Now	$33.00
1989	6	Now	$30.00
1990	6	2000	$28.00
1991	6	2002	$26.00
1992	6	2003	$24.00
1993	5	2002	$18.50
1994	6	2002	$20.00
1995	4	2000	$12.50
1996	5	2004	$14.50

WIRRA WIRRA HAND PICKED RIESLING ★★★★

before 1986		Prior	
1986	6	Now	$34.00
1987	5	Now	$26.00
1988	5	Now	$24.00
1989	5	Now	$22.00
1990	6	2002	$25.00
1991	6	2004	$23.00
1992	6	2004	$21.00
1993	5	2000	$16.50
1994	6	2002	$18.50
1995	6	2005	$17.00
1996	6	2006	$16.00
1997	6	2005	$14.50

WIRRA WIRRA SAUVIGNON BLANC ★★★★

before 1992		Prior	
1992	7	Now	$27.00
1993	5	Now	$18.00
1994	7	Now	$23.00
1995	4	Now	$12.00
1996	6	2000	$17.00
1997	5	2000	$13.00

WIRRA WIRRA SEMILLON/SAUVIGNON BLANC ★★★

before 1990		Prior	
1990	6	Now	$30.00
1991	5	Now	$23.00
1992	5	Now	$21.00
1993	5	Now	$20.00
1994	6	2000	$22.00

1995	4	Now	$13.50
1996	6	2000	$19.00
1997	6	2000	$17.50

WIRRA WIRRA SHIRAZ ★★★★

1989	5	Now	$35.00
1990	6	2001	$39.00
1991	7	2005	$42.00
1992	6	2010	$34.00
1993	5	2000	$26.00
1994	7	2004	$34.00
1995	6	2004	$27.00

Wolf Blass wines have generated an immense reputation in the last decade - a reputation for both quality and reliability. Winemakers: John Glaetzer and Wendy Stuckey.

WOLF BLASS CABERNET SAUVIGNON/SHIRAZ/MERLOT (BLACK LABEL) ★★★★★

1973	6	Now	$460.00
1974	6	Now	$420.00
1975	7	Now	$460.00
1976	6	Now	$360.00
1977	6	Now	$330.00
1978	6	Now	$310.00
1979	6	Now	$290.00
1980	7	Now	$310.00
1981	6	Now	$245.00
1982	7	Now	$260.00
1983	6	Now	$210.00
1984	6	Now	$195.00
1985	6	Now	$180.00
1986	6	Now	$165.00
1987	6	Now	$155.00
1988	6	2005	$140.00
1989	6	2003	$130.00
1990	6	2005	$120.00
1991	7	2010	$130.00
1992	6	2008	$105.00
1993	6	2010	$98.00
1994	7	2010	$105.00

WOLF BLASS CABERNET SAUVIGNON/SHIRAZ (GREY LABEL) ★★★

before 1976		Prior	
1976	5	Now	$120.00
1977	5	Now	$110.00
1978	6	Now	$120.00
1979	6	Now	$115.00
1980	5	Now	$88.00
1981	6	Now	$98.00

1982	5	Now	$76.00
1983	5	Now	$70.00
1984	6	Now	$78.00
1985	6	Now	$72.00
1986	5	Now	$56.00
1987	5	Now	$52.00
1988	6	Now	$58.00
1989	5	Now	$44.00
1990	7	Now	$58.00
1991	5	2004	$38.00
1992	6	2005	$42.00
1993	6	2006	$39.00
1994	7	2007	$42.00
1995	6	2008	$34.00
1996	7	2008	$36.00

WOLF BLASS CABERNET SAUVIGNON/SHIRAZ (YELLOW LABEL) ★★★

before 1982		Prior	
1982	7	Now	$62.00
1983	5	Now	$41.00
1984	6	Now	$46.00
1985	5	Now	$35.00
1986	5	Now	$33.00
1987	5	Now	$30.00
1988	6	Now	$34.00
1989	5	Now	$26.00
1990	6	2000	$29.00
1991	5	2001	$22.00
1992	6	2004	$25.00
1993	6	2005	$23.00
1994	5	2001	$17.50
1995	5	2002	$16.50
1996	7	2004	$21.00
1997	6	2001	$17.00

WOLF BLASS CLASSIC DRY WHITE ★★★

before 1993		Prior	
1993	6	Now	$20.00
1994	6	Now	$19.00
1995	7	Now	$20.00
1996	6	Now	$16.50
1997	6	2000	$15.00
1998	7	2001	$16.50

WOLF BLASS CLASSIC SHIRAZ (BROWN LABEL) ★★★★

before 1982		Prior	
1982	6	Now	$72.00
1983	7	Now	$78.00

1984	6	Now	$62.00
1985	6	Now	$56.00
1986	6	Now	$52.00
1987	7	Now	$56.00
1988	6	Now	$45.00
1989	6	Now	$42.00
1990	7	2000	$45.00
1991	6	2000	$36.00
1992	6	2001	$33.00
1993	7	2002	$36.00
1994	6	2003	$28.00
1995	6	2006	$26.00
1996	7	2006	$28.00

WOLF BLASS PINOT NOIR/CHARDONNAY CUVEE ★★★

before 1991		Prior	
1991	6	Now	$23.00
1992	5	Now	$18.00
1993	6	Now	$20.00
1994	7	Now	$21.00
1995	7	2000	$20.00
1996	7	2001	$18.50

WOLF BLASS RIESLING (GOLD LABEL) ★★★★

before 1989		Prior	
1989	5	Now	$24.00
1990	6	Now	$27.00
1991	7	Now	$29.00
1992	7	Now	$27.00
1993	6	Now	$22.00
1994	6	2000	$20.00
1995	6	2000	$18.50
1996	7	2002	$20.00
1997	7	2002	$18.50
1998	7	2003	$17.50

WOLF BLASS RIESLING (YELLOW LABEL) ★★★

before 1987		Prior	
1987	7	Now	$33.00
1988	6	Now	$26.00
1989	5	Now	$20.00
1990	6	Now	$23.00
1991	6	Now	$21.00
1992	Not made		
1993	7	Now	$21.00
1994	6	Now	$16.50
1995	7	Now	$18.00
1996	6	2000	$14.50
1997	6	2001	$13.00
1998	7	2001	$14.50

WOLF BLASS SHOW CHARDONNAY   ★★★★

before 1988		Prior	
1988	7	Now	$50.00
1989	6	Now	$40.00
1990	6	Now	$37.00
1991	Not made		
1994	7	2000	$37.00
1995	6	2002	$29.00
1996	6	2000	$27.00
1997	6	2000	$25.00
1998	7	2002	$27.00

Woodstock are McLaren Flat producers whose wines have rapidly been afforded prominence throughout Australia. Winemaker: Scott Collett.

WOODSTOCK BOTRYTIS SWEET WHITE (375ml)
★★★★

1984	6	Now	$36.00
1985	7	Now	$39.00
1986	6	Now	$31.00
1987	7	Now	$33.00
1988	Not made		
1989	Not made		
1990	6	Now	$23.00
1991	7	Now	$24.00
1992	6	Now	$19.50
1993	6	Now	$18.00
1994	6	Now	$16.50
1995	5	Now	$13.00
1996	6	Now	$14.50
1997	7	Now	$15.50

WOODSTOCK CABERNET SAUVIGNON   ★★★★

1981	6	Prior	
1982	7	Now	$64.00
1983	6	Now	$50.00
1984	7	Now	$54.00
1985	5	Now	$36.00
1986	6	Now	$40.00
1987	7	2000	$43.00
1988	7	2000	$40.00
1989	6	2001	$32.00
1990	6	2002	$29.00
1991	6	2003	$27.00
1992	7	2006	$29.00
1993	6	2002	$23.00
1994	7	2003	$25.00
1995	6	2006	$20.00
1996	7	2008	$21.00

WOODSTOCK CHARDONNAY ★★★

1984	7	Now	$52.00
1985	7	Now	$49.00
1986	6	Now	$39.00
1987	6	Now	$36.00
1988	6	Now	$33.00
1989	6	Now	$31.00
1990	6	Now	$28.00
1991	6	Now	$26.00
1992	6	Now	$24.00
1993	6	Now	$22.00
1994	6	Now	$21.00
1995	6	Now	$19.50
1996	5	Now	$15.00
1997	6	2000	$16.50

WOODSTOCK RIESLING ★★★

before 1992		Prior	
1992	6	Now	$17.50
1993	6	Now	$16.00
1994	6	Now	$15.00
1995	6	Now	$13.50
1996	Not made		
1997	6	2000	$12.00

WOODSTOCK SAUVIGNON BLANC/SEMILLON ★★★

before 1990		Prior	
1990	6	Now	$25.00
1991	6	Now	$23.00
1992	6	Now	$22.00
1993	Not made		
1994	6	Now	$19.00
1995	6	Now	$17.50
1996	6	Now	$16.00
1997	Not made		
1998	6	Now	$14.00

WOODSTOCK SHIRAZ ★★★

1982	6	2003	$52.00
1983	5	Now	$40.00
1984	7	Now	$52.00
1985	Not made		
1986	6	2000	$38.00
1987	6	Now	$35.00
1988	7	2000	$38.00
1989	6	2000	$30.00
1990	6	2000	$28.00
1991	6	2002	$26.00
1992	6	2003	$24.00
1993	6	2004	$22.00

1994	7	2006	$24.00
1995	6	2005	$19.00
1996	6	2005	$17.50
1997	6	2005	$16.50

WOODSTOCK "THE STOCKS" SHIRAZ
(CABERNET IN 1993) ★★★★

1991	6	2006	$40.00
1992	Not made		
1994	7	2006	$40.00
1994	6	2004	$31.00
1995	7	2008	$34.00
1996	7	2010	$31.00

Wyndham Estate in the Hunter Valley has been one of the most successful marketers in the Australian wine world, and is now part of Orlando Wyndham. Winemaker: Robert Paul.

WYNDHAM ESTATE BLANC SUPERIOR (formerly
BIN 777 SEMILLON/
CHARDONNAY) ★★

1992	5	Now	$11.50
1993	6	Now	$12.50
1994	6	Now	$11.50
1995	6	Now	$11.00
1996	6	Now	$10.00
1997	7	Now	$11.00
1998	7	Now	$10.00

WYNDHAM ESTATE CABERNET/MERLOT BIN 888
★★★

1989	5	Now	$31.00
1990	6	Now	$35.00
1991	7	Now	$37.00
1992	7	Now	$35.00
1993	7	2000	$32.00
1994	7	Now	$30.00
1995	6	2001	$23.00
1996	7	2001	$25.00
1997	6	2002	$20.00

WYNDHAM ESTATE CABERNET
SAUVIGNON BIN 444 ★★★

before 1989	Prior		
1989	5	Now	$20.00
1990	5	Now	$19.00
1991	7	Now	$24.00
1992	6	Now	$19.50
1993	7	Now	$21.00
1994	6	Now	$17.00
1995	6	Now	$15.50
1996	7	2001	$17.00
1997	7	2001	$15.50

WYNDHAM ESTATE CHABLIS SUPERIOR ★★

1992	6	Now	$14.00
1993	6	Now	$13.00
1994	6	Now	$12.00
1995	6	Now	$11.00
1996	6	Now	$10.00
1997	6	Now	$9.50
1998	6	Now	$9.00

WYNDHAM ESTATE CHARDONNAY BIN 222 ★★

1992	6	Now	$19.00
1993	7	Now	$20.00
1994	6	Now	$16.50
1995	6	Now	$15.00
1996	6	Now	$14.00
1997	7	Now	$15.00
1998	7	2000	$14.00

WYNDHAM ESTATE SHIRAZ BIN 555 ★★

before 1989		Prior	
1989	6	Now	$25.00
1990	6	Now	$23.00
1991	6	Now	$21.00
1992	5	Now	$16.50
1993	6	Now	$18.50
1994	6	Now	$17.00
1995	6	Now	$16.00
1996	7	Now	$17.00
1997	7	Now	$16.00

WYNDHAM ESTATE OAK CASK CHARDONNAY ★★

1990	6	Prior	
1991	7	Now	$26.00
1992	7	Now	$24.00
1993	7	Now	$22.00
1994	6	Now	$18.00
1995	6	Now	$16.50
1996	6	Now	$15.00
1997	6	2000	$14.00
1998	6	2000	$13.00

WYNDHAM PINOT NOIR BIN 333 ★★

1992	5	Now	$18.50
1993	5	Now	$17.50
1994	5	Now	$16.00
1995	6	Now	$18.00
1996	6	Now	$16.50
1997	7	Now	$18.00
1998	7	2000	$16.50

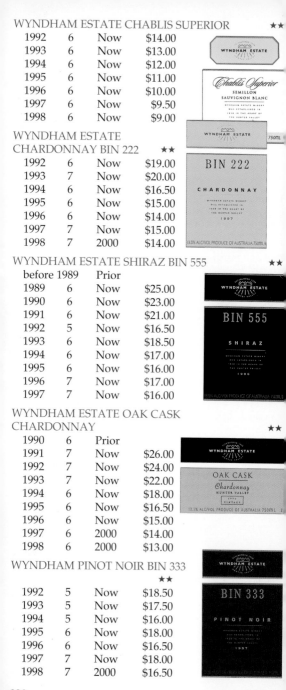

WYNDHAM ESTATE VERDELHO ★★

before 1990	Prior		
1990	5	Now	$18.50
1991	6	Now	$20.00
1992	6	Now	$19.00
1993	Not made		
1994	7	Now	$19.00
1995	6	Now	$15.00
1996	7	Now	$16.50
1997	7	Now	$15.00
1998	7	2000	$14.00

Wynn's Coonawarra Estate are leading red wine makers whose confidence in Coonawarra once saved the area as a vignoble. They are now in the immense Southcorp stable. Winemaker: Peter Douglas.

WYNNS COONAWARRA ESTATE
CABERNET SAUVIGNON ★★★★

before 1982	Prior		
1982	7	Now	$88.00
1983	3	Prior	
1984	4	Now	$43.00
1985	5	Now	$50.00
1986	7	2000	$64.00
1987	4	Now	$34.00
1988	5	2000	$40.00
1989	4	Now	$29.00
1990	7	2010	$48.00
1991	6	2005	$38.00
1992	5	2000	$29.00
1993	6	2010	$33.00
1994	6	2005	$30.00
1995	5	2003	$23.00
1996	5	2002	$21.00

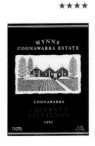

WYNNS COONAWARRA ESTATE
CABERNET/SHIRAZ/MERLOT ★★★★

before 1982	Prior		
1982	6	Now	$56.00
1983	4	Prior	
1984	5	Prior	
1985	6	Now	$45.00
1986	7	Now	$49.00
1987	3	Prior	
1988	5	Now	$30.00
1989	4	Now	$22.00
1990	7	2005	$36.00
1991	6	Now	$28.00
1992	4	Now	$17.50
1993	6	2000	$24.00

1994	5	Now	$19.00
1995	5	2000	$17.50
1996	5	2000	$16.00

WYNNS COONAWARRA ESTATE CHARDONNAY ★★★

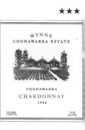

before 1991	Prior		
1991	7	Now	$30.00
1992	5	Now	$20.00
1993	5	Now	$18.50
1994	6	Now	$20.00
1995	7	2000	$22.00
1996	6	2000	$17.50
1997	6	2002	$16.50
1998	5	2000	$12.50

WYNNS JOHN RIDDOCH CABERNET SAUVIGNON ★★★★★

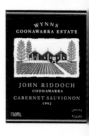

1982	7	2000	$280.00
1983	Not made		
1984	5	Now	$170.00
1985	4	Now	$125.00
1986	7	2010	$210.00
1987	6	2000	$165.00
1988	6	2005	$150.00
1989	Not made		
1990	7	2020	$150.00
1991	6	2015	$120.00
1992	5	2005	$94.00
1993	6	2010	$100.00
1994	5	2010	$80.00
1995	Not made		
1996	5	2010	$68.00

WYNNS COONAWARRA ESTATE MICHAEL SHIRAZ ★★★★★

1990	7	2005	$145.00
1991	6	2000	$115.00
1992	Not made		
1993	6	2010	$100.00
1994	6	2005	$92.00
1995	Not made		
1996	5	2010	$66.00

WYNNS COONAWARRA ESTATE RIESLING ★★

before 1994	Prior		
1994	6	Now	$15.00
1995	6	Now	$14.00
1996	6	2000	$13.00
1997	6	Now	$12.00
1998	5	2000	$9.25

WYNNS COONAWARRA ESTATE SHIRAZ   ★★★★

before 1982		Prior	
1982	6	Now	$60.00
1983	4	Prior	
1984	4	Prior	
1985	5	Now	$40.00
1986	7	2002	$52.00
1987	4	Now	$27.00
1988	5	2000	$32.00
1989	5	Now	$29.00
1990	7	2005	$38.00
1991	6	2000	$30.00
1992	4	Now	$19.00
1993	7	2005	$30.00
1994	5	2000	$20.00
1995	4	2000	$15.00
1996	5	2002	$17.00
1997	6	2002	$19.00

Yalumba is the best known brand in the S. Smith and Sons empire, which includes Pewsey Vale and Heggies. Wines from this fine family firm are honest, reliable and sometimes very good indeed. Winemaker: Simon Adams.

YALUMBA BUSH VINE GRENACHE   ★★★★

1993	5	Now	$18.00
1994	6	Now	$20.00
1995	6	Now	$18.50
1996	6	Now	$17.00
1997	6	Now	$16.00
1998	7	Now	$17.50

YALUMBA CHARDONNAY ★★★

1995	5	Now	$15.50
1996	6	Now	$17.00
1997	7	Now	$18.50

YALUMBA "D" METHODE CHAMPENOISE   ★★★★★

before 1990		Prior	
1990	7	Now	$42.00
1991	6	Prior	
1992	5	Now	$26.00
1993	6	Now	$28.00
1994	6	Now	$26.00
1995	6	Now	$24.00
1996	6	Now	$23.00

YALUMBA RESERVE CHARDONNAY   ★★★★

before 1992		Prior	
1992	5	Now	$29.00
1993	5	Now	$26.00

1994	6	Now	$29.00
1995	6	Now	$27.00
1996	6	Now	$25.00

YALUMBA SHIRAZ ★★★★

1992	6	Now	$22.00
1993	7	Now	$23.00
1994	6	Now	$18.50
1995	6	2000	$17.00
1996	6	2002	$16.00
1997	5	2001	$12.50

YALUMBA "THE MENZIES"
CABERNET SAUVIGNON ★★★★

1987	5	Prior	
1988	6	Now	$49.00
1989	5	Prior	
1990	6	Now	$42.00
1991	6	Now	$39.00
1992	6	Now	$36.00
1993	5	2000	$28.00
1994	6	2002	$31.00
1995	5	2000	$24.00
1996	6	2002	$26.00

YALUMBA "THE OCTAVIUS" (SHIRAZ)
★★★★★

1988	6	2000	$88.00
1989	Not made		
1990	6	2004	$76.00
1991	Not made		
1992	6	2006	$64.00
1993	7	2003	$70.00
1994	7	2010	$64.00
1995	6	2004	$52.00

YALUMBA "THE SIGNATURE" RESERVE
CABERNET SAUVIGNON/SHIRAZ ★★★★★

before 1985		Prior	
1985	5	Now	$64.00
1986	5	Now	$60.00
1987	6	Now	$66.00
1988	6	Now	$62.00
1989	5	Now	$48.00
1990	7	2002	$62.00
1991	6	2000	$49.00
1992	7	2005	$52.00
1993	5	2001	$35.00
1994	6	2005	$39.00
1995	5	2002	$30.00

Yarra Burn, yet another Yarra Valley maker specializing in the noble varieties, has now been acquired by BRL Hardy. Winemaker: David Fyffe.

YARRA BURN CABERNETS ★★★

before 1984		Prior	
1984	7	Now	$54.00
1985	5	Now	$36.00
1986	6	Now	$40.00
1987	5	Now	$31.00
1988	6	Now	$34.00
1989	5	Now	$26.00
1990	6	Now	$29.00
1991	6	Now	$27.00
1992	7	2000	$29.00
1993	5	Now	$19.50
1994	6	2002	$21.00
1995	7	2005	$23.00

YARRA BURN CHARDONNAY ★★★★

before 1990		Prior	
1990	6	Now	$38.00
1991	5	Now	$29.00
1992	5	Now	$27.00
1993	5	Now	$25.00
1994	5	Now	$23.00
1995	6	Now	$26.00
1996	5	Now	$20.00
1997	6	2001	$22.00

YARRA BURN PINOT NOIR ★★★★

before 1988		Prior	
1988	7	Now	$37.00
1989	6	Now	$30.00
1990	5	Now	$23.00
1991	5	Now	$21.00
1992	5	Now	$19.50
1993	5	Now	$18.00
1994	4	Now	$13.50

No longer made.

Yarra Edge are Yarra Valley makers with two very impressive wines, notable for concentrated flavours without sacrifice of elegance. Winemaker: Tom Carson.

YARRA EDGE CABERNETS ★★★★

1990	6	Now	$46.00
1991	7	2001	$49.00
1992	6	2000	$39.00
1993	6	2005	$36.00
1994	5	2000	$28.00
1995	7	2005	$36.00
1996	5	2005	$24.00

YARRA EDGE CHARDONNAY

★★★★

1990	6	Now	$45.00
1991	7	2000	$48.00
1992	7	Now	$45.00
1993	6	2000	$35.00
1994	4	Now	$22.00
1995	6	Now	$30.00
1996	7	2002	$33.00
1997	7	2002	$30.00

Yarra Ridge, *the largest producer in the Yarra Valley, is part-owned by Mildara Blass. Winemaker: Rob Dolan.*

YARRA RIDGE BOTRYTIS SEMILLON (375ml) ★★★★

1988	7	Now	$47.00
1989	Not made		
1990	6	Now	$35.00
1991	6	Now	$32.00
1992	6	Now	$30.00
1993	7	Now	$32.00
1994	6	Now	$25.00
1995	6	Now	$23.00
1996	6	Prior	
1997	Not made		
1998	7	2000	$22.00

YARRA RIDGE CABERNET SAUVIGNON

★★★★

before 1990	Prior		
1990	7	Now	$39.00
1991	6	Now	$31.00
1992	6	2000	$29.00
1993	6	Now	$27.00
1994	6	2000	$25.00
1995	5	2000	$19.00
1996	6	2001	$21.00
1997	7	2005	$23.00

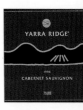

YARRA RIDGE CHARDONNAY

★★★

1992	7	Now	$37.00
1993	6	Now	$29.00
1994	6	Now	$27.00
1995	6	2000	$25.00
1996	5	2000	$19.00
1997	6	2001	$21.00
1998	6	2001	$20.00

YARRA RIDGE MERLOT ★★★★

1995	7	2001	$25.00
1996	5	2000	$17.00
1997	7	2002	$22.00

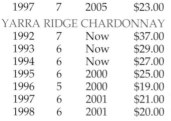

YARRA RIDGE PINOT NOIR

★★★★

1992	6	Now	$33.00
1993	5	Now	$25.00
1994	5	Now	$23.00

1995	5	Now	$22.00
1996	7	2001	$28.00
1997	6	2000	$22.00
1998	6	2001	$21.00

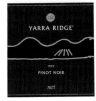

YARRA RIDGE RESERVE PINOT NOIR ★★★★★

1992	7	Now	$54.00
1993	Not made		
1994	Not made		
1995	Not made		
1996	7	2002	$41.00
1997	7	2003	$38.00

YARRA RIDGE SAUVIGNON BLANC ★★★

before 1995	Prior		
1995	5	Now	$22.00
1996	5	Now	$21.00
1997	6	Now	$23.00
1998	6	Now	$21.00

YARRA RIDGE SHIRAZ ★★★★

1994	5	Now	$20.00
1995	6	2000	$23.00
1996	Not made		
1997	7	2003	$23.00

Yarra Yering is a small, purist operation in the Yarra Valley whose wines were in the forefront of the movement towards greater elegance in Australian wines. The winemaker's ratings have been unavailable for recent years. Winemaker: Bailey Carrodus.

YARRA YERING CHARDONNAY ★★★★

before 1985	Prior		
1985	5	Now	$43.00
1986	5	Now	$40.00
1987	6	Now	$44.00
1988	6	Now	$41.00
1989	5	Now	$32.00
1990	6	Now	$35.00
1991	6	Now	$32.00
1992	5	Now	$25.00
No data since 1992			

YARRA YERING DRY RED NUMBER 1 (CABERNETS) ★★★★★

before 1984	Prior		
1984	5	Now	$50.00
1985	5	Now	$47.00
1986	6	Now	$52.00
1987	5	Now	$41.00
1988	4	Now	$30.00
1989	6	Now	$42.00
1990	6	Now	$39.00

1991	6	Now	$36.00
1992	5	Now	$28.00
1993	6	2000	$31.00

No data since 1993

YARRA YERING DRY RED NUMBER 2 (SHIRAZ BLEND)

★★★★★

before 1983	Prior		
1983	6	Now	$62.00
1984	6	Now	$58.00
1985	5	Now	$45.00
1986	6	Now	$50.00
1987	5	Now	$38.00
1988	Not made		
1989	6	Now	$40.00
1990	6	Now	$37.00
1991	6	Now	$34.00
1992	5	1988	$26.00
1993	6	2000	$29.00

No data since 1993

YARRA YERING PINOT NOIR

★★★★★

before 1986	Prior		
1986	5	Now	$58.00
1987	6	2000	$66.00
1988	Not made		
1989	4	2001	$38.00
1990	6	2002	$52.00
1991	7	2000	$56.00
1992	7	2000	$52.00

No data since 1992

YARRA YERING SEMILLON (DRY WHITE NUMBER 1)

★★★★

before 1985	Prior		
1985	5	Now	$40.00
1986	5	Now	$37.00
1987	6	Now	$41.00
1988	6	Now	$38.00
1989	4	Now	$23.00
1990	6	Now	$33.00
1991	6	Now	$30.00
1992	5	Now	$23.00
1993	6	Now	$26.00

No data since 1993

YARRA YERING UNDERHILL SHIRAZ

★★★★

1991	6	Now	$32.00
1992	5	Now	$24.00
1993	6	2000	$27.00

No data since 1993

Yarrabank is an operation dedicated to the production of extreme quality sparkling wine. Winemaker: Claude Thibaud.

YARRABANK CUVEE BRUT ★★★★★

1993	7	2000	$44.00
1994	7	2001	$40.00
1995	7	2001	$37.00
1996	7	2002	$35.00
1997	7	2004	N/R

Yellowglen was established in the Ballarat area as a specialist Champagne-style producer and have been resoundingly successful as such. It is part of the Mildara Blass group. Winemaker: Nick Walker.

YELLOWGLEN CUVEE VICTORIA METHODE CHAMPENOISE ★★★★

before 1992		Prior	
1992	5	Now	$29.00
1993	6	Now	$33.00
1994	7	2000	$35.00
1995	7	2001	$33.00
1996	7	2002	$30.00

YELLOWGLEN VINTAGE BRUT ★★★

before 1992		Prior	
1992	7	Now	$25.00
1993	7	Now	$23.00
1994	5	Now	$15.50
1995	6	Now	$17.00

Yeringberg is a tiny (2 hectare) vineyard in the Yarra Valley which annually produces 800 cases of graceful, handmade wines. Winemaker: Guill de Pury.

YERINGBERG (Formerly CABERNET) ★★★★★

before 1976		Prior	
1976	7	Now	$210.00
1977	5	Now	$140.00
1978	2	Prior	
1979	6	Now	$145.00
1980	7	Now	$155.00
1981	7	Now	$145.00
1982	6	Now	$115.00
1983	4	Now	$70.00
1984	6	Now	$98.00
1985	5	Now	$76.00
1986	6	Now	$84.00
1987	4	Now	$52.00
1988	7	Now	$84.00
1989	4	Now	$45.00
1990	7	Now	$72.00
1991	7	Now	$66.00
1992	7	2000	$62.00
1993	6	2001	$49.00
1994	6	2002	$46.00

1995	6	2003	$42.00
1996	6	2004	$39.00
1997	5	2005	$30.00

YERINGBERG CHARDONNAY ★★★★★

before 1980		Prior	
1980	5	Now	$110.00
1981	5	Now	$100.00
1982	4	Prior	
1983	4	Now	$72.00
1984	5	Now	$82.00
1985	7	Now	$105.00
1986	5	Now	$70.00
1987	5	Now	$66.00
1988	7	Prior	
1989	5	Now	$56.00
1990	6	Now	$62.00
1991	6	Prior	
1992	6	Now	$54.00
1993	7	Now	$58.00
1994	7	Now	$54.00
1995	5	Now	$35.00
1995	5	Now	$33.00
1996	5	2000	$30.00
1997	5	2001	$28.00
1998	6	2002	$31.00

YERINGBERG MARSANNE/ROUSSANNE ★★★★

1979	5	Now	$120.00
1980	3	Now	$66.00
1981	5	Now	$100.00
1982	5	Now	$96.00
1983	2	Prior	
1984	7	Now	$110.00
1985	6	Now	$90.00
1986	2	Prior	
1987	7	Now	$90.00
1988	7	Now	$84.00
1989	3	Prior	
1990	6	Now	$62.00
1991	5	Prior	
1992	6	Now	$52.00
1993	6	Now	$49.00
1994	5	Now	$38.00
1995	5	Now	$35.00
1996	6	Now	$39.00
1997	6	2000	$36.00
1998	6	2001	$33.00

YERINGBERG PINOT NOIR ★★★★

before 1978		Prior	
1978	4	Now	$100.00
1979	5	Now	$115.00
1980	7	Now	$150.00

1981	7	Now	$140.00
1982	7	Now	$130.00
1983	7	Now	$120.00
1984	5	Now	$80.00
1985	6	Now	$90.00
1986	7	Now	$96.00
1987	5	Now	$64.00
1988	6	Now	$70.00
1989	6	Now	$66.00
1990	6	Now	$60.00
1991	6	Now	$56.00
1992	6	Now	$52.00
1993	5	Now	$40.00
1994	5	2000	$37.00
1995	5	Now	$34.00
1996	6	2000	$38.00
1997	6	2001	$35.00

Yering Station *is a 1988 replanting of part of the first Victorian vineyard of Paul de Castella, originally established in the Yarra Valley in 1838. Winemaker: Tom Carson.*

YERING STATION CABERNET SAUVIGNON(/MERLOT) ★★★★

1991	7	Now	$36.00
1992	5	Now	$23.00
1993	5	Now	$22.00
1994	6	Now	$24.00
1995	7	2002	$26.00
1996	6	2001	$21.00
1997	7	2002	N/R
1998	7	2004	N/R

YERING STATION CHARDONNAY ★★★

1991	5	Now	$27.00
1992	6	Now	$30.00
1993	7	Now	$32.00
1994	6	Now	$25.00
1995	5	Now	$20.00
1996	6	2001	$22.00
1997	7	2002	$24.00
1998	7	2003	$22.00

YERING STATION PINOT NOIR ★★★

1991	6	Now	$34.00
1992	6	Now	$31.00
1993	5	Now	$24.00
1994	5	Now	$22.00
1995	7	2000	$29.00
1996	7	2001	$27.00
1997	7	2002	$25.00
1998	7	2003	$23.00

Zema Estate is a painstakingly purist red wine vineyard in Coonawarra. Winemakers: Nick and Matt Zema.

ZEMA ESTATE CABERNET SAUVIGNON ★★★★

before 1990		Prior	
1990	7	2000	$40.00
1991	6	2000	$31.00
1992	7	2000	$34.00
1993	7	2000	$31.00
1994	7	2002	$29.00
1995	5	2000	$19.50
1996	7	2004	$25.00
1997	6	2004	$20.00
1998	7	2006	N/R

ZEMA ESTATE CLUNY
(CABERNET/MERLOT/MALBEC/ CAB.FRANC)
★★★★

1993	5	Now	$23.00
1994	6	Now	$26.00
1995	6	Now	$24.00
1996	7	2000	$26.00
1997	7	2001	$24.00
1998	7	2003	N/R

ZEMA ESTATE FAMILY SELECTION
CABERNET SAUVIGNON ★★★★★

1988	7	2000	$92.00
1989	Not made		
1990	7	2002	$78.00
1991	6	2002	$62.00
1992	7	2004	$66.00
1993	6	2004	$52.00
1994	7	2006	$58.00
1995	Not made		
1996	7	2008	$49.00
1997	Not made		
1998	7	2010	N/R

ZEMA ESTATE SHIRAZ ★★★★

1982	7	Now	$78.00
1983	5	Prior	
1984	7	Now	$66.00
1985	5	Prior	
1986	6	Now	$49.00
1987	5	Now	$38.00
1988	7	Now	$49.00
1989	6	Now	$39.00
1990	7	2000	$42.00
1991	6	2000	$33.00
1992	7	2001	$36.00
1993	6	2001	$28.00
1994	7	2002	$31.00
1995	5	2000	$20.00
1996	7	2004	$26.00
1997	6	2004	$21.00
1998	7	2006	N/R